A Spencer
Love Affair

A Spencer Love Affair

EIGHTEENTH-CENTURY
THEATRICALS AT BLENHEIM PALACE
AND BEYOND

ALLAN P. LEDGER

FONTHILL

A Spencer Love Affair is dedicated to my loving wife Brenda,
for her unfailing support during its birthing and the 200th
anniversary of the publication of *Mansfield Park* by Jane Austen

Frontispiece: Fig. 1 Blenheim Palace from an eighteenth century print, entitled *Blenheim Castle.*

Fonthill Media Limited
www.fonthillmedia.com
office@fonthillmedia.com

First published in the United Kingdom 2014

Copyright © Allan Ledger 2014

ISBN 978-1-78155-352-7

Typeset in 10pt on 13pt Minion Pro

Printed and bound by CPI Group (UK) Ltd, Croydon, CR0 4YY

Contents

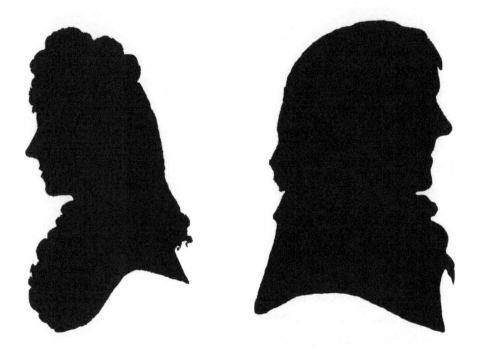

Fig. 2 Silhouettes drawn by Lady Charlotte Spencer of Edward Nares and a self portrait.

List of Illustrations

Picture Credits

His Grace the Duke of Marlborough for his kind permission for the images of George, 4th Duke of Marlborough by G. Romney; the Spencer family portrait by Reynolds; Lady Charlotte Spencer's drawings and silhouettes; *False Delicacy* by J. Roberts; The Theatre, Blenheim Palace; Conduct when Behind the Scenes and playbill for the *Deaf Lover*.

The Duke of Bedford and the Trustees of the Bedford Estates for their kind permission for the image of Signorina Caterina Galli.

The Earl of Derby for his kind permission for the image of the 12th Earl of Derby by Reynolds – *licence granted courtesy of The Rt Hon. The Earl of Derby 2013.*

The Trustees of the Weston Park Foundation for their kind permission for the image of Duchess Caroline's ivory theatre box key fobs.

Ilchester Estates for their kind permission for the image of The Indian Emperor by Hogarth.

The National Portrait Gallery for permission to include the image of The Young Fortune-Teller, after Sir Joshua Reynolds, mezzotint, [*c.* 1774–75] © National Portrait Gallery, London.

The Garrick Club and the Art Archive for permission to include the image of the playbill of *Lovers' Vows.*

The Warden and Fellows of Merton College, Oxford, for their kind permission for the image of the portrait of the Revd Edward Nares by A. Dovetin, Lady Charlotte Spencer's silhouettes, play tickets, playbills and items of Nares memorabilia, including the first volume of Edward Nares' memoirs.

The Beazley Archive and the Governing Body of Christ Church College, Oxford, for their kind permission for the image of Cupid and Psyche by Gillray.

The Warden and Scholars of New College, Oxford, for their kind permission for the image of the Siege of Blenheim by Gillray.

The Headmaster of Magdalen College School, Oxford, for his kind permission for the image of the school production of *The Critic*, performed at Blenheim Palace, 2011.

Oxfordshire County Council, Oxford History Centre, for permission to include the image of Hart Street, Henley-on-Thames, 1820.

The Berkeley and Spetchley Estates for their kind permission for the image of the Berkeley family portrait, by O. Humphry.

De Vere Venues Ltd of Eversley for their kind permission for the images of Warbrook House.

Christmas Archives International, courtesy of Andrew Hubert von Staufer, for permission to include the image of Mansfield Park, 1895.

Oliver Nares for his kind permission for the image of Edward and George Nares by J. Hamilton Mortimer.

Francis E. B. Witts for his kind permission to include the images of the Witts family by J. Hamilton Mortimer and Agnes Witts by Joseph Wright of Derby.

Paula Byrne for her kind permission for the image of A Scene from *Lovers' Vows*, private collection of the author of *The Real Jane Austen*.

Fonthill Media for permission to include images from *The Diary of a Cotswold Lady* and *The Diary of a Cotswold Parson*.

Richard Cragg, David Ross and Howard Sherwood for their kind permission for images relating to both Blenheim Palace and Merton College.

Acknowledgements

I am most grateful to His Grace John Spencer-Churchill, the 11th Duke of Marlborough, for consenting to write the Foreword and for kindly encouraging me to persevere over the last five years with my researches into his ancestor Lady Charlotte Spencer and her husband, the Revd Edward Nares. My thanks also go to the following:

John Forster, archivist at Blenheim Palace, for his assistance concerning Lady Charlotte Spencer's drawings, the Scharf Catalogue, the Residuary Accounts of the 6th Duke of Marlborough and the Parson Woodforde Society's article on the Revd Edward Nares.

The Dowager Duchess of Devonshire for her kind permission to publish extracts from her book *The House: A Portrait of Chatsworth*, the staff at Chatsworth for their help and advice, and Helen Marchant for her invaluable assistance.

The Duke of Bedford and the Trustees of the Bedford Estates for allowing the reproduction of the drawing of Signorina Caterina Galli and for permission to quote from the Woburn Archives, HMC8, volumes 24 and 45; Chris Gravett, curator at Woburn; and Ann Mitchell, archivist, for their time and expertise.

The Earl of Derby for permission to view and include the portrait of the 12th Earl of Derby, and Dr Stephen Lloyd, curator of the Derby Collection, for all his kindness and assistance at Knowsley Hall.

Lord and Lady Saye and Sele for a delightful visit to Broughton Castle.

The late Adrian White for his transcribed copy of Edward Nares' life and the Nares family tree. This had been in the possession of Edward's great-great-granddaughter, Margaret Bratt, née White, born 1928, who lived in Saskatchewan, Canada. Margaret's father, Arthur (1891–1969), was Edward's great-grandson and brother to Agatha White and Marion Fisher, née White.

My brother, Paul Ledger, Postmaster of Merton College, without whose determination the two journals written by Edward Nares would have lain undisturbed in the college archives.

Julian Reid, the archivist of both Merton College and Corpus Christi College, for his unfailing help and expertise since 2005 concerning the Nares memorabilia lodged at Merton.

Julia Walworth, librarian of Merton College, for her time and for allowing me access to Merton's unique library; also for permission to photograph selected items belonging to Edward Nares, left by Miss Agatha White and deposited at Merton in 1961/62.

The Warden and Fellows of Merton College for allowing me access to the Senior Common Room to view the portrait of Edward Nares by Anna Dovetin, and Mikhail Kizilov in *The Treasures of Merton College* concerning Russian treasures.

The Governing Body of Christ Church College, Oxford, for permission to photograph items in an exhibition in the Upper Library concerning the 4th Duke of Marlborough's intaglios; Claudia Wagner, curator of the Beazley Archive, Oxford, for permission to include these photographic items; and Cristina Neagu for her assistance and photographic expertise.

The staff at The British Library for their advice and assistance concerning archive newspaper reports from The Charles Burney Collection on private theatricals at Blenheim Palace.

Eleanor Taylor, Jane Handol and David Bowd-Exworth at Berkeley Castle for their time and assistance.

The staff at The Wellcome Library, London, with regard to Edward Nares' Commonplace Book.

Lavinia Wellicome for permission to quote from *The Ladies of Woburn*.

James Peill, at Goodwood, for his enthusiasm and assistance concerning the Dukes of Richmond, and Rosemary Baird for kindly allowing me to quote from her comprehensive history of Goodwood.

The staff at the Bodleian Library, Oxford, for their help with the journals of the Jane Austen Society and Edward Nares' notebooks on twelve lectures in political economy.

Amanda Foster at The Prince of Wales and Duchess of Cornwall's press office.

Mrs Gilliam, the archivist at OxHistory, concerning the letter of I. Pigot, 1785.

Helen Lefroy for her many kindnesses concerning the Lefroy family and Jane Austen.

Deirdre Le Faye, Evelyn Howe and Betty Askwith of the Jane Austen Society for their expertise concerning Jane Austen and the theatre and amateur theatricals.

Elizabeth Semper O'Keefe, Herefordshire County Records Officer, for permission to quote from the diary of Lady Anne Bateman.

Marcus Risdell, librarian of the Garrick Club, London, for allowing me access to the Garrick's Library.

Kent History and Library Centre, Maidstone, for permission to include The Biddenden Maids, Kent.

The librarians at the Society for Theatre Research, London.

The librarians of Bath City Library, and Sharon Kitchener, for their help regarding *The Bath Chronicle* of 1802.

Elizabeth Newport and Ruth Gillingham at Milton-under-Wychwood Library for their patience and help over the years.

The staff of De Vere Venues at Warbrook House Hotel in Hampshire, the Nares family home in the eighteenth century.

Penny and Richard Corbett of Shobdon Court, Herefordshire, who informed me of further possible correspondence in the County Library at Hereford and told me of Ivor Pfuell's book *A History of Shobdon*.

Richard and Diana Way, antiquarian booksellers of Henley-on-Thames, for assistance concerning Henley and the Dukes of Marlborough; and the librarians of Henley Library for help with Henley church records.

Madeleine Gilpin, Secretary of St Mary's Parochial Church Council at Ardley with Fewcott, Oxfordshire, for assistance regarding the Spencer memorials in the church.

Susan Gunter of Begbroke for her knowledge on Begbroke and its priory.

Barry Simon for his expertise on the history of Swindon Village, Cheltenham.

David Ross of Cheltenham and Richard Cragg of Woodstock for permission to use photographic items, and Howard Sherwood for his professional expertise and advice concerning all illustrations, including a possible cover design.

Nick Carter for alerting me to the Magdalen College School production of *The Critic*.

Nicholas Allen and John Edwards for helpful advice; Robert Hastings and Clive Reynard for publishing advice; and Laura Wilkins at the Writers' Workshop, Charlbury, for her valuable time and assistance concerning publishing.

My cousin Gillian Jenkins for kindly allowing me to stay in Oxford while researching at Merton College.

My sister-in-law Jenny Ledger for allowing me to stay *en famille* during visits to the British Library.

Francis E. B. Witts of Upper Slaughter for kindly permitting me to include Witts family portraits and extracts from his ancestors' diaries.

Victoria Huxley for kindly permitting me to include the Leigh and Austen family tree.

Anne Braithwaite for her patience and fortitude in deciphering my researches and for typing out the manuscript.

My wife Brenda for her support and encouragement, and her considerable knowledge concerning the French Court at Versailles during the eighteenth century, which was to lead in time to publication. For which my thanks go to the editorial team at Fonthill Media, from whom I have received much helpful advice. In particular to Alan Sutton, Sarah Parker and Richard Ley, who have guided me through the unfamiliar process of publication.

Last, but by no means least, for financial support from The Greening Lamborn Trust, whose aim is to promote public interest in the history, architecture, old photographs and heraldry of Oxford and its neighbourhood by supporting publications and other media that create access to them.

Fig. 3   Merton College from the Oxford Almanac 1737.

Foreword by His Grace the 11th Duke of Marlborough

I am pleased to welcome this new addition to the Blenheim Library. I congratulate Mr Allan Ledger for having written this fascinating and well-informed love story concerning my eighteenth-century ancestor Lady Charlotte Spencer, the 4th Duke of Marlborough's favourite daughter.

In this affectionate story, he has managed to combine the essence and feel of life at Blenheim in that golden era of private theatricals. He has unravelled the complexities of the principal characters involved, whether at Blenheim or at other great country houses. His searches have thrown up some delightful vignettes concerning the world of private theatricals, including Jane Austen's own childhood experiences at her family home. I welcome this splendid story, based on many years of research.

Marlborough

Blenheim Palace

Preface

This touching love story between Lady Charlotte Spencer and the Revd Edward Nares is set against the backdrop of eighteenth-century private theatricals at Blenheim Palace, the family home of the Dukes of Marlborough. It was the 4th Duke of Marlborough, George Spencer, and his wife Caroline's Georgian obsession with creating a suitable home environment for their ever-growing family that led to Caroline's refurbishment of Blenheim. Not long after their marriage in 1762, the Spencers employed 'Capability' Brown to landscape the grounds and parkland with the creation of a vast lake, and with the general embellishment of the palace by the architect Sir William Chambers, Blenheim was to become a fairy-tale family home for the Spencer children, for the Spencers were part of that Georgian world of glittering parties, of fortunes lost and won on the racecourse and at the card table.

As George and Caroline's family grew so did the Spencer problems, especially when it came to the question of marriage for the children of one of England's noblest families. Marrying well not only gave women stability, it also gave them status, for in Georgian times no one contemplated equality and all were expected to accept their place on the social ladder that had been ordained by God. Love was not the prime purpose of marriage, which was why Duchess Caroline was to persecute her daughter Lady Charlotte for making a love match with an impecunious parson, putting both the Spencer family's reputation and her daughter's status in society at risk. Rebelling against her mother's marriage wishes meant in time that having a palace as a home would no longer be an option for Charlotte.

After his wife's death in 1811, George Spencer would become increasingly more reclusive and silent. It may be that the loss of his favourite daughter, Charlotte, in 1802 preyed on him so heavily that he added a codicil to his will to have her re-interred in the family crypt of Blenheim's private chapel. Perhaps even Sir John Vanbrugh (see Appendix G), who designed Blenheim more as a stage set than a family home, would have appreciated the irony of Blenheim being the backdrop of a true love affair at a time in our history when Great Houses ruled our lives. As George Sand wrote in her novel *Indiana*:

> Love is woman's virtue, it is for love that she proudly accepts the consequences of her acts, it is love which gives her the heroism to face her remorse. The greater the cost of her misdemeanour, the more she deserves from the man she loves.

The inspiration for this book's original title *Leading to Love* was due to His Grace, the Duke of Marlborough. It was indeed appropriate, as it is similar to the title of the poet John Dryden's play, *All for Love*, which was performed at Blenheim in 1719 for His Grace's great ancestor John Churchill, the victor of the Battle of Blenheim, fought in the year 1704, during the War of the Spanish Succession. In his play, Dryden (see Appendix G) wrote these lines:

> Errors like straws upon the surface flow;
> He who would search for pearls must dive below.

After much soul-searching, it was decided that *A Spencer Love Affair* would be a more appropriate title.

A similarly critical approach is required when writing about a subject of which one has no previous knowledge. The starting point was the unexpected affair that developed during the era of Blenheim's private theatricals between the Revd Edward Nares and Lady Charlotte Spencer, and the discovery at Merton College, Oxford, of Edward's memoirs, in his own handwriting, in two leather-bound journals. These memoirs explained from Edward's point of view his friendship with the Spencer family at Blenheim, his role in the private theatricals of the 1780s, and the love affair that led to his marriage with Charlotte Spencer.

T. S. Eliot, one of Merton's many illustrious undergraduates, described culture as 'that which makes life worth living', and writing this book has certainly made life well worth living for its author. As the Ledger family motto *Finis Coronat Opus* (The end crowns the work) implies, to do a job satisfactorily one needs to see it through to its conclusion. A point that would have been appreciated by Sir Winston Churchill, who was born at Blenheim, and wrote, 'Writing a book is like having a friend and companion at your side to whom you can always turn for comfort or amusement.'

I trust that it will give you the reader as much pleasure.

Introduction to Eighteenth-Century Theatre

During the eighteenth century going to the theatre was one of England's most popular pastimes and an important part of fashionable society life in the late Georgian era. Everybody went, from royalty to the aristocracy, from the gentry to middle-class tradesmen, as well as the rougher elements of the lower classes. There were theatre boxes for those who could afford them, while those less well off sat squashed in the pit. In the lower gallery were the townsfolk, while in the upper gallery were the rougher elements and the servants of the aristocracy.

The average entertainment ran for up to four hours. Following an overture performed by the orchestra came the main play, which might be a comedy, a drama, a musical or an opera. In the interval there would be music and dance, and afterwards, if there was room available, one could get in for half price. To complete the entertainment a shorter after-piece, which tended to be of a farcical nature, was performed.

The theatre itself was in great measure that which we know today, with a proscenium arch and stage, the play being performed, as it were, 'in a frame' and the actors cut off from the public but costumed more or less in conformity with the parts they were playing.[1] Clothing was as important as scenery, and sometimes aristocratic ladies gave the actresses their clothes to wear, usually cast-offs that were no longer required. However, it was only towards the end of the eighteenth century that theatre lighting was considered to be of any real importance with regard to the stage – previously, theatres were lit entirely by candles and oil lamps – and it was David Garrick (see Appendix G) who, in 1765, introduced footlights or floats. He placed oil lamps with attached tin reflectors in the wings, which could be directed towards or away from the stage. House lights were kept on during the entertainment, as the audience came to the theatre as much to observe each other as the play.

The custom of allowing the liveried footmen of the aristocracy in for a free place in the galleries after having procured seats for their masters led to so much rioting and brawling that it was abolished in 1780. In Garrick's day, the disorders were so great that his friends hired a body of professional bruisers who waded into the pit and galleries, cracking skulls left and right until they had established some sort of order. With this type of behaviour it might seem strange that the upper classes were not deterred from visiting the theatre.

However, due principally to Garrick, Sheridan and Kemble (see Appendix G), going to the theatre not only had the seal of respectability but was a way of emulating London's High Society, or the Ton as they were known, inhabiting Mayfair.

London's theatre lovers tended to go to the theatre not just to be seen but also to see their favourite actor, and certain actors became the Ton's favourite celebrities, which in turn encouraged playwrights to write with a particular actor in mind, all of which was encouraged by clever theatre managers such as Garrick and Kemble. This applied not only in London but in the provinces as well; when the London theatres were shut, the theatrical companies travelled all over Great Britain drumming up business. So it was that most literate people were within reach of some kind of theatrical performance by companies of strolling players.

According to Garrick, in a letter to his brother Peter, after their visit to see strollers act in Lichfield, these players had hardly changed since 1737. This was the year when a new Licensing Act introduced a check on plays satirising the government. This Act also confined legitimate theatrical performances in London to only two theatres: the Theatre Royal in Drury Lane, and Covent Garden. Both these theatres had had the seal of royal approval from the time of Charles II and the Restoration and were the only theatres licensed to produce serious drama. The Haymarket Theatre had a partial licence, which permitted the production of plays in the summer, when the two main theatres were shut. There were also smaller fringe theatres that avoided the licensing laws by billing a concert and performing a play in the interval. Other theatrical stages included Astleys and the Lyceum, both of which presented grandiose spectacles, the latter specialising in ballad operas, musical farces and melodrama.

The custom of offering a double bill gave the audience full value for their money. Even professional actors such as Edmund Kean, famous for his performance of Macbeth, might then follow on in a production of Aladdin. The popularity of going to the theatre had grown considerably during Garrick's time, which was no doubt why most of London's high society were present at his funeral in 1779. After Garrick's death, Sarah Siddons (see Appendix G) and her brother John Kemble dominated the London stage. These two actors had cause to be grateful to Garrick for many reasons, including stopping the audience from sitting on the stage – a custom that Voltaire, well before Garrick, introduced to the French theatre. During the last quarter of the eighteenth century, plays about high society life were favoured, partly due to King George III and Queen Charlotte's love of the theatre, especially of Georgian comedy.

In the mid-eighteenth century a craze for building theatres in England had spread from France. One of the best preserved of these Georgian theatres is the Theatre Royal in Bristol, the oldest continually operating theatre in Britain, built in 1766, following the plan of Garrick's own theatre at Drury Lane. Another is at Richmond in Yorkshire, built by the actor-cum-theatre manager Samuel Butler in 1788. Richmond's Georgian theatre was reopened after restoration in 1963. A more recently restored Georgian theatre is the Theatre Royal, Bury St Edmunds. Built in 1819 by William Wilkins, who designed the National Gallery in London, it is possibly the best preserved of all England's Georgian theatres, even when compared to London's Drury Lane, Covent Garden and the Old Vic. Now in the care of the National Trust, it is one of the most significant theatre buildings in England.

By 1805, there were 279 public theatres officially recognised as places for theatrical entertainment in England. Whether private or public, going to the theatre had become a firm part of the English nation's entertainment by the end of the eighteenth century, a phenomenon that had also been a part of French culture a century earlier, in the age of Louis XIV.

ACT I

The French Love of Theatre

The theatre-mad age of Louis XIV was due in part to the creation of Versailles as a theatre set in which the Sun King could play out his role of kingship.

For the wedding of Louis XIV in 1660, the largest theatre in Europe, 226 feet long, was built by Gaspare Vigarani, called the *Salle des Machines*. However, it was not until 1755 that the first true production in a public theatre occurred, with Voltaire's *L'Orphelin de la Chine* (The Orphan of China) in Paris. Before then, amateur dramatics or charades acted in French châteaux by the French aristocracy were the vogue, a temporary stage often being set up in a salon, a gallery or an orangery, or out of doors in the garden. It was this French fashion that was to pioneer the development of English private theatres by the English aristocracy in their country houses during the eighteenth century.

At one time France had at least fourteen purpose-built private theatres compared to England's four. The fashion in France for having one's own private theatre was started in 1722 at the Château de Malle near Bordeaux by its owner Alexandre-Eutrope de Lur-Saluces, but if anyone was truly responsible for the vogue of amateur dramatics in private theatres it was Voltaire, whose views epitomise the 'Age of Enlightenment' and who in the 1730s created his own private theatre at Cirey. Early in 1727, Voltaire had been imprisoned following political differences with the Royal Court at Versailles, and in May of that year he chose to be exiled to England for three years. Voltaire saw England as a land of civil liberties, and it was at this time, the year of the coronation of King George II and Queen Caroline, that he visited Blenheim Palace. On seeing Blenheim, he commented that it was *'une grosse masse de Pierre, sans agrèment sans gout'* [a great mass of stone, without charm or taste], to which the first Duchess of Marlborough, Sarah Churchill, replied, 'He is either mad or a philosopher.'[1]

On his return to France, Voltaire was to become the literary adviser to Madame de Pompadour, who was married to Charles Guillaume Le Normant d'Étoilles. This French nobleman had built his own private theatre for his wife, but, as Louis XV's mistress, Madame de Pompadour had her own private royal theatre at Versailles. Known as The Little Theatre, this opened in 1747 with Molière's play *Tartuffe*, written in 1667. The theatre was so small that it could accommodate only fourteen people, but due primarily to the cost of running it, it closed after only three years.

The most famous of all royal French private theatres was the Queen's Theatre, built in 1778 by Richard Mique assisted by Hubert Robert (see Appendix G) for Marie Antoinette and completed a year later. The Queen's Theatre was inaugurated in 1780, when royal festivities were held at the Trianon. Marie Antoinette even formed her own theatrical company and enjoyed participating in productions at Versailles performed for Louis XVI. One of her favourite roles was that of a laundry girl or village maiden in the escapist fantasies that were in vogue right up to 1785. Following the success of the Queen's Theatre, Marie Antoinette asked Mique to design a whole village for her, complete with artfully dilapidated thatched cottages, a mill and a dairy, which became known as *L'Hameau* [The Hamlet]. Even today, the buildings of *L'Hameau*, which have been restored to something of a theme park or film set, appear contrived. No real French hamlet would have anything as whimsical as the Tour de Marlborough, with its balconies and spiral staircases, and it is indeed strange that this tower should be named after one of France's greatest foes, John Churchill, the victor of the Battle of Blenheim in 1704. Perhaps the explanation lies in the sentiments of brotherhood that followed the signing of the treaty between France, Britain and America in 1783, which was to bring the American Revolutionary War to a close. English tourists and diplomats now flooded back into France, the result being that polite society in France was in the grip of rampant Anglomania. However, this was to be short-lived, for after 1789 and the French Revolution, polite society's enthusiasm for everything English was to dwindle, along with the fashion for private theatricals.

The English Passion for Private Theatricals

During the eighteenth century, private theatricals became the favourite diversion not only of the English aristocracy but of the gentry and clergy also, the rage continuing into the following century until around 1810. But before the eighteenth century, one of the most famous of all amateur productions was that of Cavalli's opera *La Calisto* in 1675.[1] The principal parts in this lavish production were enacted by children, including two royal princesses, Mary and Anne, the daughters of James II, together with a number of court ladies, who included the 1st Duchess of Marlborough, Sarah Churchill, née Jennings, aged fifteen years. Following the Interregnum of Oliver Cromwell in the seventeenth century, between 1660 and 1700 there were fourteen women patrons named as the objects of dedication in plays of the time, including the two princesses and various aristocratic ladies such as Sarah Churchill, Elizabeth Godolphin and the Duchess of Richmond.

It was in 1675 that Sarah first met John Churchill; they married two years later. Sarah had first gone up to court in 1673, when Princess Anne was eight years old. Their friendship lasted for almost thirty years, even through the difficult political times of the Catholic James II, both of the royal princesses being Protestants. On 4 November 1677, Princess Mary married William of Orange, who was to reign jointly with his wife after the overthrow of James II in 1688, when England ceased to be a French satellite, John Churchill committing himself to help England by changing his allegiance from James to William.

During the War of the Spanish Succession, John and Sarah Churchill became the power behind the throne of Queen Anne. Blenheim Palace was the reward given by the Queen to John Churchill for outfighting the forces of Louis XIV, depicted in a glorious series of tapestries at Blenheim telling this story of war and ultimate victory that would eventually lead to Britain becoming a superpower. All of this Vanbrugh was to portray in his theatrical design of Blenheim for His Grace John Churchill, the 1st Duke of Marlborough.

In the first half of the eighteenth century there were few private theatricals in England. The earliest was at Blenheim Palace, when the Duke and Duchess moved into rooms in the east wing in the summer of 1719. These theatricals were put on by the grandchildren and their friends for John and Sarah Churchill in a room in the private east wing dining room, known as the Bow-Window Room. Here they were entertained in a production of John Dryden's *All for Love*. This had been thoughtfully censored and bowdlerised by the

Duchess, with the cast gorgeously dressed in rolls of material soon to be cut for curtain and covers. The Duke was so taken by this story of Antony and Cleopatra that having seen it twice, he asked for it to be repeated a third time, particularly as it included watching his two granddaughters Lady Anne and Lady Diana Spencer.

Another dilettante theatrical production with children took place in London, an example of which can be seen in Hogarth's painting of a children's performance of Dryden's *The Indian Emperour*. In 1731, this play had been successfully revived at Drury Lane before it was performed at a house in Great George Street, Hanover Square, the home of John Conduit, the Master of the Royal Mint. The production was directed by the theatre manager Theophilus Cibber and the part of Cydaria was played by the 2nd Duke of Richmond's daughter, Lady Caroline Lennox, aged nine. The audience included not only Lady Caroline's parents but the Duke of Cumberland and his sister as well. A repeat performance of this play was later given in front of the King and the Queen at St James's Palace. It was then decided to commemorate the occasion by having Hogarth paint a conversation piece of the young actors, all aged about ten years, in front of an audience, which is why the children are the focus of the main attention while the audience's background is enhanced by the inclusion of paintings, sculpture and architecture.

In 1737, a new Licensing Act was passed regarding the theatre and actors. As a result, other aristocratic ladies patronised certain star actresses of the time, including Clive, Cibber, Pritchard and Woffington. These aristocratic ladies included Mary Churchill, a daughter of the 1st Duke of Marlborough and now Duchess of Montagu, and Susannah Ashley Cooper, Countess of Shaftesbury, who were members of The Ladies Shakespeare Club. Another wealthy female patron was Georgiana, Duchess of Devonshire.

A few years later, on 26 September 1740, the 3rd Duke of Richmond, Charles March, presented with his sisters Caroline and Emily a production of Boissy's *Les Dehors Trompeurs* (*False Appearances*) before a small but select noble audience at Goodwood, possibly in the Long Hall. At the time Caroline was seventeen, Emily nine and Charles five years old. It may have been for this that the actor-manager Colley Cibber came to stay, writing to the Duke, 'Good God! How I will rejoice with you! For who can want spirits at Goodwood? Such a place, and such company!'[2]

On another royal private theatrical occasion in 1740, in an open-air theatre (still in use today) at Cliveden House, Buckinghamshire, built for the 2nd Duke of Buckingham, George Villiers (see Appendix G), *Rule, Britannia!* was first sung during a performance of James Thomson's masque *Alfred*. This was given before Frederick, Prince of Wales, who was living partly at Cliveden. This seal of royal approval may have led in time to the building of specially erected indoor private theatres, one of the most famous being at Wargrave, Berkshire, built in 1789 for Richard Barry, 7th Earl of Barrymore (see Appendix G). This theatre was rectangular and held up to 400 spectators. It had two tiers of boxes, as well as two stage boxes, unusually placed over the orchestra's well, and was provided with a series of workrooms with an adjoining salon for refreshments. After ruining its owner, it was demolished in 1792. In her journal in 1790, Caroline Powys (see Appendix G) wrote, 'Lord Barrymore had last summer a very elegant playhouse at Wargrave and had a Mr. Young from the Opera-House to paint the scenes.'

One of the earliest private theatres built was for the young Sir Watkin Williams Wynn (see Appendix G) at Wynnstay in Denbighshire. Lacking an interest in parliamentary politics, he turned to theatricals in the 1770s as a means of making a name for himself, becoming Garrick's patron. Wynn invited Richard Sheridan and George Colman (see Appendix G) to witness and sometimes to act in his productions, which lasted over seventeen years. The Wynnstay theatricals were notable for the involvement of the family servants, particularly of the butler Sidebotham, who was responsible for the allocation of tickets. It was this relationship between master and servant in the Georgian household that Jane Austen drew attention to in *Mansfield Park* by describing its disruptive effects on the servants. Wynn's private theatre, converted from an old kitchen wing of the house, had no boxes or galleries, merely a commodious pit in which professional actors, family members and household servants acted together. It was used for annual performances from 1771 to 1789, with its stage décor by John Inigo Richards (see Appendix G). Plays performed included such favourites as *The Beaux' Stratagem* and *High Life Below Stairs*.

Whether this theatre was due to the coming of age in 1770 of Sir Watkin Williams Wynn is not known, but what is certain is that a great celebration took place, according to the diary of Elizabeth, Duchess of Northumberland:

> At noon, not less than twenty thousand visitants were assembled … among the heca-tombs sacrified to his friends, an enormous ox was roasted whole, which being placed upon a kind of triumphant car, ornamented with garlands and streamers, was drawn, by six little mountaineers, to the amphitheatre in the midst of which was erected a Bacchanalian altar, crowned with a cask, the size of which presented a suitable emblem of that unbounded hospitality so long renowned at Wynnstay … When Sir Watkin, from an eminence, gave his guests a general salute in a bumper, their repeated acclamations, mixed with the thunder of cannon, might fairly be said to make the adjacent Welsh mountains tremble. While the populace were regaled, the numerous visitants of superior rank were summoned, by sound of trumpet, to dinner …[3]

Not so long after this celebration, Robert Nares (see Appendix G), Edward Nares' cousin, was employed as a tutor by the Wynn family. It was while he was at Wynnstay that Robert wrote both prologues and epilogues for the Wynn private family theatricals.

John Montagu, 4th Earl of Sandwich (see Appendix G) was another English aristocrat to create his own private theatre at Hinchingbrooke, near Huntingdon. Montagu was held responsible for mismanagement at the Admiralty during the American War of Independence and the fall of North's government in 1782, and after his retirement from politics he partly devoted himself to the world of private theatre. In 1786, the Prince of Wales was invited to watch the theatricals at Hinchingbrooke, the actors subsequently being known as 'His Royal Highness's Company of Comedians' – the only instance of a private theatrical company being taken under royal protection. In 1787, Samuel Foote's *The Liar*, more of a children's theatrical, was performed at Hinchingbrooke, the part of Young Wilding being played by Major Arabin, a famous amateur actor. Comparing Hinchingbrooke with the Blenheim productions of 1787, *The Times* on 15 November wrote:

Whereas the latter [Blenheim] excelled in magnificence of decoration and in acting, the former was without rival for good humour, vivacity, and acquaintance with the interior business of theatrical arrangement.

These theatricals were however approached from a musical rather than from a dramatic point of view. And although Georgian society prided itself on its sophistication and culture, as far as many members of society were concerned, the theatre was simply an arena for flirting, for seeing and for being seen; the play and the actors came a poor second.

James Wyatt was employed by the 3rd Duke of Richmond in 1787 to construct a private theatre at Richmond House in London. This was not a new building, as it was constructed from two rooms that held about 100 spectators. The Duke of Richmond employed the well-known scene painter Thomas Greenwood (see Appendix G) to paint the scenery backdrops. Private theatricals reached their apogee in the late 1780s, when occasions such as those at Richmond House caused a sitting of the House of Commons to be postponed in order that MPs could attend.

One of the oldest private indoor working theatres still in existence is at Chatsworth in Derbyshire, the ancestral home of the Dukes of Devonshire. This was completed in 1832, well after the death of the 5th Duke (1748–1811), who had bought 1,347 volumes of plays from John Kemble, Sarah Siddons' brother, for his library at Chatsworth. These plays were sold by the 9th Duke in 1912 to the Huntington Collection in California. However, it was the theatre-loving 6th Duke, the 'Bachelor Duke', who seems to have had a greater interest in private theatricals, even if his theatre was on the whole used primarily for family charades. He wrote an extensive account of life at Chatsworth that included a description of the Ballroom or the Theatre of Charades. The 6th Duke also put on private theatricals at his London home in the nineteenth century.

In her book *The House: A Portrait of Chatsworth*, the Dowager Duchess of Devonshire describes the theatre as it was in the 1980s:

> For some years after we came to live here the Theatre was a store and had the depressing smell and feeling of a place which is locked and dead except to searchers for forgotten furniture. It was very dirty as well, from years of neglect. In the early sixties we covered the walls with red rep and hung curtains of red velveteen and blue silk lining, trimmed with bobbles dyed in tea to correspond with the painted curtains framing the stage – all made by Miss Feeney, of course.
>
> The two backdrops, which let down by a complicated series of pulleys, are a desert island and a drawing-room, which presumably cover all possibilities known to theatre. There is a trap-door in the stage for devils to come up or down according to the piece. As I am a complete failure when it comes to entertainment before footlights, this pretty theatre has never been used for the purpose for which it was intended, except for a memorable concert given to inaugurate a local orchestra. Every seat was occupied, but mostly by people who were unpractised in the art of listening to music, and there was clapping when there should not have been at those false stops between movements when the unwary wake up and clap out of good manners.

The Temple Attic or Belvedere above would most probably have been pulled down by my father-in-law but for the outbreak of war in 1939.[4]

The theatre, formerly the Ballroom or Banqueting Room, was designed by Sir Jeffry Wyatville as a ballroom for the 6th Duke and completed in 1832. The ceiling is decorated with late seventeenth-century painted panels by Sir James Thornhill and Louis Chéron. These were removed from the walls of the 1st Duke's Long Gallery and adjacent Little Dining Room when they were converted into the Library and Ante Library by the 6th Duke. The two boxes and the gallery above are part of the original furnishing of the room. One was used by Queen Victoria when she attended a ball here in 1843. The room was subsequently used for entertainment of various kinds. In 1896, the 8th Duke commissioned William Hemsley, a leading London designer and supplier of 'theatrical scenery and appliances', to fit the room out as a theatre. He provided a permanent stage, stage equipment, a painted proscenium and front drop curtain, and a number of sets. Most of these remain, and are extremely rare survivors of late-nineteenth-century scenery.

The theatre was used so regularly between 1898 and 1907, during the winter visits of the Prince and Princess of Wales (later King Edward VII and Queen Alexandra), with performances of plays, dance and music to entertain the royal house party, that the press of that time dubbed it the 'Theatre Royal'. From 1989 to 2005, the room was used for textile conservation. In 2005, Chatsworth was the backdrop for the film *Pride and Prejudice* and became Jane Austen's Pemberley.

At Craig-y-Nos Castle in Powys, the theatre built in the nineteenth century for the famous singer Adelina Patti still exists. The private theatre at Loton Park, Alberbury, near Shrewsbury was built in the 1870s by Sir Baldwin Leighton, nearly doubling the size of his house. The present owner of Loton Park is the 11th Baronet, Sir Michael Leighton. Another theatre still in use is at Buscot Park, Lord Faringdon's house in Oxfordshire. Other theatres built in the twentieth century, such as the late John Christie's opera house at Glyndebourne in Sussex, though founded by private individuals are open to the public and charge for admission so cannot be strictly classed as private theatres, as is the case at Buscot.

Further north, at Seaton Delaval in Northumberland, Lord Delaval built a theatre in the hall. His theatricals included all members of the Delaval family as well as estate workers and family servants. One of the epilogues for a play ends with the words 'In Love and Friendship, but one Family' – a suitable motto for all aristocratic families who were indulging in the world of private theatricals.

At Home with the Spencers at Blenheim Palace

In provinces, where scarce a church is found
These well-frequented theatres abound
And should we go to Blenheim or Winstay [Wynnstay]
It would not be to act, but see a play.

From the Prologue of Richard Graves' comedy The Coalition or the Opera Rehearsed

Throughout the eighteenth century going to the theatre continued to grow in popularity. It was said that even before 1800, every market town, however small, had its own specially built theatre. In the summer, these theatres were visited by London actors or even troupes of actors from the big towns nearby. However, the relatively limited theatre-going audience meant that plays rarely ran for long and there was a constant demand for new plays. Over two thousand plays were written and produced between 1750 and 1800, some of which may have been written for the aristocratic country houses and the guests and friends of the aristocracy who lived there. Others were written for all kinds of theatre, including the provincial theatres that often functioned as a place of assembly, thus taking on a political as well as a cultural role. The acquisition of a royal patent for these provincial playhouses was regarded by the local gentry as a considerable coup.

Having your own private theatre to entertain your guests and friends was considered to be the height of fashion. In *A Collection of Playbills, Notices and Press-Cuttings* by Charles Burney, which deals with private theatrical performances between 1750 and 1808, over fifteen such private theatres are described, including Wynnstay and Blenheim. It is interesting that both theatres are mentioned by Graves in the prologue of his comedy *The Coalition or the Opera Rehearsed*, written in 1793, even though by then both had been closed down.

As well as having her own private theatre at Blenheim, the 4th Duchess of Marlborough, Caroline (see Appendix G) enjoyed going to the London theatres, as evidenced by her ivory theatre box key fobs of the 1780s era, some of which have survived and are at Weston Park, Shropshire, the home of the Bridgeman family. In 1777, Duchess Caroline went with some female friends to visit Garrick, who at the age of sixty had just retired from a glittering stage career. It was said that his performances 'drew a dozen dukes a night'. Later, while Garrick was staying at Althorp with the 1st Earl Spencer and his wife Georgiana Poyntz, a good and generous friend of Garrick and his wife, the Viennese dancer Eva-Maria Veigel, he suffered an attack of kidney stones. Returning to his house at Adelphi Terrace, London, Garrick lingered until his death on 20 January 1779. The funeral procession on 1 February reached all the way from his house to Westminster Abbey, and among the pall-bearers was the 1st Earl Spencer.

In the year Garrick died a new magazine entitled *The Macaroni and Theatrical Magazine* was published. The Macaronis were the young fops of the time, who aped foreign fashions with their dandified dress and manners. Their trade marks were the wearing of white silk shoes with red heels and highly elaborate wigs offset by a miniscule hat. The original twenty-seven members of Brooks's, the famous London club founded in 1778 by William Brooks, were all Macaronis, their average age being twenty-five, and they had all made the Grand Tour, an aristocratic rite of passage for many young noblemen and gentlemen. During the tour the traveller would inspect classical architecture as well as paintings and statuary in the galleries of foreign royalty and noblemen. This corpus of knowledge could then be employed later by the young aristocrat when he embarked on acquiring his own collections of paintings and sculpture.

Caroline's father, the 4th Duke of Bedford, had employed Garrick in 1744 to put on a production of Dryden's *All for Love* at Woburn Abbey, the Duke's family home. The two ducal families of the Bedfords and Marlboroughs were not only related but were also good friends. Lady Elizabeth Keppel, who married Francis, Marquess of Tavistock (see Appendix G), heir to the Dukedom of Bedford, often went to Blenheim to see Francis's sister, Caroline. Blenheim was a favourite place for Elizabeth, as it was there that Francis proposed to her in 1764. When Francis became engaged to Elizabeth, he wrote to his friend Thomas Robinson saying, 'I dare not say how happy I am ... I feel for her an attachment equally binding with the utmost love ... I have a tenderness for her which I did not think my heart capable.'[1]

The Breakfast Room at Woburn contains a painting of Elizabeth Keppel that is considered to be one of the best known compositions of Sir Joshua Reynolds (see Appendix G). Sir Thomas Lawrence thought it the most beautiful portrait he had ever seen. This marvellous painting is a reminder to both the Dukes of Bedford and the Dukes of Richmond that they are related, as Elizabeth was the Duke of Richmond's first cousin. Sadly for Elizabeth, in 1767, Francis went out with the Dunstable Hunt and was thrown from his horse, which fell on him, kicking him in the head as it struggled to get up and fracturing his skull.

In 1771, the 4th Duke of Bedford died and, as far as is known, no more theatricals were acted at Woburn until 1777, when the tragedy *Panthea* by Francis Beaumont and John Fletcher was performed. The cast for this production included the Duke of Bedford, aged twelve, Lords John and William Russell, his brothers, Lady Caroline Fox, aged ten, and her brother Lord Holland, who was only four years old. Whether Duchess Caroline attended this performance is not known. In the 1790s, the Duchess of Bedford revived theatricals in a newly decorated theatre, the play *John Bull* being first performed to the servants, then to tenants and then to high-society friends. The Duke played Dennis Brulguddery and his wife and children other parts.

In 1803, after the death of his first wife, the 6th Duke of Bedford married Lady Georgiana Gordon. Having taken part in theatricals at Gordon Castle in Scotland in 1792, Lady Georgiana was the new driving force, improving the theatre at Woburn, which was to survive until 1872. Among other plays staged at the Bedford ancestral home was Samuel Foote's popular farce *The Mayor of Garratt*, which was performed there in 1805.

At Woburn there are two rooms in the family wing, the Green Room and the Theatre Room, which were part of the house's private theatre used in 1848 during the 7th Duke's time, when, among others, the French play *Les Arbres Célestes* was performed. The Duke's wife Anna Maria loved theatricals and performing in them, and is also remembered for starting the habit of taking afternoon tea in 1841, Catherine of Braganza, the wife of Charles II, having introduced the drinking of tea to England in 1662. Anna Maria even had her own travelling tea service, which can be seen at Woburn today. At the time, only the wealthy could afford to drink tea; the Woburn archives contain a receipt, dated 1685, showing that tea cost £100 per pound weight. Some of the plays performed during the 7th Duchess's time were written by family members and were generally enacted around Christmas and the New Year. A small display case in the Blue Drawing Room is filled with programmes and plays performed in the 'Woburn Theatre'.

After Caroline's marriage to George Spencer, 4th Duke of Marlborough, she may well have been strongly influenced by the theatrical performances at her family home of Woburn Abbey to create her own theatricals at Blenheim, and was also emulating Sarah Churchill, the 1st Duchess of Marlborough, who in 1719 had created her own private theatricals at Blenheim Palace. The first of Duchess Caroline's theatricals appears to have taken place in 1773, during a large house party, when an epilogue to the play *High Life Below Stairs* by the Revd James Townley was recited (see Appendix K). No further theatrical performances at Blenheim are known about until after Caroline's visit to the theatre in Oxford in 1786. This was reported on by Fanny Burney (see Appendix G) in her diary:

> Drove to the theatre. At the inner court to the door of the theatre, stood the Duke and Duchess of Marlborough, the Marquess of Blandford in a nobleman's Oxford robe, and Lady Caroline and Lady Elizabeth Spencer ... Once the royal party had gone in the Spencers followed on and when the whole was over everyone left the theatre in the same manner as we had entered it. The Duke and Duchess of Marlborough, the Marquis and the Ladies Spencer attended the King and Queen to their carriages, and they went back to the theatre to wait for their own.[2] (See Appendix Q.)

At the time, King George III and Queen Charlotte were staying with the Harcourt family at Nuneham Courtenay near Abingdon. Fanny Burney did not herself accompany their majesties in 1786 on the occasion of the royal visit to Blenheim, during which the Queen famously remarked that Duchess Caroline was 'the proudest woman in England', and it may have been this royal visit that triggered the development of a private theatre at Blenheim.

Caroline's royal connections stemmed back to 1761, when she was one of Queen Charlotte's bridesmaids. As a result of marrying England's most eligible bachelor, the 4th Duke of Marlborough in 1762, Caroline's pride knew no bounds, although she was probably disappointed that her new husband had previously refused the honour of carrying the sword of state during the coronation in Westminster Abbey.

It was also in 1786 that the American statesman Thomas Jefferson, the principal author of the Declaration of Independence and third president of the United States from 1801 to 1809, visited Blenheim. Greatly impressed by what he saw, particularly the lake, he wrote, 'The water here is very beautiful and very grand.' He also gave an accurate account of the size of the park and gardens of the time:

> ... 2500 ac, of which 200 is garden, 150 water, 12 kitchen gardens and the rest park. 200 people employed to keep it in order, and to make alterations and additions. About 50 of these employed in pleasure grounds. The turf is mowed once in 10 days in summer. About 2000 fallow deer in the park and 2000 sheep.[3]

The 4th Duke of Marlborough had summoned Lancelot 'Capability' Brown (see Appendix G) in 1764 to design a landscaped park at Blenheim, Brown entrusting his foreman Benjamin Read to carry out this work. Included in the remodelled landscape were classical temples, one of which, the Temple of Diana, was designed by Sir William Chambers (see Appendix G). It was in this temple that Winston Churchill proposed to Clementine Hozier in 1908. Its portico was inscribed with verses from the *Hippolytus* of Euripides.

Amongst other visitors who enjoyed Brown's beautification of the park at Blenheim, enclosed by seven and a half miles of walls, were two of Jane Austen's brothers, James and Henry. At the time of their visit in 1787, Jane's favourite brother Henry was up at Oxford University at St John's College. Both brothers were keen on acting and playwriting, and were mainly responsible for the Austen private theatricals at the rectory at Steventon in Hampshire. Perhaps the reason for their visit was to find out more about Blenheim's private theatricals and to see its theatre, which had completed its first successful season the previous year. Accompanying them was another keen thespian, their cousin Eliza de Feuillide. Writing about their visit, Eliza said how much they had all enjoyed riding round the park, but was less enthusiastic about the interiors of the palace. According to the Austen Papers of 1704–1856, edited by R. A. Austen-Leigh, she found them old-fashioned and shabby.

Blenheim was a favourite place for other local visitors, such as Mrs Caroline Powys, who was related to the Austens. A tireless country house visitor for over half a century, she had first visited Blenheim in 1759, the year after the 3rd Duke of Marlborough's death. Caroline was married to an Oxfordshire squire and the couple lived at Hardwick House overlooking the Thames. In her diary she wrote, 'In this part of our county there are more fine houses near each other than in any I believe in England, nineteen within a morning's airing worth seeing.' In 1759, she travelled to Bath for the first time, visiting the Pump Room, the Abbey and the Assembly Rooms, where she met Elizabeth, Duchess of Marlborough, who had married the 3rd Duke in 1732. Elizabeth died in 1761, and was visiting Bath in her old age presumably for therapeutic reasons.

Caroline Powys's visits to Blenheim are revealing not only about the estate but also about the Spencer family:

> The environs of Blenheim have been amazingly improved by ['Capability'] Brown since I was last there, many rooms furnish'd and gilt, and as there are many fine pictures, must be always worth seeing. A fine ride round the park of five miles, which we went, and afterwards three round the shrubbery. The Duke, Duchess and many of their children with other company were driving about in one of those clever Dutch vehicles call'd, I think, a Waske, a long open carriage holding fifteen or sixteen persons. As forms [benches] are placed in rows so near the ground for the horses to step out, it must be very heavy, but that, as it was drawn by six horses, was no inconvenience and 'tis quite a summer machine without any covering at the top.

Her remarks emphasise that it was not until the 4th Duke's time that Blenheim became a true home to the Marlborough family. The 3rd Duke, Charles Spencer, had preferred Langley, near Windsor, in order to be nearer to royalty. In those times it was possible to see Langley Park from the north terrace at Windsor Castle through a telescope.

Several members of the family have been made Knights of the Garter over the years: the 1st Duke of Marlborough in 1702, the 3rd Duke in 1741, the 4th Duke in 1768, the 9th Duke in 1902, and Sir Winston Leonard Spencer-Churchill in 1954. The names and the heraldic arms of all Knights of the Garter are inscribed in St George's Hall, Windsor Castle, which for six centuries has been associated with the Order of the Garter, the ceiling being decorated with the family coat of arms. The thousandth Knight of the Garter was HRH Prince William in 2008.

Among the 'many fine pictures' referred to by Caroline Powys was the Spencer family portrait painted by Sir Joshua Reynolds in 1778. Reynolds had set out for Blenheim on 13 August that year, returning to London on 4 September. Most of his time at Blenheim seems to have been spent drawing the children, and it was on one of these days that the Duchess ordered a servant to bring a broom and sweep up the snuff that had been dropped by Reynolds on the carpet. Reynolds informed the servant that 'the dust raised by the broom would do more injury to my picture than the snuff could possibly do to the carpet'.

The Spencer family portrait was shown at the Royal Academy Exhibition of 1778, afterwards being returned to Blenheim's Great Hall where Reynolds made several improvements to it. The frame for the painting was designed by Chambers, and the painting was later hung in the family dining room.

In the painting, the 4th Duke is seated, holding his favourite sardonyx, engraved by Francesco Bartolozzi, an Italian engraver (1727–1815) and one of the original members of the Royal Academy in 1769. The sardonyx shows the cameo head of the Emperor Augustus, responsible for the death of the last Pharaonic Egyptian Queen, Cleopatra. The Duke rests his right hand on the shoulder of his oldest son George, Marquess of Blandford, and wears a sumptuous costume. His blue velvet Garter mantle is draped over one shoulder and on the far left can be seen his Garter hat trimmed with white ostrich feathers and a black heron feather. The Duke had in fact been granted this coveted honour on 12 December 1768, although he was not installed at Windsor until 25 July 1771. His oldest son is clothed in a suit of red velvet lined with squirrel fur, with a frilled shirt collar that is open, and on his feet he wears white silk shoes with red heels. The Marquess holds one of the ten crimson cases containing the fabulous Zanetti gems, purchased in Venice by his father in 1762. When these were sold at Christie's on 28 June 1875 by the 7th Duke they fetched 35,000 guineas.

The most famous of the Marlborough gems is 'The Marriage of Cupid and Psyche' which was once owned by Lord Arundel, to whom it had been given by Rubens, and is now in the Boston Museum of Fine Arts. In the eighteenth century it became a popular subject, being used on the decoration of mantelpieces and bedheads, and was also copied by Wedgwood for decorative plaques and pottery. There is at Blenheim a beautiful marble fireplace with this classical relief, carved with exquisite skill, which is a copy of the Marlborough gem. The 4th Duke's collection of intaglios was the largest and most important of all the eighteenth-century English gem collections.

The Marquess's mother, Duchess Caroline, stands in the centre of the painting, wearing a classical cross-over shoulder white gown, with a gold fringe on the shoulders and sashed at the waist and a blue mantle lined with ermine. Her towering hair is lightly powdered and topped with a gold gauze scarf, and she rests her hand lightly on her husband's arm.

On the extreme right is her oldest daughter Lady Caroline, who wears a tight-bodiced robe in creamy-pink satin trimmed with a blue ribbon and gold lace. She rests her left hand on the shoulder of her youngest sister Lady Anne, shrinking back in alarm at the theatrical mask being held up teasingly by her older sister Lady Charlotte, who looks out mischievously at Reynolds. Lady Anne is wearing a white muslin dress with cross-over stitching, and round her waist she wears a blue silk sash. Apparently Lady Anne was intimidated by the presence of Reynolds and had told her governess that she did not want to be painted, which is why Reynolds may have asked Lady Charlotte to hold up the mask to distract her sister's attention away from the artist. Lady Charlotte wears a pink taffeta dress with a white silk over-gown, over which her long tresses dangle. The motif of Lady Charlotte holding the mask was engraved as an independent picture by Luigi Schiavonetti in 1790 and later by Turner, entitled 'The Ghost'.

Standing slightly behind and to Lady Charlotte's right is her young brother Lord Henry, wearing a red velvet suit lined with squirrel fur with a white open-collared frilled shirt, who looks up at his oldest sister Lady Caroline. The last of the Spencer children is Lady Elizabeth, who wears a low-cut whitish dress, the bodice of which is edged with gold and fastened with a blue bow. Like her older sister, her hair has been piled fashionably high. Round her neck dangles a pendant on a long black silk ribbon, and she is also watching her older sister.

In the background can be seen Blenheim, as well as typical Reynolds barley twist pillars and other classical architectural effects. This painting is included by the Revd William Mavor (see Appendix G) in his book *New Description of Blenheim* published more than ten years later, in 1789:

In the Dining Room hangs a painting of the present Duke, Duchess and six children. Ladies
Caroline, Elizabeth, Charlotte and Anne – the Marquess of Blandford, and Lord Henry: – the
two youngest, Lord Francis and Lady Amelia, were born since this very capital picture [which
cost seven hundred guineas] was painted by Sir Joshua Reynolds.

This painting portrays not just the family but their way of life, and shows the Spencers to be
still living a formal and aristocratic life at Blenheim. The 4th Duke as a young man would
have considered himself closely aligned to the cultured society to which he belonged.
By marrying Lady Caroline Russell, daughter of the ultra-aristocratic Duke of Bedford,
George Spencer had endorsed the old style of formality rather than the more liberal era of
the 1760s and 1770s.

And so life at Blenheim went on as before. Visitors were able to choose from two different
circuits in the parkland: a short circuit of the pleasure grounds for walkers, where they
could admire the tigress sent to the 4th Duke by Clive of India, Governor of Bengal, or the
new flower garden, described in 1787 as oval in shape with geometric beds and radiating
paths, said to be after the plan of Madame de Pompadour's gardens at Versailles. Those
choosing the walking circuit could admire the Temple of Flora and Health by John Yenn
(see Appendix G) that stood in the centre of the Duke's new pleasure grounds. This temple
was designed in 1785 and built to celebrate one of George III's temporary recoveries from
porphyria.

Fig. 4 Blenheim Palace, the family home of the 4th Duke and Duchess of Marlborough, where Lady
Charlotte Spencer lived till her marriage to Edward Nares.

However, while the 4th Duke was busy on the park and grounds, Duchess Caroline had turned her attention to Blenheim's interior. Mavor's book gives a flavour of what Duchess Caroline had achieved regarding the interiors of the palace with the assistance of William Chambers and John Yenn. It appears that Caroline was probably responsible for the main state rooms being redecorated blue, a fact commented on by Horace Walpole (see Appendix G) in his memoirs. The addition of new chimney pieces by Yenn and pier glasses by James Moore enhanced the rooms, making Blenheim more of a family home.

Mavor, who was for many years a loyal champion of the Spencer family as well as being one of the tutors to the Spencer children, gives a detailed account of the interiors, especially concerning some of the paintings and *objets d'art* at Blenheim:

> In the Bow-Window Room there is a small pendant cabinet, with a miniature painting by Lady Caroline Spencer. In the East Drawing Room there is a charming picture by Sir Joshua Reynolds, representing Lady Charlotte Spencer in the character of a gypsy, telling her brother Lord Henry his fortune. In the Blue Drawing Room, named presumably because the hangings were of blue damask, hang pictures of the Ladies Caroline and Elizabeth Spencer by Romney; the latter is represented as playing on her harp, the former in the act of taking a sketch of her sister. In the Green Drawing Room hanging above the chimney piece is a highly finished and inexpressibly attractive picture of her Grace, the Duchess of Marlborough, in an elegant white dress, by Romney. In the State Drawing Room one of the principal ornaments however of the room is a most superb picture of His Grace, the Duke of Marlborough, in his Garter robes by Romney; it is placed over the chimney. From this beautiful painting Jones has executed a very happy mezzotint: another of the Duchess from Romney paintings has likewise been finished by the same artist. The prints of the theatrical characters, painted by Roberts, are also by Jones.[4]

Of particular interest is the Reynolds painting in the East Drawing Room of Lady Charlotte with her young brother Lord Henry. Painted in 1774–75, it was entitled *The portraits of a young nobleman and his sister* when exhibited at the Royal Academy. At the time, Lady Charlotte would have been nine years old and her brown hair contrasts sharply with her simple white dress, while her favourite brother Lord Henry, aged eight, wears a red Van Dyck dress, a black hat decorated with pink and white feathers, and blue shoes. The painting was sold before 1888 by the 8th Duke via Agnew's to Sir Charles Tennant. It was subsequently purchased in 1923 by the Huntington Collection in San Marino, California.

Having completed the interiors of Blenheim, Duchess Caroline may have decided that the time had come to undertake a new project – that of creating a private theatre. Apart from the fact that she enjoyed the world of the theatre, her own family were growing up fast and would soon be of a marriageable age, and it would provide an opportunity to invite friends and relations to the plays and supper parties. Certain family members could even be invited to join in with the acting, especially if they themselves were of a marriageable age. Her daughters had all the right qualities to attract men: they were beautiful, rich and gifted, being able to dance well, sing beautifully and even play a musical instrument. Thus, in 1786, the stage was set for her to advance her plans, which she realised would cost herself and the Duke dearly.

Duchess Caroline was not the only aristocratic lady to create a private theatre as an integral part of her home. Albinia Hobart (see Appendix G), later Countess of Buckingham, was a case in point. Her husband, the 3rd Earl, was in part a theatre manager. Creating your own private theatre provided an opportunity to show off one's family home and its estate, as well as being a useful method of airing publicly some of the preoccupations of contemporary Georgian society. These included the education of young people and the cultural divide between different levels of society. Importing the metropolitan culture of the theatre world to the provinces contributed to the easing of the social divide between these great families, their tenants and their servants. Such was the success of these private theatres that the professional theatres in London and Bath now found that their winter bookings in 1787 were fewer than usual. At the time, the press reported that 'audiences of a hundred and fifty were not uncommon following the spectacular performances at Richmond House, Hinchingbrooke and Blenheim'.

No doubt Caroline was delighted that her private theatre was considered to be as successful as those of the Duke of Richmond and the 4th Earl of Sandwich. Perhaps it was her pride that blinded her to any dangerous intimacies that might result from having one's own private theatre, especially as Georgian amateur dramatics provided a perfect opportunity to further romantic liaisons.

ACT IV

Scene I:
The Untold Story of Blenheim's
Private Theatricals

Blenheim's private theatricals were planned to coincide with the Spencer family's Christmas festivities of 1786. One of the plays chosen, probably by Duchess Caroline, was Oliver Goldsmith's *She Stoops to Conquer*. Goldsmith wrote the play in 1773, the year before he died, and it became a great favourite at the time with Georgian theatre audiences. A few years later, in 1777, Richard Sheridan was to revive another comedy of manners in *The School for Scandal*. At Blenheim the first act of Sheridan's play *The Critic or A Tragedy Rehearsed*, written in 1779, was included as part of the entertainment, as was Garrick's adapted Massinger's play *The Guardian*. These three plays would have been considered by Caroline as suitable for aspiring young actors to perform, as well as giving good all-round entertainment for her aristocratic friends. The playbills of some of these plays performed at Blenheim are in the British Library, Merton College, Oxford, and in 'The Untold Story' visitor display at Blenheim Palace.

Edward Nares was born in Carey Street, London, on 26 March 1762, the third and youngest son of Sir George Nares (1716–1786), who was a serjeant-at-law, having been called to the Bar in 1741. Edward was educated at Westminster School before going up to Christ Church College, Oxford, in 1779. While at Oxford he met Lord Henry Spencer, who invited him to the first season of Blenheim's private theatricals. Although Edward chose not to be a part of the cast, he was no doubt extremely pleased to have been invited to join the select audience to watch *She Stoops to Conquer*. The play includes one of the great moments of eighteenth-century comedy in which the local squire drills his menservants in how to behave correctly before they wait on his guests at dinner. On the front of Edward's playbill are these words:

BLENHEIM
On the 27th December 1786
will be performed
She Stoops to Conquer, or
The Instructions of a Night

Hardcastle	Lord Henry Spencer
Sir Charles Marlow	Lord Charles Spencer
Young Marlow	Lord Blandford
Hastings	Lord William Russell
Tony Lumpkin	Mr. Edgcumbe
Mrs. Hardcastle	Miss Pigot
Miss Hardcastle	Lady Elizabeth Spencer
Miss Neville	Lady Caroline Spencer

Of the eight members of the cast only two were not family, Richard Edgcumbe (see Appendix E), who played Tony Lumpkin, and Miss Pigot (see Appendix E), who played Mrs Hardcastle. Edgcumbe was an enthusiastic amateur actor and a musician who matriculated at Christ Church in 1781, while Miss Pigot was an old and trusted friend of Duchess Caroline.

In the year before the plays were first put on, Caroline received a letter from her old friend Isabella Pigot. Isabella lived in London and knew all the court gossip, especially concerning the Prince of Wales. In 1785, she wrote to Caroline from Althorp, expressing regret that she had missed seeing her at Blenheim, although she had seen her son Lord Blandford, who was up at Oxford, aged nineteen, Isabella reporting that Caroline's son was behaving himself at university. She praised the beauty of the Oxfordshire countryside around Blenheim and sent her love to the Spencer daughters. At the time, Isabella may well have already been invited by Caroline to take part in the plays.

At Althorp perhaps Isabella also saw the bible given by William III to the 1st Duke of Marlborough. In this bible since 1700, every member of the Spencer family at Althorp has had their name entered, showing where they were born, where they were baptised, who the godparents are, and who they married. Also at Althorp is Kneller's portrait of Duchess Sarah, who cut off her long auburn hair when she was in a rage with her husband. It was not until after the Duke's death that Sarah found that John Churchill had preserved her hair.

Today visitors at Blenheim can see in a glass cabinet in 'The Untold Story' three admission tickets given to Lady Caroline Spencer, Lord Henry Spencer and the Hon. Richard Edgcumbe, all of whom acted in Goldsmith's play on 27 December 1786. Heading the programme for *She Stoops to Conquer* was Lord Henry (see Appendix E), aged sixteen, the youngest member of the cast, playing the part of Hardcastle. He seems to have been a keen actor, participating in most of the productions at Blenheim between 1786 and 1790. His uncle, Lord Charles Spencer (see Appendix E), brother of the 4th Duke, who played the part of Sir Charles Marlow, lived at Wheatfield near Thame in Oxfordshire. It was Lord Charles's son, John Spencer (see Appendix E), born in 1767, who was later persuaded to act alongside his father. In 1790, John married another member of the 1786 cast, his cousin Lady Elizabeth Spencer. Lady Elizabeth, who played the part of Miss Hardcastle, had in fact just celebrated her twenty-first birthday at the time. Her brother George, who as the Duke's eldest son had inherited the family title of Lord Blandford, was twenty-two when he played the part of Young Marlow. His cousin, Lord William Russell (see Appendix E), aged nineteen, played the part of Hastings.

Five of the cast for *She Stoops to Conquer* were to appear the following day in two other plays: *The Guardian* and the first act of *The Critic*, a comedy by Richard Sheridan. *The Critic* was written at a time of great national importance when Britain's empire had expanded with victories over the French in the Seven Years War (1756–63). In 1773, the Boston Tea Party, provoked by the British Government's taxation of tea, was the spark that ignited the American Declaration of Independence in 1776. A year later, the British were defeated at Saratoga and were to suffer further defeats when the French and Spanish officially joined the War of Independence on the colonists' side in 1778–79, precisely when Sheridan was working on *The Critic*. The cast for *The Guardian* was as follows:

Mr. Heartley	Lord William Russell
Sir Charles Clackit	Lord Blandford
Young Clackit	Mr. Edgcumbe
Miss Harriet	Lady Caroline Spencer
Lucy	Miss Pigot

Edgcumbe as Young Clackit was perfect in the role for 'the early coxcombry of the gentleman born when compared with the extravagant buffoonery of the public stage', according to a press report of the time.

The Guardian was to be performed again at Blenheim in 1787, but before that took place the Duke and Duchess decided to create a proper theatre in what was termed 'the greenhouse', originally Vanbrugh's conservatory. Today known as The Orangery, it is used primarily for corporate hospitality and is situated on the south side of the original kitchen courtyard.

By October 1787, the new theatre was ready, and *The World* reported on 4 October 1787:

Theatricals at the Duke of Marlborough's. The arrangement of the Blenheim Plays is finally settled, and in the best style.

On the 17th the House opens with two full dress rehearsals. The first on that day will be given before the Corporation of Woodstock. The second, on the 18th, will be given before the Corporation of Oxford.

Subsequent to this, each piece will be represented twice before all the gentry of the adjacent seats – who may receive invitations on this occasion.

The Theatre, which is very beautiful, contains with great ease to the number of one hundred and sixty persons.

The Cast of the Characters is very judicious, as being well adapted to the talents of the performers.

With every proper speed, the time has been employed in preparing for these festivities; and as the rehearsal of Private Plays is frequently amongst the pleasanter parts of the entertainment – the hours are not to be held as lost.

> To add to the gaiety of these scenes, the Princess de Lamballe [see Marie-Thérèse Louise de
> Savoie-Carignan, Appendix G] last Friday arrived at Blenheim. After passing two days there
> – she went to Oxford, to view the beauties of that scene – and speaks, everywhere most highly,
> as all must – of the splendid hospitalities of the House of Spencer.

On two further occasions *The World* made reference to these private theatricals. On
10 October, it reported that a prologue, written by Mr Berkeley (see Appendix G), was to be
spoken by him before the play *False Delicacy* was performed, and that an address was to be
delivered by the Hon. Mr Edgcumbe; on 15 October, *The World* reported that 'the portraits
of all the performers are to be painted in character' by Roberts of Oxford. It then gave the
cast list for *The Guardian* and *The Liar*, and informed its readers that, on the second night,
the plays *False Delicacy* and *Who's the Dupe?* were to be performed.

The *World*'s critic Bellendenus wrote an account of the plays that included a description
of Lady Charlotte as Miss Rivers. He praised her acting abilities and the musical ability of
her sister Lady Elizabeth, who sang an Italian air with grace and sweetness.

In his early guide book to Blenheim, William Mavor describes Blenheim's improved
private theatre as being:

> … fitted up in a style of peculiar elegance, and with appendages correspondent to the
> munificence and fortune of the owner. The stage is large and is furnished with proper changes
> of scenery and fixtures: the seats for the audience are easy and commodious, and capable of
> accommodating two hundred persons, without including the side-boxes. The whole has a
> grand and pleasing effect.

The side-boxes in the newly designed theatre would have been situated on each side of
the stage and would have been reserved for those in the audience considered by Duchess
Caroline to be socially superior. In fact, the Duchess was only following other great country
houses in their imitations of the London playhouses.

To celebrate the opening of the theatre Mavor composed a lengthy poem entitled 'To His
Grace – The Duke of Marlborough, on converting his green-house into a private theatre'.
He describes the theatre as dove grey, with the niches and friezes in pale blue and the
ornaments and the pilasters in white, with the stage situated at the west end, and the motto
'Laugh where you may, be candid where you can' ribboned above it. Mavor even informs
us that:

> … a new experiment in lighting was made in the shape of reverberators or lens and reflectors,
> which were placed at the extremity of the boxes on each side of the stage and served the
> proscenium, instead of footlights.

This new experiment in lighting was the invention of Pierre Patte, who publicised it in his
Essai sur L'Architecture Théatrale in 1782. Mavor also tells us that the machinery for the
stage was 'contrived by Mr. Austen of Woodstock and a Mr. Talbot led the orchestra of

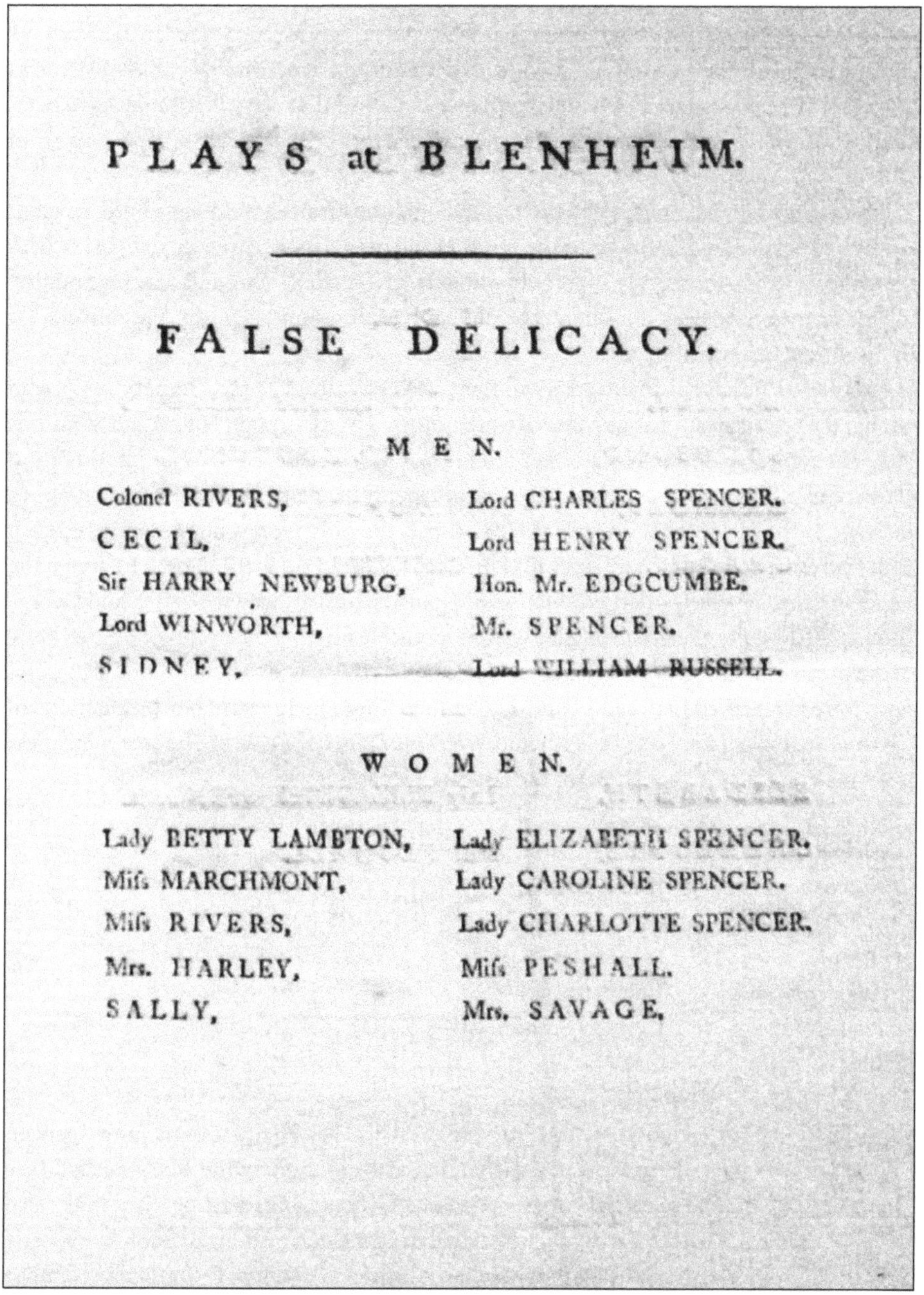

PLAYS at BLENHEIM.

FALSE DELICACY.

M E N.

Colonel RIVERS,	Lord CHARLES SPENCER.
CECIL,	Lord HENRY SPENCER.
Sir HARRY NEWBURG,	Hon. Mr. EDGCUMBE.
Lord WINWORTH,	Mr. SPENCER.
SIDNEY,	Lord WILLIAM RUSSELL.

W O M E N.

Lady BETTY LAMBTON,	Lady ELIZABETH SPENCER.
Miss MARCHMONT,	Lady CAROLINE SPENCER.
Miss RIVERS,	Lady CHARLOTTE SPENCER.
Mrs. HARLEY,	Miss PESHALL.
SALLY,	Mrs. SAVAGE.

Fig. 5 The playbill of *False Delicacy* with Lady Charlotte Spencer playing the role of Miss Rivers in 1787 in the newly created theatre at Blenheim Palace.

professional musicians'. It is of interest that when Miss Pigot wrote to the Duchess in 1785 from Althorp she made an appointment with a Mr Austen. It seems likely that Austen was employed at Blenheim as a carpenter or handyman and that Miss Pigot may have been partly responsible for the installation of the scenery for the theatricals first performed in 1786.

The orchestral music played by the professional musicians would have been selected carefully in order to demonstrate the musical talents of those Spencer daughters who performed in these theatricals, especially with regard to their singing and dancing abilities. The music may have been chosen by one of Oxford's most famous musical professors, Dr Philip Hayes (see Appendix G).

Another professional involved was Michael Angelo Rooker (see Appendix G) who painted the ten scenery changes, one of which showed Marlborough House and St James's Park. No complete designs by Rooker are known to have survived, although there is a watercolour showing him working on a landscape in his paint shop or scene loft above the stage at the Haymarket Theatre *c.* 1788. This is the only representation of an English paint frame or scene known up until 1874. Rooker had been the artist chosen to design the scenery in the Covent Garden production of Goldsmith's play, which Garrick and George Colman the Elder as theatre managers were responsible for.

The theatrical season at Blenheim held later on in 1787 was an extensive one, as several plays were performed between 19 and 27 October. These included major productions of *The Guardian, The Liar, False Delicacy* and *Who's the Dupe?* The cast of *The Liar*, which was performed on every night except for the last two, was as follows:

Wilding	Hon. Mr. Edgcumbe
Old Wilding	Lord H. Spencer
Sir J. Eliot	Lord W. Russell
Papillon	Mr. Spencer
Miss Grantham	Lady E. Spencer
Miss Godfrey	Lady Car. Spencer
Kitty	Miss Peshall

The only new actor included in these private theatricals at Blenheim was John Spencer, who played the part of Papillon in the Blenheim production, while Mary Peshall (see Appendix E), who had been in previous productions, played the part of Kitty. Mary also recited the epilogue to *The Guardian*, which had been written by John Randolph, formerly professor of poetry at Oxford University and later Bishop of London. Oxford's most famous hotel, The Randolph, is named after the venerable professor.

On 26 and 27 October 1787, *False Delicacy* and *Who's the Dupe?* were performed. Such was their popularity that they were performed again on 17 November, when Lady Charlotte appeared as Miss Rivers and the role of Sally in *False Delicacy* was played by a Mrs Savage. This was once more reported by *The World* in November, it also stating that on the last night Countess Harcourt attended with a foreign nobleman. *The World* not only commented on the colour scheme of the theatre but also described in detail the costumes worn by the actors in *False Delicacy*: 'Lady Charlotte's dress as Miss Rivers was à la bergere. Her hat in a new style of elegance – her gown a Devonshire brown – a white petticoat.'

However, there is a more detailed account of these theatrical performances by Frederick Reynolds, who was invited as a friend of Monck Berkeley (see Appendix G). Reynolds was a playwright, educated at Westminster School, where he became a friend to the son and heir of the Duke of Bedford. This connection with the Bedfords would have eased his invitation to Blenheim, as Duchess Caroline was the 4th Duke of Bedford's daughter. Reynolds was a gregarious person with many theatrical, literary and political friends; a keen cricketer, he was also a member of the MCC. He wrote some hundred theatrical pieces over forty years in a profession that was financially precarious, and it is possible that the title of his play *Laugh Where you Can*, written in 1798, is a memory of the motto set above the stage at Blenheim. In 1826, he published his autobiography entitled *The Life and Times of Frederick Reynolds*, which is a lively portrayal of mainly late eighteenth- and early nineteenth-century theatrical life, including the performances at Blenheim. In it he describes how Monck Berkeley came with two other actor-dramatists, Joseph Holman and Miles Peter Andrews, to see the private theatricals at Blenheim in October 1787:

> We arrived at Woodstock, about seven o'clock in the evening October 19th, 1787. Presenting our tickets to the officers at the lodge we were immediately admitted. Advancing along the avenue we reached the River Glyme, over which was thrown a handsome bridge. Crossing to the other side, we approached the statue of the great Duke of Marlborough. Entering the quadrangle of the palace we were conducted towards the theatre, originally a green-house, but then enlarged and embellished and capable of accommodating up to two hundred spectators. Our friend Monck Berkeley was the author and speaker of the prologue and had taken care to secure us places. We seated ourselves and in a few minutes the play commenced. During the performance the Duke who heard the clattering of cups concluded that refreshments needed to be served and just at the moment when the hero played by Lord Henry was on the point of rushing into the heroine's arms the Duke addressed the performers by exclaiming, 'Stop – some of the company want tea,' and added, 'Ladies and gentlemen, you shall be served immediately.'

This was the first time, says Reynolds, that refreshments were given in the middle of a play. After this a short dance ensued by the actors, much to the delight of the audience. During the farce *Who's the Dupe?*:

> Andrews became so impatient, except for the singing of an Italian air by Lady Charlotte, which she sang most delightfully, all my exertions would barely have restrained him from leaving the theatre. Our friend Berkeley conducted us to meet the Duke and Duchess where Andrews was heard to say, 'My dear friends, for your own sakes, I speak my mind – your theatre is too cold and you have chosen a dull obsolete play. Even real sterling talent would have done nothing with the heavy walking ladies and gentlemen in *False Delicacy*. To be sure I liked the dancing and the Italian air, yes my dear friends, and I liked the servant with a letter.'[1]

This was a reference to the Duke's porter, who in a minor role spoke his one line so naturally and audibly that Andrews had applauded. Reynolds also stated that he was unable to hear one line of the twenty that these really private actors uttered!

The account is interesting in stating that Lady Charlotte sang some Italian airs. A gifted musician, she was painted in her costume by James Roberts of Oxford in 1787. The following year, the oil painting was reproduced as a mezzotint by J. Jones. In Hugh Kelly's play *False Delicacy*, her character, Miss Rivers, is persuaded by Sir Harry Newburgh, played by Edgcumbe, to elope with him, thus going behind her father's back. This plot was more than prophetic, as ten years later Charlotte was to elope from Blenheim in order to marry Edward Nares, one of the actors of the 1789 productions, –a dangerous liaison indeed for a daughter of such illustrious parents.

Frederick Reynolds' description of his visit to Blenheim concludes by stating that the main refreshments were served on trays by ten footmen, so that the audience could enjoy tea, coffee and orgeat (a cooling drink made from barley or almonds and orange-water). Owing to Andrews' outspoken remarks to the Spencers, the young men were not invited to stay after the show and dine at Blenheim. On their way back to Oxford, Holman was heard to say, 'Andrews, you ought to acknowledge that there was one great actor in the Marlborough family.'

'Which, which, my dear Sir?'

'Why their heroic ancestor – the glorious consumer of gun powder.'

Whether Reynolds deliberately included the gunpowder reference is of interest, as Andrews' hobby concerned the manufacture of gunpowder. Later in his life he set up his own gunpowder company near London.

Of these four young men, Holman and Reynolds achieved celebrity status in their life, while Andrews rose in society from being an actor and dramatist to become a commander of a Westminster contingent of the Prince of Wales's Loyal Volunteers in October 1803. There is a painting of the Duke of Kent with his staff at Horse Guards Parade, with Andrews suitably attired in military uniform at this time of political unrest with France amidst the real threat of a French invasion.

On the night 20 October 1787, *The Guardian* and *The Liar* were performed. *The World* reported that the former 'had been presented with more taste and delicacy, and the scenes between Young Clackit [Edgcumbe] and Harriet [Caroline] would scarcely ever again be so well finished'. In *The Liar* Edgcumbe made a hit with the audience as Young Wilding, 'rousing incessant laughter in the last scene'.

Monck Berkeley had written another prologue for this play:

> The night our laughing Muse will paint a youth
> At constant war with heaven descended truth.
> Yet still she hopes by candor's rules you'll try her,
> Nor kill with frown severe, one harmless Lyar.

Jones's mezzotint of *The Guardian* shows that the scenery was virtually the same as in the last scene of *False Delicacy*, with the addition of a draped curtain and an additional view through a door.

On 23 October, the programme was varied by performing *False Delicacy* and *The Liar*, which was watched by the Vice-Chancellor of Oxford, two bishops and three deans. The *Morning Chronicle* commented, 'May the example of encouraging this most noble and rational amusement be followed by patrons equally capable of doing honour to it.' All of which would have been greatly appreciated by the Duke and Duchess and by these young, aspiring actors.

Two days later, on the fourth night, *The Guardian* and *The Liar* were again performed. Among the audience was another local enthusiast of private theatricals, Lady Saye and Sele. She lived at Broughton Castle, situated to the north of Blenheim near Banbury, which is still in the Saye and Sele family. A skilful harpist, Lady Saye and Sele was also an accomplished actress and performed in private theatricals at Adlestrop House, near Stow-on-the-Wold in Gloucestershire, in 1787. Adlestrop House was owned by the Leigh family, cousins of Jane Austen's mother.

For the final two performances on the nights of 26 and 27 October, *False Delicacy* and *Who's the Dupe?* were performed. After this Mary Peshall spoke a farewell address and Duchess Caroline announced that there would be a further theatrical season at Christmas. In fact, it was not to be until after the new year of 1788 that the season really got under way, due to further improvements being made to the stage and the auditorium. Once again, Mavor describes this makeover of the theatre in his publication on Blenheim:

> Many valuable improvements and decorations, several beautiful scenes by Rooker have been added to the former suite; and new arrangements made for the accommodation of the spectators are such as judgement and experience united have evidently dictated.

On 10 January 1788, *The Guardian* and *The Liar* were performed and two new plays were introduced into the repertoire of plays on 18 January: George Colman's *The Musical Lady* and General John Burgoyne's *The Maid of the Oaks*. When *The Maid of the Oaks* was performed in London in 1775, the actress Frances Abington played the part of Lady Bab Lardoon. The play included these words for Lady Bab, 'You shall see what an excellent actress I should have made, if fortune had not unluckily brought me into the world an Earl's daughter.' Whether Lady Elizabeth Spencer, who played this role, shared these lofty sentiments is doubtful, though her younger sister Charlotte may well have harboured such thoughts, particularly before her marriage. John Burgoyne (see Appendix G) was a soldier turned dramatist, *The Maid of the Oaks*, written in 1775, and *The Heiress*, in 1786, being among his best known plays. Duchess Caroline had specially requested that Frances Abington should play Lady Bab masquerading as the shepherdess Philly Nettletop: 'On seeing Mrs. Abington perform Lady Bab Lardoon, at the Request of Her Grace, the Duchess of Marlborough, spoke these lines in the play:'

> Nature and fashion now no more
> Shall disagree as heretofore,
> But both their force unite

Convinc'd one female can display
Th'extended pow'rs of either's way,
And variegate delight.[2]

Colman's play *The Musical Lady* must have been successful at Blenheim, as it was performed again in October 1788. The playbills for these plays still exist and show that the cast was virtually identical for both plays:

The Musical Lady
Men

Old Mask	Lord Henry Spencer
Mask	Hon. Mr. Edgcumbe
Freeman	Lord Charles Spencer
Rosin	Mr. [John] Spencer
Servant	[unnamed]

Women

Sophy	Lady Elizabeth Spencer
Lady Scrape	Lady Caroline Spencer
Laundress	Mrs. Savage [crossed out and played by Lord William Russell]

The Maid of the Oaks
Men

Mr. Oldworth	Lord Charles Spencer
Old Groveby	Hon. Mr. Jenkinson
Sir Harry Groveby	Mr. [John] Spencer
Mr. Dupeley	Hon. Mr. Edgcumbe
Harry	Lord Henry Spencer

Women

| Lady Bab Lardoon | Lady Elizabeth Spencer |
| Maria | Lady Caroline Spencer |

The one new addition to the cast was Robert Banks Jenkinson (see Appendix E) who was up at Christ Church College with Lord Henry. Jenkinson, who went up to Oxford at the age of sixteen, would have worn the distinctive gold-laced nobleman's gown and was known as Jenky by his graduate friends. In *The Maid of the Oaks*, Edgcumbe sang an Italian air, the evening concluding with a ballet in which Lady Caroline and Lady Elizabeth danced with Richard Edgcumbe and John Spencer. The music for this was provided by the Duke's own band. For the first three nights of the performance the audience was drawn from the inhabitants of Woodstock, Witney and Oxford respectively, and for the last two nights the university and the gentry and clergy of the county were given tickets on application. Holders of tickets who were unable to utilise them were asked to return them the day before the performance.

On 7 February 1788, *The World* reported on James Roberts' paintings of the actors in *False Delicacy*. In fact, Roberts painted three scenes, one from *The Guardian* and two from *False Delicacy*, which hang in the Smoking Corridor of Blenheim's private east wing. All three paintings were engraved by J. Jones of Marylebone, and published on 8 December 1788; his mezzotints hang nearby and can be admired by today's visitors to Blenheim.

In his painting of *The Guardian*, taken from Act 1 Scene 1 which was performed in 1786 and 1787, Young Clackit was played by Richard Edgcumbe, Mr Heartley by Lord William Russell, and Miss Harriet by Lady Caroline Spencer. Roberts' second painting from *False Delicacy* is taken from the last scene of Act 3. This included the part of Cecil played by Lord Henry Spencer, Betty Lampton by Lady Elizabeth Spencer, Lord Winworth by John Spencer and Mrs Harley by Miss Peshall. The third painting, also from *False Delicacy*, Act 4, Scene 2, shows that the part of Colonel Rivers was played by Lord Charles, and Miss Rivers by Lady Charlotte dressed in the latest French fashion as a shepherdess.

Despite *The World* reporting on 21 August 1788 that 'the theatrical at the Duke of Marlborough's will be in November next', it was in fact in October that a further theatrical season got under way. More additions had been made to the scenery by James Roberts and by Thomas Greenwood the Elder. Greenwood was chief scene painter at Drury Lane, and his bill for painting the scenery for the plays still exists and reads as follows:

> By order of her Grace the Duchess, Painted the Frontispiece with Pillasters,
> Curtains and Cornice (5 gns); Painted two busts in circular frames (2 gns);
> Painted an Architect drop with a View of a Garden thro' an Arch (10 gns).

This is interesting in that it appears to support the premise that it was Duchess Caroline who was responsible for establishing the private theatre at Blenheim, particularly as she held the purse strings.

On the nights of 17, 18, 20 and 21 October 1788, two plays were performed: *The Musical Lady* and *The Provok'd Husband*. The former play is a farce premiered in London in 1762, the other being written by Sir John Vanbrugh but left unfinished and entrusted to Colley Cibber for completion. This play was originally in five acts and had first been performed in 1728, the Blenheim version having been shortened to three acts. The cast for *The Provok'd Husband* was once again dominated by the Spencer family:

Men

| Lord Townly | Lord William Russell |
| Mr. Manly | Lord Charles Spencer |

Women

Lady Townly	Lady Elizabeth Spencer
Lady Grace	Lady Caroline Spencer
Mrs. Trusty	Mrs. Savage

On 20 October, *The World* reported as follows:

> The very pretty theatre of this magnificent palace opened on the 16th and the performances
> of the plays both passed with as much elegance and ingenuity as at last year's theatrical. Lady
> Elizabeth was very animated in each characteristic quality of Lady Townly in *The Provok'd
> Husband*. From grave to gay – from lively to severe – and Lady Caroline Spencer acted the part
> Lady Grace, if acting it can be called, where the pure repose of the scene harmonises so exactly
> with the native charms of the performer.

Describing *The Provok'd Husband* as a comedy and *The Musical Lady* as an entertainment,
The World went on to say:

> This truly elegant theatre has received great additions and improvements since last year in its
> scenery, decorations and accommodation … the distribution of tickets at Blenheim is very
> liberal and for five nights [these performances] are but the prelude to a more magnificent
> theatrical expected about Christmas.

On 24 October, it reported that there was a 'commodity of good names' at the Blenheim
theatrical, which included the 'Duchess of Bedford, Lady Jersey, Lady Di Beauclerk, the
Marquis of Worcester, Sir Harry Englefield, Sir G. and Lady Beaumont, Sir John and Lady
Skinner, General Rooke – all were there – the Dean of CCC was not there'.

The Dean of Christ Church College at the time was Cyril Jackson, who had replaced
Lewis Bagot in 1783. In 1784, James Blackstone was a Commoner of Christ Church College
and was granted the use of the library by the Dean, who vouched that 'the indulgence
would be advantageous to him and would not be abused'.[3] Later in his life Blackstone would
be appointed as the 4th Duke of Marlborough's steward. Of particular interest is the visit
of Lady Diana Beauclerk, the oldest daughter of the 3rd Duke of Marlborough and thus
the aunt of the Spencer children, who was to befriend Lady Charlotte after her marriage to
Edward Nares. Lady Diana was a gifted artist and her exquisite pastels are much admired
today by both the Marlborough family and visitors to Blenheim.

On 25 October, *The World* reported:

> The Marlborough Theatrical is to be painted by Roberts; but whether in a series of portraits,
> as in the former performance of *False Delicacy*, or in one group, the Duke has not yet
> determined.

The cast of *The Musical Lady* on this occasion was as follows:

Men
Old Mask	Lord William Russell
Mask	Mr. Spencer [John]
Freeman	Lord Charles Spencer

Rosin	Mr. Robinson	
Servant	[unnamed]	
Women		
Sophy	Lady Elizabeth Spencer	
Lady Scrape	Lady Caroline Spencer	
Laundress	Mrs. Savage [crossed out and played by	Lord William Russell]

The only new actor, Mr Robinson, may have been Frederick Robinson (see Appendix G), son of a friend of the 4th Duke of Marlborough. In 1785, Frederick married Catherine Gertrude Harris, the eldest daughter of James Harris, 1st Earl of Malmesbury (see Appendix G), who was a well-known musician at that time. As the daughter of such a man, she would have been brought up knowing some of the celebrated musicians of that time, such as Handel, but whether Catherine was involved at all musically in the private theatricals is uncertain. It is curious, though, that the farce chosen was entitled *The Musical Lady*, which was a satire on sentimentality and English tastes. In a letter George Spencer, when a bachelor, wrote to Robinson, he confided about his love for Lady Caroline, daughter of the Duke of Bedford:

O my dear Robinson, since we last met strange things have happened to your poor friend. I have lost the greatest prospect of happiness I ever formed to myself, but in lieu of it I have gained a certain philosophical apathy, a sang-froid upon the events of this world that partly recompense the severity of my loss. You may guess that love alone can have wrought such a change of sentiments.[4]

While on the Grand Tour in Italy, George Spencer had written to Robinson that he would keep clear of love, 'for if it once gets hold of me I can no longer answer for myself'. All of this showed the anguished state of his feelings once he had fallen in love. George and Caroline were to live together happily as husband and wife for nearly fifty years.

At the performance of *The Provok'd Husband* and *The Musical Lady* on the first night of the event, on Friday 17 October 1788, was Agnes Witts. She was married to Edward Witts (see Appendix V), who had inherited the family wool stapling business in Chipping Norton, Oxfordshire. In 1775, at the time of his marriage, Edward Witts bought Swerford Park, near Chipping Norton. The following is an entry from his wife's diary:

1788 Friday Oct. 17th. The same kind of weather but cloudy till the afternoon when it was beautifully bright & clear. Mr. Witts went early to a Justice Meeting at Adderbury the rest walket about till time to Dress when my Bro' went to see Mrs. Rollinson, & Mrs. Naper & I to adorn ourselves for the Play at Blenheim, Mrs. Penyston coming in the meantime was unable to receive her. Dined early & reach'd Blenheim by seven, a genteel & crowded House, the performance of three acts of the Provok'd Husband & the Musical Lady most amusing. Lady Elizabeth a capital performance, came home by two o'clock much pleased with our entertainment. Rec'd Letters from Mrs. Rollinson & Mrs. Granville.[5]

The genteel people were in fact the local gentry who had been invited to watch the performance and partake of the supper afterwards. The highlight of the evening seems to have been Lady Elizabeth Spencer's role as Sophy in *The Musical Lady*. Although Agnes Witts does not mention her friend Mrs Savage, it is of interest as Mrs Savage had originally been cast to play the part of a laundress. For some reason or other she was unable to perform and the part was played by Lord William Russell. Quite what the 'genteel' audience thought of this cross-dressing role is unknown.

Just before the theatre reopened in August 1789, Agnes visited Blenheim in order to 'Dine at the Public Day'. This is what she wrote in her diary:

> 1789 Tuesday Aug. 18th. No change of weather quite as fine, Mr. Evans breakfasted here, & we went to Dine at the Public Day at Blenheim, rather warm going there, the Dutchess not being well did not appear till Ten, but the young Ladies amply supplied her place at Dinner where was 28 in number, only 9 Ladies & those not very resplendent but I fell into a very pleasant party & liked it very well, home between 10 & 11 by the finest light of the stars I ever saw.[6]

Preparing for the private theatricals and the Public Day supper party seems to have been all too much for Duchess Caroline, which is why she did not appear until ten o'clock. Fortunately, the Spencer girls were able to entertain the twenty-eight people. Perhaps the hot weather also accounted for her comment as to why the ladies were 'not very resplendent'.

Earlier that year, the play *The Deaf Lover* by Frederick Pilon (see Appendix G) had been performed on Wednesday 18 March at Blenheim 'by special desire of His Grace the 4th Duke of Marlborough'. Among the cast of players was Edward Nares, in the role of Captain Meadows, Lady Charlotte playing Betty Blossom. Other well-known personalities who performed in the play included Sir William Chambers, John Yenn, Lady Susan Stewart (see Appendix E) and Lady Fitzroy (see Appendix Y). Edward certainly seems to have heeded the eighteenth-century notice concerning 'Conduct when Behind the Scenes', which advises the players to maintain silence at all times in the wings of the theatre. In his journals he kept silent about this play and the role that his future wife Lady Charlotte played.

The theatre reopened on 21 August for just two days during a heat wave, when fewer tickets were distributed than normal. Among the audience as reported in *The World* on 26 August was Charles Bowles (see Appendix G), who lived quite close to Blenheim at The Hall, North Aston, just off the main Oxford–Banbury road. The Bowles family were well known locally for the private theatricals held at their home. Bowles was also invited to the November performances in 1789.

The first play performed in August 1789 was a new one in the Blenheim repertoire, the comedy *False Appearances*, which had been translated into English by General Henry Seymour Conway (see Appendix G) from Boissy's French play. Conway had also written a prologue for a play performed at Richmond House in 1787, Arthur Murphy's *The Way to Keep Him*, in which the general supported amateur dramatists 'as a retreat from the bustle of the public theatres'. At the time, public theatres were playing to diminishing audiences due to the growing popularity of private theatricals. The aristocracy held the view that by supporting private theatres they were only doing what the lower orders of society did with their support for public entertainment. Conway's prologue does seem to support this view. It reads:

> While here, in this fair Garden's calm retreat
> At once the Virtues, and the Muse's seat;
> Where friendly suns their kindest influence shed
> Each tender plant may dauntless raise its head.

The cast for *False Appearances* was as follows:

Men	
Baron	Mr. [John] Spencer
Marquis	Lord Henry Spencer
Governor	Lord Charles Spencer
Abbé	Mr. Nares
Robert	Servants
Champaign	
Women	
Countess	Lady Elizabeth Spencer
Lucile	Lady Caroline Spencer
Caelia	Miss Peshall
Lisette	Mrs. Savage

On 25 August 1789, *The World* reported that 'Mr Nares, son of the late judge, was the only new recruit, and a very valuable acquisition he makes. His Abbé could not be surpassed.'

When Edward had first been invited by Lord Henry to participate in the theatricals, he had felt unable to due to the death of his father in 1786, but he finally succumbed following repeated invitations from the whole Spencer family. As a loyal son, he would have considered it totally inappropriate in the circumstances to accept invitations to join the Blenheim cast, although socially correct to attend as a spectator. This accounts for the tickets in the Nares memorabilia at Merton for theatricals at Blenheim in which he did not take part. The Duchess told Edward that it was impossible for her to express how much they appreciated the pleasure of his company, and that the more he could make it convenient to be at Blenheim, the more happy he would make them.

Marian Fowler in her book *Blenheim: Biography of a Palace,* states that in 1787 'the Blenheim young people, feeling the growing silence and inertia inside Blenheim house oppressing them, persuaded their parents to mount some theatricals'. She goes on to say that in 1789 a new player joined the cast: 'He was a friend of Lord Henry's called Edward Nares, and was very short and very sprightly, with a large nose, blue eyes and fair, wavy hair.'[7] In his memoirs Edward wrote that 'those who have been at Blenheim since can have no idea how princely the whole establishment was at that time, and yet how little the family moved with the world at large'.

A popular play for amateurs at the time was *Who's the Dupe?* by Hannah Cowley (see Appendix G), which was considered to be not too demanding for the actors. At Blenheim the cast for this play was:

Men

Doiley	Lord Henry Spencer
Sandford	Lord Chas. Spencer
Granger	Mr. [John] Spencer
Gradus	Mr. Nares

Women

Elizabeth	Lady Eliz. Spencer
Charlotte	Miss Peshall

Reporting on 26 August 1789, *The World* stated, 'Mr Nares, as an *élève* [pupil] of the Wynnstay Theatre, does it infinite credit.' Whether Edward as a young man took any part in the private theatricals at Wynnstay he does not state in his memoirs, although he does write about his clever academic cousin Robert, who was tutor to the household at Wynnstay from 1779 to 1783. At Wynnstay private theatricals were performed from 1770 onwards, during the time of the 4th Baronet, Sir Watkin Williams Wynn, and also during the 5th Baronet's time. In his journal Edward also wrote about his experiences as an actor at Blenheim and even about the part of Gradus in *Who's the Dupe?* Apparently he suddenly assumed so grotesque an attitude that Lord Charles Spencer not only missed his cue but had to run laughing from the stage! Fortunately, Edward managed to keep the audience amused until Lord Charles was sufficiently recovered to return on stage. Edward's verdict on these 1789 theatricals confirms the opinion of Frederick Reynolds of the 1787 productions:

> The newspapers of the day gave us credit for being capital actors; but I am persuaded none of us pretended to be so; it would have been absurd and preposterous. As comic actors we were satisfied to make people laugh, and whatever our lack of histrionic talent it was fully compensated by the elegance of the theatre and the scenery, the splendour of the dresses, and the good management of the whole.

Edward fully understood that it was the setting and the environs of private theatres that compensated for such amateur performances. Even though socially he may have felt out of his depth, he knew he could more than hold his own. In his memoirs Edward also discusses his embarrassment and diffidence as an actor, but writes:

> Once on stage to my utter surprise, much of my embarrassment entirely vanished. The glare of the lamps in front of the stage prevented my seeing the audience and the dress of the character I personated made me feel as if I was the character itself.

The glare of lamps to which Edward refers would have been the new footlights created by Pierre Patte.

A second performance was proposed in November 1789, but Edward was laid up with what he terms 'a dangerous illness from which I was not fully recovered'. This meant that he would act in only one of the two plays to be performed, *False Appearances*, but not in *The Maid of the Oaks*, for fear of fatigue. Lord Henry was also prevented from acting and instead the role was taken over by George Spencer, Lord Blandford (see Appendix E), his older brother, who had last acted in the plays in 1786 and had recently returned home from the Grand Tour. The only new actor to participate in the November 1789 season of private theatricals was Thomas Parker (see Appendix E), brother of the Earl of Macclesfield, who took over Robert Jenkinson's role as Old Groveby in *The Maid of the Oaks*. This farce had been written in 1775, in honour of the marriage in 1774 of Lady Elizabeth Hamilton to Edward Stanley, 12th Earl of Derby (see Appendix G), whose family home was at Knowsley Hall, near Liverpool. The plays in which Parker performed ran for five successive nights, starting on 26 November and ending on 30 November 1789.

Amongst the audience on one of these nights were not only the two distinguished generals Conway and Burgoyne but Caroline Powys's two older sons, who were given a lift in Conway's carriage all the way from Henley to Woodstock. Caroline Powys's diary records, 'Young Phil and Tom went with General Conway to the Blenheim play. We were all offer'd tickets but the weather was so bad we declined going.' Phil and Tom were no doubt only too happy to accompany their distinguished neighbour in his carriage. While Conway was looking forward to seeing his old military friend Burgoyne, it is known that later in his life Tom Powys was an admirer of Jane Austen's sister Cassandra. In his journal Edward Nares describes how the two old generals sat side by side, 'uncritical and beaming', immediately in front of the stage, and 'it was reported to us that they express'd themselves well pleas'd. It might be so, but they could hardly be expected to say otherwise.'

The cast had expected to meet Conway at supper, 'but were disappointed as he returned to his seat near Henley'. Quite what treats the invited guests from the audience had for supper Edward does not say, but the hospitality of the 4th Duke and Duchess was legendary, especially early on in their marriage. For example, the birth of their second son was marked by a gargantuan supper of roast beef, mutton and pork, chicken, ducks, geese, a boar's head, an apple pie and two plum puddings.[8] Supper was taken any time after nine in the evening; thus there would have been nothing unusual in serving the meal after the performance. The invitation to supper for such favoured guests as the 6th Duke and Duchess of Beaufort and the Earl and Countess of Abingdon and their families was all part of the entertainment of attending the theatricals.

Edward took his role of the Abbé seriously in *False Appearances*. His part had in fact been added onto Boissy's original French comedy by Conway, a fact that Edward would have been only too well aware of. In his memoirs he continues:

> As to my own performance, it was so extoll'd in the newspaper that had I been capable of being deluded by such exaggerations, I might have fancied myself a Roscius … Some who acted with me deserved the compliment. Fine acting we none of us pretended to.

Edward emphasises that they are only amateurs when it comes to acting, while at the same time giving most of the credit to his fellow actors. In addition, he stresses the uncritical attitude of a friendly audience, when he writes:

> It may easily be suppos'd that we had only good-natur'd audiences to witness our performances, that we play'd light pieces, and made no attempt at tragedy. The theatricals offer'd opportunities of entertaining their neighbours, of which the Duke and Duchess gladly availed themselves.

The guests on the night of 26 November were members of the corporations of Oxford, Woodstock and Witney with their wives and families. The following night was for the university, and the third night was reserved for the Duchess's invitations to the county and neighbourhood. The final night, when the audience consisted solely of friends and family of the cast, was the most select of all.

Just after Christmas, two more evenings of entertainment were given, on 28 and 29 December 1789, the doors for the performances opening at half past six and the performances beginning at seven. Two new plays were performed: *The Deaf Lover*, and *Cross Purposes* by William O'Brien (see Appendix G). Edward wrote an additional scene for the farce *Cross Purposes*, with a glee to be sung at the end. As previously, the names of household servants who took part did not appear on the playbill. The scenery was again painted by James Roberts of Oxford, with ten scene changes. In his journal Edward wrote that it had been hoped that 'their majesties would have been present, but public business prevented it', adding that 'these two pieces were the last we performed as the theatre was from this time shut up'.

In 1789, the whole of England was gripped in doom and gloom by the momentous events taking place across the Channel with the onslaught of the French Revolution. In his memoirs Edward emphasised this:

> From the busy state retiring
> Now our mask'd disguise is o'er
> Mimic scenes no more admiring
> Smiles of truth may we implore.
> No cold critics here intrude
> No proud judges prone to blame,
> Here no censors harsh and rude
> Check our blameless hopes of fame.
> Whilst the stage of life we range
> Sure from trouble to be free,
> Harmless is th' attempt to change
> Gloomy hours for mirth and glee.

In late December 1789, *The World* reported a rumour that the Blenheim theatricals would reopen with Lord Henry's support, but nothing came of this. Whether it was the French

Revolution, or George III's illness of 1788–89, or the imminent marriages of some of the cast that led to the closure of the private theatre Edward does not state in his journal.

The first of the family to marry was Lady Elizabeth, in March 1790, to her cousin John Spencer. The romance between them must have developed during the time they were performing in the private theatricals. According to a letter dated 24 January 1790, written by George Leveson-Gower to his aunt Lady Stafford, 'the romance had been going on for a year' and 'Lady Elizabeth's marriage was a surprise but the knowing ones say that they liked each other over this last twelve months'. He goes on to say that the Duchess of Bedford approved of this 'charming match' and that the Duchess thought 'Mr. Spencer a good actor, good musician and a good composer and that they will be very happy'.[9]

Lady Elizabeth's wedding was to be closely followed by two other members of the cast of Blenheim's theatricals. In 1791, the Marquess of Blandford, the oldest Spencer son, married Lady Susan Stewart, and in November of that year Leveson-Gower wrote a letter to his mother about one of the balls he attended at Blenheim, presumably to celebrate the wedding:

> There was on Thursday a very splendid ball at Blenheim, made splendid by the variegated lamps and colours of the frames at supper. The company was by no means beautiful and the ladies Spencer about the only girls with whom I was acquainted. Lady Caroline being the first dancer, I thought proper to ask Her Ladyship and figured away three dances with her.[10]

It was also in 1791 that Hannah Humphrey published *The Siege of Blenheim* or *The New System of Gunning Discovered* by James Gillray (see Appendix G). At that time, Gillray's cartoons were so popular that there were often queues outside the print shop in London where he worked. Gillray died in 1815 while still in his fifties, a victim of hard drinking and overwork.

The amateur novelist Mrs Gunning had been, as Lady Henrietta Spencer writes:

> … so keen to marry her daughter to the Marlborough heir that she forged a score of love letters, purportedly from George to her daughter, in an attempt to blackmail him. The ruse failed and George, still reeling from the experience, speedily married Lady Susan Stewart, the daughter of the 7th Earl of Galloway.[11]

Perhaps Mrs Gunning was not the only mother keen to marry off her daughters as speedily as possible. Certainly, Duchess Caroline would have felt she had achieved most of her marriage objectives with regard to her own children by marrying them off into other aristocratic families, and there was therefore no need to continue with the expense of private theatricals. By 1790, the Duchess was left with just two daughters of a marriageable age, Lady Charlotte and Lady Anne, as her youngest daughter Amelia Sophia, born in 1775, was only fifteen years old.

Quite when the relationship between Lady Charlotte and Edward Nares developed is difficult to fully ascertain from Edward's memoirs. He gives a mixed account of the events, covering up the true state of affairs by admitting that during the four years he was the bursar of Merton College he was encouraged to stay at Blenheim by Duchess Caroline as frequently as possible. It seems that he was particularly popular with the two youngest of the Spencer children, and both Lady Charlotte and Edward seem to have spent a good deal of time devising games to play with the children. In time, all this would lead Edward and Charlotte to the altar in 1797, followed by the birth of their first child in 1798. Edward never fully explained in his memoirs what happened to his wife during the difficult births of their children, and these events may have hastened his wife's premature death in 1802. Perhaps when he wrote his memoirs it was still too painful, or maybe he felt it was better to leave an account suitable for posterity to read. Nor does he explain how he met his second wife Cordelia Adams, whom he married in 1803, other than to say that she was from a local family and a good mother to all his children.

By the time William Mavor published his *Oxford University and City Guide* in 1819, Edward had been the rector of Biddenden in Kent for twenty years. Mavor included a short description of Blenheim and its private theatre in his guide book, stating that 'the theatre is a neat room, well suited for the purpose of Drama and contains good scenery. It has not been used for many years.'[12]

Whether it was Duchess Caroline's decision to put an end to the theatre at Blenheim is not explained in Edward's memoirs. Neither does Edward elaborate on the blossoming relationship with Lady Charlotte, which would in time lead to even greater dramas in the Spencer household at Blenheim in the 1790s.

Scene II:
Romance and Marriage

Edward Nares kept a detailed journal of his life, which he wrote up in two leather-bound volumes. These were presented to Merton College, Oxford, by his great granddaughter Miss Agatha White, who lived at The Lawn, Holybourne, near Alton in Hampshire. Exactly when and why Edward decided to compile these journals about his life, apart from his concerns for his children and their descendants, he does not fully explain, but it is probable that they were written sometime after 1808. In the introduction to his first journal Edward writes:

> Since life is above all things precarious and God only knows how long I may live, and as I have at present children so long that though it should please God to spare their lives, I may not live to see them come to maturity; and as it is reasonable to think, that when they grow up they will be anxious to know who they are descended from; and yet may have none to tell them; for these reasons, and no other, I have resolv'd to put together such particulars of my life and connections as may satisfy from enquiries, and serve to inform them who and what their Father was, as far as such knowledge can be honestly and correctly communicated by frail man.

Edward's father, Sir George Nares, had been appointed Town Clerk of Oxford in 1746 and made a King's Serjeant in 1759. In May 1768, he was elected as MP for the city of Oxford, with the 4th Duke of Marlborough's backing, and appointed its Recorder. In 1771, he vacated his seat for Oxford and resigned as its Recorder when he became a judge in the Court of Common Pleas, as the Duke's younger brother, Lord Robert Spencer, wished to represent the city of Oxford, which he did in due course. Edward's mother, Mary Strange (1726–1782), was the third daughter of Sir John Strange, Solicitor General to George III and later Master of the Rolls and a Privy Councillor. Curiously, Edward's maternal grandmother Lady Strange was, as Edward wrote:

> … one of the 4 Daughters … of Mr. Edwd. Strong [see Appendix G] – a very eminent Mason, who was particularly concerned in the building of St. Pauls, of which he laid the last Stone upon the Lantern, Oct 26th, 1708.

As a stonemason, Strong would have known of the architect Nicholas Hawksmoor (see Appendix G), who had worked not only at Blenheim but also on St Paul's Cathedral and Greenwich Hospital.

Edward came from a distinguished family of highly regarded professional people. His uncle, James Nares (1715–1783), became a well-known composer of church music and was appointed as deputy organist of St George's Chapel at Windsor Castle. In 1734, he moved to York Minster as the cathedral organist, serving there until 1756, before subsequently moving to London where he was Master of the Children of the Chapel Royal, as organist and composer for George III. Another distinguished member of the Nares family, and one of James Nares' children, was Edward's cousin Robert, a clergyman and a famous philologist. As a young man, he had acted as tutor to the younger sons of Sir Watkin Williams Wynn and his wife Lady Charlotte Wynn. Between the years 1779 and 1783, Robert worked for the Wynn family both in London and at Wynnstay Hall. It seems that both the Nares cousins from an early age shared an enthusiasm as budding playwrights and actors, their literary talents being recognised at Wynnstay and Blenheim.

Colman, the theatre impresario, saw the theatre at Wynnstay in 1779, describing the lighting, 'which came from a more natural direction and did not throw the wrong way like foot lights'. But it could not be adopted, writes Colman, 'where there were upper boxes and galleries because it would prevent the occupants from seeing the stage'.[1] The private theatre at Blenheim in the 4th Duke of Marlborough's era solved the problem of 'the tormenting line of lamps at the front of the stage which wrong everything it illuminates by the use of reverberators at the extremity of the boxes', wrote the *Morning Post* of the time.

In 1779, George Colman and his sixteen-year-old son, also named George, took part in the Wynnstay theatricals. However, according to George junior, his father did not think much of the amateurs' efforts. At this time, Robert Nares was one of the new actors at Wynnstay, writing some prologues and epilogues for the plays, as well as an elegy on the death of Garrick that he recited during the Wynnstay theatre season. In 1785, *Who's the Dupe?* was performed at Wynnstay on 28 December, but this was after Robert Nares' departure from Wynnstay, as by then he had taken holy orders.

When Sir Watkin died in 1789, the long series of theatricals came to a stop. It was not until 1803 when his son, Master Watkin Williams Wynn, succeeded to the title that the theatricals were revived. These were performed at Christmas house parties from 1803 to 1810, mainly in the old Wynnstay theatre, which was to survive as a theatre until 1840.

Edward Nares' oldest brother John (1754–1814) was educated at Eton and became the family lawyer. John was the grandfather of Sir George Strong Nares, famous for the narrative he wrote entitled *A Voyage to the Polar Sea*, published in 1878. Sir George was promoted to Vice-Admiral in 1892 and died in 1915. Edward's other brother, also named George, was born in 1759 and went to Westminster School before going up to Christ Church College, Oxford. In the painting by J. Hamilton Mortimer (see Appendix G) *c.* 1772, Edward can be seen in his Westminster School uniform and George in his scholar's uniform. The boys are standing at the front gates of Warbrook House at Eversley in Hampshire, the country residence settled on by his father following his promotion to the Bench. After university

George joined the Army, and as Captain of the 70th Regiment of Foot he distinguished himself at the taking of Martinique but died of a fever after its surrender. On his deathbed, he gave these instructions: 'I beg Edward Nares to be a guardian to my child, he being the Man on Earth I most revere.' This child was christened Edward and was the offspring of George's marriage to a Miss Heard.

In his memoirs Edward wrote not just about his brothers and their careers but also about his four sisters and their marriages. Edward's oldest sister Mary married the Revd Thomas Treacher in 1779. The previous year, Treacher had been appointed the rector of Ardley in Oxfordshire by the 4th Duke of Marlborough, the year that Reynolds painted the Spencer family portrait at Blenheim. The Duke also held the advowson of four other ecclesiastical livings – Bladon, Woodstock, Wheatfield (from 1807) and Waddesdon (1789–1825). Treacher served as a Church Commissioner with William Mavor, who, as we have seen, wrote the first guide books to Blenheim and the city of Oxford.

Edward wrote of Mary that she was 'a religious, good woman and generally esteemed by all who knew her'. About his other sisters he wrote less in his memoirs, partly because Mary played a greater role in Edward's life, especially when he was at Oxford and Blenheim. Edward's second sister, Susanna Letitia (1760–1818) married Charles Masterman Henning from Dorset in 1799. His third sister, Anne, was born in 1765 and died in Bristol in 1795. His youngest sister Sophia (1768–1847) married D'Arcy Preston of Askham in Yorkshire at Begbroke near Woodstock in 1792. D'Arcy as a young man accompanied Lord St Vincent to the West Indies in 1794. After the taking of Martinique, D'Arcy was sent home with the dispatches, which led in time to his appointment as master and commander. Eventually in 1796 he was appointed Post Captain. After the death of his father, D'Arcy lived on his father's estate at Askham with Sophia and their five sons and two daughters.

When Edward was a small boy he was taught to read and write by his mother, to whom he was devoted. When he was eight he was sent to Westminster School, 'the only school I ever went to'. Edward believed that boys should be educated at school but favoured private education at home for daughters. He writes in his memoirs, 'My first years at Westminster were certainly not happy ones. I was short for my age and not of a strong constitution.' In fact, Edward was so small that one of the senior boys, Charles Chetwynd (later Lord Chetwynd, Earl of Shrewsbury), carried him up the stone steps of the lobby every morning in his teeth, with the addition 'of my satchel of books on my back'. At Westminster, Edward was often punished for his inattention and idleness: 'I could not apprehend the real importance of learning.' After a time, Edward ceased boarding at Westminster and as a day boy he was able 'to dine and relax' at home, where he spent much time in his father's study reading. He especially enjoyed reading Goldsmith's *History of England* in the form of letters from a nobleman to his son. After reading Milton, Edward decided that he would write an epic poem and later on, with his father's encouragement, he wrote two plays as well as a burlesque novel, which may have been an earlier version of his adult novel *Thinks I to Myself* (see Appendix M).

In 1774, Edward and his father received an invitation from the radical John Wilkes, then Lord Mayor of London, to dine at the Mansion House; Edward was just twelve at the time.

Wilkes even drank to Edward's health 'and spoke highly of his endeavours as a writer'. All this was music to young Edward's ears and boosted his confidence considerably, so much so that before he left Westminster he learnt Hebrew with the King's Scholars of Westminster, whose duty at coronations is to shout out the 'Vivat' during the ceremony. In 1779, at the age of seventeen, Edward was entered as a commoner at Christ Church College, Oxford, under Dr Bagot, while his tutor was Dr John Randolph, later Bishop of Oxford. At Oxford, Edward was appointed the first president of the Union Club, which consisted at that time of four Westminster men, four from Stowe and four from Harrow. The Oxford Union is of course famous today for its debates and for its influence on affairs of national importance.

Although Edward was primarily an academic, he was also fond of dancing and during his life 'could never resist an invite to a dance', writing that 'the balls of the rich and great always began with Minuets'. In his memoirs he discusses how rigid society was, especially in terms of dress, between the 'higher and lower orders' and how as a vicar he saw 'many poor families in reduced circumstances still wearing their best in Sunday church'.

In 1782, Edward's mother died of a dropsical disorder at the age of fifty-five. On her deathbed Mary told her children 'to be most attentive to your father after I am gone'. She was buried in the family vault at Eversley, Hampshire. A year later, in January 1783, Edward was awarded his BA. In the same year he wrote a comedy in five acts and with this script in his pocket, he went to London to see Mr King, the famous theatrical manager of Drury Lane. King returned his manuscript, saying that it was 'unfit for the public', much to Edward's great disappointment.

Also in 1783, William Pitt (see Appendix G) became Prime Minister at the age of twenty-four, which caused Edmund Burke to call Pitt 'the young minister in disguise'. Edward had met Pitt while accompanying his father on his judicial circuits and had even dined privately with him. He says in his memoirs that he often saw Pitt walking in St James's Park early in the morning and that Pitt always recognised him.

Having gained his BA, it appears that Edward was undecided as to what career he should pursue. He had hoped that playwriting would provide an income, but when his hopes were dashed by Mr King he went on a touring holiday in 1784 with his Christ Church friend, Greenhill, touring Wales and Ireland. In Dublin they saw a man who had been tarred and feathered by a mob and witnessed two men being shot at in front of a theatre. Dublin at that time was not a good place to visit, as the import of English goods into Ireland had made English visitors most unpopular. Not long after this incident the two friends returned to England. At Whitehaven in Cumberland they saw the coal galleries that stretched under the Irish Sea, and this was followed by a tour of the Lake District before they returned to their respective homes.

Edward was to pass his time at home pursuing another of his interests – ballooning. In his memoirs he writes that he was 'a keen supporter of the Montgolfier Brothers' successful venture of 1783'. Edward may have been at Oxford in October 1784 when James Sadler made his first ascent by balloon from the meadow south of the city wall, near Merton College. Sadler was a local man who at the time worked as a technician at one of the University of Oxford's laboratories.

On 30 November 1784, Edward was present at the ascent of a balloon from Grosvenor Square in London by Dr Jean-Pierre Blanchard and Dr John Jeffries. The following year, the two doctors were the first to cross the English Channel by balloon. According to Edward, 'these two men attempted to cross the Channel between Dover and Calais, but Blanchard went off on his own much to the annoyance of Jeffries, who then attempted to go abroad with the help of a posse of sailors'. A neighbour of Edward's father read about this in the newspapers and suggested to Edward that it would be a good subject for an epic poem. The result was a 1,000-line mock epic, *The Ballooniad*, which he had published and was later translated into French for the King of France's son, the Dauphin.

It appears that at the time he wrote *The Ballooniad* Edward was in love with a lady called Maria and being of a romantic nature he composed some verses on love. These verses were then written on the back of a lady's fan and inscribed with the question, 'Do you love me?' However, Maria answered, 'No, pray excuse me.' Not long after this rejection, in September 1785, Edward and his brother, now Captain George Nares, went on a tour of the continent. On 17 September they went to the theatre in Calais but were not amused when in the middle of the night, three armed men, officers of the French police, barged into their bedroom enquiring in French 'who I was and whither I was going'.

Another incident at Calais happened in a hotel where they met two English naval officers, a Captain Oakes and a Captain Williams, who knew where George and Edward were staying. Oakes and Williams had been challenged to a duel by some French officers, who alleged that 'they had been given an affront to be fought with pistols and swords'. Fortunately for all, it was, as one of the French officers described it, '*en mal entendu*' (a misunderstanding). As a result of this, the commander of the French garrison, the Duc de Rochambeau, who fought in the American War of Independence, invited them to dine with him. A distinguished soldier, he had been sent out to America in 1780 to support the American cause against the British. In 1781, he rendered effective help at Yorktown before returning to France in 1783. He later served with the Napoleonic army and was made a marshal by Napoleon in 1803.

After Calais, Edward and George went to Lille where they met Isaac Barré, MP for Calne in Wiltshire. At St Omer the coach carrying Barré and his travelling companion, the Revd W. Perry, overturned. Barré was a remarkable and uncomplaining man who achieved much despite his blindness. In parliament he was an opponent of Lord North, who, on discovering that Barré was blind, remarked, 'There were no two men in the kingdom who would be more happy to see each other.' In Lille the brothers were entertained by a French garrison of over 12,000 men. On Sunday they attended a grand military parade, where they were amazed at the appearance of the commandant, who wore pattens (metal undershoes that were a type of galosh), had his hands in a muff and wore ear-rings. On 10 October, Edward returned to England by the packet boat, which was stranded twice on the dreaded Goodwin Sands. Once home, he wrote a parody about the dangers of ballooning for a Christmas party to which he had been invited. This poem was published in a newspaper and was entitled *New Year's Ode*.

The year 1786 was 'a melancholy one' due to his father's poor health. Eventually Edward and his sister Susanna persuaded their father to leave their London home in Carey Street and move to Ramsgate in Kent. In his memoirs Edward describes the Ramsgate house with its narrow staircase leading up to his father's bedroom. As the final days of his father's life approached and he lost his appetite, Edward wrote, 'He shows great fortitude and spirit.' On his last night, 20 July 1786, his father asked a servant for some cider to drink, his final words being that it was 'a hard trial to die, but that it was a trial that came but once and would now soon be over'. No wonder that Edward wrote of him, 'He was a religious, good man, so good that I have never known any better.' Sir George was interred in the family vault at Eversley church and a memorial to him was placed above the Nares family pew. In his father's will, Edward was left an amethyst ring set with diamonds 'as a token of the great love I bear him for the uninterrupted comfort I have derived from his excellent behaviour to me and diligence in his studies'.

After Edward's death this ring was owned by Cordelia, his second wife, and had been set as a locket. The ring has an interesting history, as in the 1760s his parent's London home was burgled and all of his mother's jewellery was stolen, including the ring. The culprits were caught and sentenced to death. While the men were in Newgate Prison awaiting their fate they wrote to Sir George, sending the ring as evidence, saying that if he could get the king, George III, to pardon them, they would make certain all the jewellery was returned. Sir George wrote back saying it was not possible, and all three men were hanged.

Another family death occurred on 11 August 1786 when Thomas Treacher died at Begbroke, near Blenheim, leaving his wife Mary, Edward's sister, to look after their five children. Treacher was buried at St Martin's church, Carfax, Oxford. Unfortunately for the Treacher family, the youngest daughter Sophia was not old enough to consent to the will, with the result that it was contested in the Court of Chancery. This was so prohibitively expensive that it quite ruined the Treacher family and led to their move from Begbroke parsonage to Henley.

In the summer of 1787, Edward was chosen for a future Fellowship of Merton College, Oxford, although it would take another three years before he was to achieve his goal of a church or university career. This is probably why, in April 1788, Edward with his friend, a fellow of All Souls College, Oxford, a Mr Clitherow of Boston House, Brentford, Middlesex, set off for the continent. This tour started in Paris with a visit to the French parliament on 16 April 1788. Only a few days later:

> Two members were sent to Prison & the Duc D'Orleans banish'd; this was, I believe, generally regarded as the first measure of force on the part of the Government and the grand preliminary of all the dismal scenes & Events that followed … I was able however to attend the Court at Versailles and … I believe it was the very last day on which their Majesties Louis XVI and his Queen Marie Antoinette dined together in public … At dinner we were plac'd next to them for some time … Her Majesty was certainly a most Majestic figure, graceful in her Manners, and her features handsome. She did not appear quite at her ease and there was, I apprehend, too much cause for her to be otherwise. She eat [*sic*] nothing, but had a plaited Napkin plac'd before her. Little cd. I suppose when I saw her in such splendour … that I was looking upon a person doom'd so soon to suffer on a Scaffold. If she was really chargeable with the faults

imputed to her it shd. be recollected that she was the queen of a very voluptuous and most unprincipled Nation. She sat on a Throne surrounded by profligate Ministers, servile Courtiers and the most abject Flatterers.

The King's countenance was mild and benevolent and had in it, to my Judgement, more marks of an honest sincerity in it than falls to the lot of the French in general. He made but a hasty meal, spoke but little and seem'd heartily glad when the ceremony was ended. Numerous dishes were plac'd successively on the table of most of which he tasted, but eat [*sic*] little. None but the Queen sat at the table with him. After we had withdrawn we were conducted to the apartments of his second Son, the Duc de Normandie, afterwards Louis XVII, at that time only three years old. The Dauphin was yet living, but too ill to receive us.

After Paris the young men travelled on to Lyons where Edward became unwell. Their travels were abandoned and they returned to England in late May 1788. In his memoirs Edward wrote, 'The whole of the Bourbon monarchy who survived the revolution of 1789 sought political refuge in England ... the French now bow down to the greatest tyrant that ever wore the crown.' The fall of the Bastille in Paris caused both political and social shock in Britain, creating panic among the landed classes in England, due in part to the sudden influx of refugees. Thousands of French aristocrats who fled to England in the wake of the terror added a new dimension to English society. One estimate has put the number of refugees as high as 40,000 by the end of the eighteenth century.

It was a good thing for Edward that he had returned to England, for on 2 August 1788, he was elected as a Fellow of Merton College. At the time of his election, the Head of Merton was the Revd Dr Henry Barton. Edward informs us in his journals that it was now his intention to go into the church and also to keep up his studies in chemistry, mineralogy, botany and anatomy. At least the doors of Oxford University were now open to him and he could look forward to an effective future in an Oxford college he had long admired, 'as among the most ancient and respectable in the University'. Other doors also opened for him, this time at Blenheim Palace, when he acted in *The Deaf Lover* on Wednesday 18 March 1789, with Lady Charlotte Spencer.

Later that year, in August, Edward made reference in his journals to how Lord Henry Spencer made the request for him to go to Blenheim 'to take part in a play to be acted at the Duke's private theatre'. In the Nares memorabilia at Merton there are tickets for two productions of the play he saw as a spectator, one of which has his name inscribed on it. As we have seen, Edward at first refused, partly out of shyness and because:

The extreme elegance of the Theatre, high rank of fashion of the performers, choice selection of company and superb manner in which everything was conducted were certainly particularly striking so that, except what I felt on the Score of shyness, it was impossible not to be gratified with so distinguished an invitation. I did not however venture to accept it immediately, nor till after repeated solicitations from the family; but these were urg'd with so much civility and so many compliments that it wd. have been a great piece [*sic*] of rudeness not to have consented to make a trial of my abilities.

It was fortunate for Edward that he did accept Lord Henry's invitation, as 1789 was the last of the private theatre seasons at Blenheim.

Whether in his journals Edward deliberately tried to conceal *The Deaf Lover* performances of March 1789 is difficult to tell, and whether the roles that Charlotte and he performed led to the early stages of their relationship is not discussed. Edward, however, would have been all too aware of the dangers that can beset actors when they become involved with their fellow actors, as well as of the great social divide between the aristocracy and the clergy in eighteenth-century England.

The following year was to be even more momentous for Edward's career. On 17 July, he obtained his MA, and, following the death of Dr Henry Barton, the Warden of Merton College, was appointed Principal of the Postmasters at Merton for four years. The new warden, Dr Scrope Beardmore, was a close friend and supported Edward's nomination to the post, which meant superintending the scholars of Merton but involved no teaching. (The title 'postmaster' was a corruption of 'portionista', the name given to certain men who had gained a financial bursary, known an Exhibition, at Merton; in the original endowment of Merton in 1380 there were fourteen postmasters.) This appointment resulted in Edward being much in demand by lords, dukes, bishops and even princes of the blood, hoping that their sons would be awarded an exhibition.

Edward's time as Principal of the Postmasters was a happy one:

> The temporary importance which my situation at Merton gave me ... was certainly heightened by the frequency of my visits to Blenheim, the shutting of the theatre having by no means put an end to my acquaintance there.

So despite the private theatre at Blenheim being in disuse by 1790, Edward continued to be a guest at Blenheim, often staying for considerable lengths of time. He even wrote stories for the Spencer children, claiming they were written by Revd Le Docteur Snares.

Although Edward carefully avoids saying anything about his relationship with Charlotte in his journals, he does write about visiting his sister at Begbroke, just south of Blenheim. Certainly, Mary Treacher was still living in Begbroke in 1791 with her children, all of whom were christened in Begbroke church. After her husband's death in 1786, Begbroke Parsonage became a boarding school for young ladies, the rent being annually paid by Mrs Wyatt from 1786 to 1801. From 1810 to 1821, a Miss Matilda Smith and her brothers ran a boarding school for young gentle-ladies, rented from the Duke of Marlborough. This house is today known as St Philip's Priory and was primarily used as a novitiate for an Order of Roman Catholics, having been sold by the Blenheim estate in 1895. The 9th Duke of Marlborough turned to Catholicism later in life, and in his will bequeathed a silver paten (communion plate) to the Order in gratitude for the hours spent at religious services in the priory.

Edward took holy orders in June 1792, being ordained as a deacon at Christ Church Cathedral by Bishop Smallwell of Oxford on 30 December 1792. In November, Edward had been a witness at the marriage of his youngest sister Sophia to D'Arcy Preston at Begbroke, as were John and Anne Nares, who signed the marriage register.

In August 1793, Edward resigned his office of Principal of the Postmasters, and on 15 November, Merton presented him to the curacy of the college living of St Peter-in-the-East, Oxford, now the library of St Edmund Hall, across the High Street from Merton. In 1266, this church had been presented to Merton College in a perpetual advowson. It served Magdalen College, New College, Queen's College, University College, Hertford College and the halls of St Edmund and Magdalen. In August 1794, Edward was appointed bursar of Merton College. Apart from his new duties in the college, much of his time in 1794 and 1795 seems to have been spent with the Spencer family either at Blenheim or at Brighton. In his memoirs Edward wrote that he was 'still enjoying the attention of the Spencer family' and that he was at this time 'very much at Blenheim, and frequently served my church from thence, having the use of one of the Duke's carriages to do so'. It seems probable that it was in 1794 that Edward and Charlotte's love for each other deepened, especially as he had stayed with the Spencers at fashionable Brighthelmstone (Brighton) during the summer.

Sea bathing was popular for many visitors at Brighton in the 1790s, the experience of a quick, total immersion in sea water being intended as a medical treatment. The bather took off all his or her clothes in a bathing machine and was then plunged into the sea by attendants known as dippers. The hiring charge for a bathing machine in the 1770s varied from 9*d* for two or more gentlemen bathing themselves, to 1*s* 6*d* for a gentleman taking a machine with a dipper. Naked bathing continued until the 1860s, when a by-law was passed stating that male and female bathers were to be segregated by not less than sixty feet, and that female bathers would be provided with gowns or dresses, with drawers or similar for male bathers.

According to his journals, Edward spent much of his time at Blenheim during the winter of 1794/95. In January 1795, one of the Archbishop of Canterbury's chaplains advised him to apply for the Merton College living of Denton in Norfolk, which had to be given to a Fellow of Merton. However, Edward was then 'wrongly advised not to apply for this'. Quite why he failed to follow the Archbishop's advice he does not elaborate on, but perhaps he felt that it might put an end to invitations to Blenheim and that being at Denton would have made visits to Blenheim to see Lady Charlotte almost impossible.

Edward also writes about Lady Charlotte officiating as a bridesmaid at the royal wedding of George, Prince of Wales (later George IV) and Princess Caroline Amelia of Brunswick, in the Chapel Royal at St James's Palace. According to Edward, the princess eventually arrived in England from Germany in early April, and Lady Charlotte was given very little time to get to London for the wedding, which took place on 8 April 1795. In Sir William Hamilton's sketch of the marriage, the prince and his bride stand with their hands joined before the Archbishop of Canterbury, John Moore, and near the altar stands the Bishop of London, Beilby Porteus (see Appendix G). Under a gallery in which the choir is placed stand the princess's bridesmaids, with George III and Queen Charlotte seated either side of the bridal pair. Apart from Lady Charlotte Spencer, the other bridesmaids were Lady Mary Osborne, aged eighteen and daughter of the 5th Duke of Leeds; Lady Caroline Villiers, aged twenty-one and daughter of the 4th Earl of Jersey; and Lady Charlotte Legge, daughter of the 2nd Earl of Dartmouth, who was only fifteen.

Princess Caroline, who was twenty-seven years old, met her husband for the first time on her wedding day, when the couple took an immediate dislike to each other. The Prince of Wales was under pressure to marry, not just from his parents but from the rest of the nation. The following year, after the birth of Princess Charlotte Augusta, the prince deserted his wife for good. After the death of George III in 1820, Princess Caroline returned to England and was publicly humiliated by being excluded from the coronation of her husband and threatened with a Bill of Divorce. She is said to have died of a broken heart in 1821 at Brandenburg House, Hammersmith, which she had rented from the Margravine of Anspach.

On 3 May 1795, not long after the royal wedding, Edward accompanied his sister Anne to the therapeutic waters of the Hotwells at Bristol. Anne had caught a chill in the winter and this had led to a severe cough. Sadly for Edward, Anne died on 20 May. He had been close to her all his life, and at the time of her death she had been engaged to one of his best friends. Edward wrote that 'a purer person, I believe, never ascended to Heaven'. Anne was buried in the family vault of Eversley church in Hampshire.

Later in the year, Edward was to be affected by another bereavement when, on 26 September, Lord Henry Spencer, Edward's friend from his Oxford days, died in Berlin of a fever, aged twenty-four. His death was a great blow to the whole Spencer family and in particular to his sister Lady Charlotte. When she decided to leave Blenheim in 1797, all she took with her were her brother's letters and a few of his possessions. On hearing of Henry's death, Edward quoted from Horace '*multis ille bonis flebilis occidit, nulli flebilior, quam mihi*' (He died wept over by many good people, missed by nobody more than me). Lord Henry was buried at St Mary's church, Ardley. The Ardley Estate had been purchased in 1753 by Charles, 3rd Duke of Marlborough, and was held by the Marlborough family until 1894, when the 9th Duke sold it by auction. Between 1753 and 1778, when the rector of Ardley was Benjamin Holloway, the parish was served by curates who lived at the rectory there and each received a stipend of £30 per annum. This was at a time when many of the aristocracy and clergy merely paid lip-service to the spiritual needs of parishioners and the practice of underpaid curates performing the religious duties of absentee clergy was commonplace.

However, 1795 was not all doom and gloom at Blenheim, as a curious book concerning geographical games was published by Abbé Gaultier, whom Edward had met at Blenheim. The book was dedicated to Lady Amelia Spencer. One of these games was invented by Lady Charlotte, it being played with counters on skeleton maps, the idea being to make the study of geography more interesting, especially for young children. There was also a popular card game called 'Casino', written out in Charlotte's neat copperplate handwriting, which is among the Nares memorabilia at Merton College. The rules for the game were:

Humbly inscribed to Her Grace the Duchess of Marlborough, by whose indulgence and frequently at her Grace's own cost, the Inventor was permitted to make repeated trials of his system at her Grace's card table at Marlborough House, Blenheim and Sion …

The death of Edward's sister Anne in May 1795 is the last event described in his memoirs that year. The next three pages have been carefully cut out and destroyed, and the following six pages have been crossed through, making it virtually impossible to decipher what was written about the romance between Edward and Charlotte during the year 1796. It is probable that at some later stage Edward cut out these pages. In her book *Blenheim: Biography of a Palace* Marian Fowler states:

> Little Edward Nares had fallen in love with Charlotte, and she with him. Edward asked the Duke, ever so politely, for his daughter's hand. The Duke, however, had no intention of giving his favourite daughter in marriage to a commoner whose unpretentious home, Warbrook House, at Eversley, Hampshire, would fit into Blenheim's kitchen court, and have room to spare.[2]

In fact, Warbrook House is a handsome Georgian house dating from 1727 and set in extensive grounds. It was designed by John James (see Appendix G), a pupil of Sir Christopher Wren.

In 1797, the mores of courtship and marriage were firmly fixed. Either parent or offspring could suggest a match but both had the power of veto. Parents should not force a daughter to marry against her will, nor should a daughter go against her parents' wishes, for filial disobedience was a major sin. It was indeed ironic that Lady Charlotte, playing the part of Miss Rivers on Friday 19 October 1787, on her eighteenth birthday, had stood on The Orangery's stage at Blenheim and had spoken these haunting words from *False Delicacy*: 'when a woman flies from the protection of a parent who merits the utmost return of her affection'.

On 10 December 1796, Lady Anne, Charlotte's younger sister, married the Earl of Shaftesbury's brother, Cropley Ashley-Cooper. Whether it was this marriage that was the catalyst for Charlotte's decision to leave Blenheim, or Edward's departure from Blenheim, is difficult to ascertain. We do know, however, that on 18 March 1797, Edward left Blenheim, having spent much of the winter there, after declaring to Charlotte that he 'would not return until their mutual attachment had been disclosed'. In the meantime, Charlotte had refused to broach 'their attachment' to her parents, and in the margin of his journal Edward writes, 'We in no way planned to cause a family rift.' After the crossed-out pages, there are a further four pages in which Edward gives his version of what happened next, and there is then yet another page that has been removed. The following page of the journal states that 'Charlotte really was alone at the inn in Henley and a fugitive from Blenheim'.

It appears that after Edward's ultimatum to Charlotte in March 1797, he went to stay with his sister Mary, who by then had moved to Henley-on-Thames. The rector of Henley was a personal friend of the Nares family and offered both Edward and Mary support and hospitality. Whilst it is unclear what Edward planned to do next, he was profoundly taken aback by events that took place a few days later. On the evening of 21 March, 'this impasse was shattered in an abrupt manner', wrote Edward, when he received a note from Charlotte. Edward's memoirs continue:

When I was sitting with my Sister after dinner I receiv'd a note from Lady Charlotte, informing me that she was *alone* at one of the Inns in the Town. I was never in my whole life more astonished or distress'd. On repairing to the Inn my grief was great, to find that she had quitted Blenheim unknown to any Body, walk'd from thence to Oxford, and proceeded undiscovered in a Chaise to Henley. How much she had suffered from agitation of spirits and fatigue of Body need not be related. Few persons, I conceive, were ever placed in circumstances more distressing than myself at that moment. I felt that her flight wd. be imputed to my suggestion, tho', before God, I declare I had never entertained a thought of the kind and that it was on both sides wholly & entirely *unpremeditated*.

It appears that after Edward's ultimatum to Charlotte she had discussed their relationship with her mother while her father was away. On the Duke's return, her parents had refused to consider it, and Charlotte, fearing that she would be barred from further association with Edward, had left Blenheim in a distressed state. Exactly when Charlotte arrived at Henley is difficult to ascertain from Edward's journal. The probability is that it would have been during the afternoon of the 21st, after a journey of forty miles or so. She could have caught the London coach from Woodstock to Henley, which passed through Oxford, Nuneham Courtenay, Dorchester-on-Thames and Nettlebed. But worrying that she might be recognised, she had first walked to Oxford and then caught chaises to Henley.

The Revd Francis Witts wrote in his diary about Henley and the journey from the town to Oxford, which would have been similar to Charlotte's journey there in 1797:

> The Town of Henley is after Oxford the largest in the County: it is well built, & possesses a handsome Town House. We alighted at the Bell Inn, whence we took Horses to Benson. The Country for these eleven Miles is not so picturesque but sufficiently bears the mark of fertility & industry. Benson seems marked only by the number of coach-makers, & two good Inns. The first mile from Henley, the Road being planted on either side with trees, is named the fair mile. From Benson to Oxford are twelve miles, the road moderate. Pass thro' the Village of Dorchester, The Church Yard of which containing a large Church is in Shropshire. We arrived in the King's Arms Oxford by six & partook of excellent Veal cutlets.[3]

The comment regarding the churchyard at Dorchester can be explained by the fact that prior to the Local Government Act of 1888 it was not unusual for small islands of land or parishes of one county to be geographically situated in another. For a small part of Dorchester in Oxfordshire to be part of Shropshire was taking this historical oddity to its most extreme, and was therefore considered noteworthy by Witts.

In his memoirs Edward states that it was 'Lady Charlotte who had evinced an extraordinary attachment to me'. Charlotte's attachment, extraordinary as it was to Edward, might not be so to her, especially as she was now twenty-eight and both her older sisters and her younger sister and brother were married and her favourite brother Henry was dead. She might well feel that she was alone at home at Blenheim, with only her two younger siblings for company. By telling Charlotte that he would not return to Blenheim until she had discussed it with her parents, Edward had brought it all to a head, as she must have realised only too well what her parents' reaction to her marrying a commoner would be. Above all, she now missed Edward's witty and clever personality, and thus he had become indispensable to her.

As Madeline Barber wrote in *A Man of Many Parts: Professor or Bishop?*:

> The arrival of Lady Charlotte, unaccompanied, at the Red Lion Inn in Henley, today an hotel, was a source of acute embarrassment to Edward and his family. On hearing the news, his sister immediately went to the inn and brought the young woman back to her house, where Edward's sister Mary made arrangements for Lady Charlotte to sleep in the guest bedroom of her house, whilst Edward prepared to spend the night on a sofa in a room on the ground floor.[4]

The Red Lion is situated opposite the bridge over the River Thames in the centre of the town. In 1786, a new stone bridge replaced Henley's old wooden bridge which had been washed away in a flood earlier that year. One of the sponsors of the new bridge was Charlotte's uncle, Lord Charles Spencer.

Edward sent for his sister Mary to come to the inn and 'convey Charlotte to Mary's home'. Meanwhile he immediately dispatched an express letter to the Duke at Blenheim, expressing his concern at what had happened. His journal continues: 'At about 9 at night on 21 March one of the Duke's most confidential servants arrived at his sister's house and insisted upon being admitted.' Edward went to the front door and declared:

> … unless he would listen to me patiently, I would have him committed, for as to any right to enter, he had none – the man then told me he would hear me patiently, upon which I explained things to him exactly as I have explained them now and admitted him into the house.

It is possible that the Duke's manservant had brought a letter for Edward, though at the time Edward makes no mention of it. In this letter the Duke had imputed that Edward had not behaved in a gentlemanly manner. However, in his memoirs Edward did say that he asked the manservant to tell the Duke that 'neither he nor Charlotte intended to treat the Duke and Duchess without respect' and that the servant was 'a good man who showed warmth towards his master'.

The stresses and strains of the day were now catching up with Charlotte, for Edward states that 'around 11 at night Lady Charlotte retired to rest'. Realising that the day was by no means over, Edward wrote that events were 'unfolding fast and I lay down on a sofa awaiting what would happen'. He did not have long to wait, for at midnight the Marquess of Blandford arrived at Henley, having come, as Edward states, 'from his seat Bill Hill near Wokingham'. As well as the Marquess, another member of the family arrived at Henley – Lord Henry, 2nd Viscount Clifden, who was married to Lady Caroline Spencer, Charlotte's oldest sister. Lord Henry sent a note asking Edward to come to the inn where he was staying. This was probably once again the Red Lion, where the 1st Duke had a room which seems to have been kept solely for use by the Marlborough family. Edward continues in his journal that Lord Henry 'had sent a carriage to fetch him to the inn'. When Edward arrived there he was met by both men. Edward writes, 'Lord Blandford listened to him with great candour' and that Lord Henry Clifden 'expressed a wish to see his sister-in-law'. Apparently Lord Blandford in his talk with Edward had stated that 'the connection would be ruinous to both Edward and Charlotte'. Edward replied that 'even if all the family and friends advised against it' he did not think that 'Charlotte would abandon me or should I in that case ever abandon her'. Both the Duke's son and son-in-law then went in a carriage to see Charlotte. The outcome was that Lord Blandford informed Edward that 'Charlotte was willing to go with him, provided that I had no objection'. So, with the consent of all parties, Charlotte went to Bill Hill, her brother's home near Wokingham, and, in Edward's words, 'Thus ended this memorable day.'

On the following day, Wednesday 22 March, Edward wrote to Lord Blandford to explain matters more fully. On the same day, he received Lord Blandford's reply, that he 'could do nothing until he knew what the Duke and Duchess thought'. Edward also received a letter from Charlotte which 'strongly encouraged him to hope that everything would turn out well'. Edward now wrote an impassioned letter to the Duke, 'emphasising his good faith and honourable conduct throughout'. This letter was duly dispatched to Blenheim on the same day. After staying a few days at Bill Hill, Charlotte then went up to London with her brother and met both her older sisters Lady Caroline and Lady Elizabeth. She even had a meeting with the Archbishop of Canterbury, John Moore. After these meetings Charlotte wrote to Edward saying that all who had seen her had 'expressed themselves favourably towards us' and that she had a letter 'from her F[ather] and M[other] asking her to return to Blenheim to discuss the matter'. This Charlotte had agreed to. On her return to Blenheim she continued to write to Edward each day, hoping that 'all would be resolved amicably'. What happened to all this correspondence is unknown.

Unfortunately, not only did the newspapers suggest Edward's complicity but Edward wrote of 'over officious people at Oxford, who were eager to make their court at Blenheim and who were said to have inferred that they were in no manner displeased with me but attributed everything to Lady Charlotte'. These two factors when combined were to cause enormous damage between the young couple and Charlotte's parents. The immediate consequence was that a servant was sent from Blenheim to Henley with an express letter, signed jointly by the Duke and Duchess, in which they expressed themselves 'shocked beyond measure at my conduct and resolved never to give their consent to a match on all accounts so improper'. This letter arrived sixteen days after Charlotte's flight from Blenheim and, as Edward continues, 'up till then not one word of reproach had he received'.

Edward goes on to say that the Duke had also been informed wrongly about his financial state of affairs, and that he had been left not £2,000 by his father but £4,000, and that Charlotte was well aware of this. It was this false information concerning his financial affairs that caused him to write to the Duke, saying that 'he would confer with no one on the subject of Lady Charlotte, since he was liable to misrepresentations and that he had not realised he had caused the Duke so much displeasure'. Edward later regretted writing this letter, which he said he had composed in haste and while under duress. It is true that

Edward was misrepresented by the press, for the papers at the time were full of the affair. It had even been reported that Edward was the Duke's chaplain and at one time the tutor to the family. The result was that the Duke and Duchess refused their consent to the marriage, although Charlotte was 'invited to stay at the palace till the day fixed for our marriage'.

All of this of course would have been extremely stressful for both Charlotte and Edward, which is why in his memoirs Edward vividly recalls all the various details that were still etched in his memory long after they occurred. Thus Charlotte returned to Blenheim knowing that her parents would have no part in her wedding arrangements, despite pleas from the Archbishop himself. The date and timing of the ceremony were not to be revealed to them, no carriage was to be provided, and there was to be no money for her wedding expenses.

Time and again in his memoirs Edward writes that 'it was the newspapers who were mainly to blame for inaccuracies concerning both Charlotte and myself and the Duke and the Duchess'. Edward adds, 'I have never ceased to resent all imputations cast on them by the newspapers.' At the time, he was the object of hostile criticism for his supposed connivance on the issue of the marriage, a charge which he vigorously denied.

Edward's next journal entry states:

On the morning of 16 April 1797 [which was a Monday] my eldest sister [Mrs Treacher] went in her carriage to Blenheim to fetch Lady Charlotte to Henley, where the marriage ceremony was to be performed. We all arrived early at the church [St Mary's] and were married very privately.

In the Henley marriage register for the year 1797 is written:

April 16 Nares Edward o.t.p. [of this parish] Bach.Lic
Spencer Blenheim spn. [spinster]
Witnesses John Nares
Susannah Nares

'Bach.Lic.' refers to bachelor licence, which meant that the banns had not been called, money having been paid instead.

An 'Act for the Better Preventing of Clandestine Marriages' had been passed in 1753, which required four weeks' residence in the parish before the date of the ceremony, evidence of such residence to be produced, and two witnesses to be present at the marriage. All this meant that Edward, who had left Blenheim on 18 March, would have been resident in Henley for the necessary four weeks and that the marriage could now legally take place on 16 April. The marriage ceremony was performed by Edward's friend from Oxford, Dr Landon, the Provost of Worcester College. In fact the Vice-Chancellor of Oxford and Head of Merton had also offered to marry them, but Edward declined, as 'it might appear as an affront to the Duke'. Landon had also kindly offered Edward his parsonage house in Herefordshire at Croft, near Leominster, as a honeymoon retreat, and, as Edward wrote, 'We went there immediately after the ceremony.'

However, for Edward and Charlotte the press were once more on their trail, the newspapers carrying various reports stating that 'the young couple had gone to Yorkshire or to Wales'. When the truth finally came out about their honeymoon destination the papers published a story about how they had lost their way and that Charlotte had had to walk two miles without shoes. In reality the driver of their carriage to Croft had gone two miles further along the road from the 'proper turning to Doctor Landon's house at Croft, two miles of as wretched a road as I ever travell'd'. In order to retrace the two miles, Edward and Charlotte had decided to walk back along the road and on the way one of Charlotte's shoes came off. Luckily for them, the weather was fine and the road was dry.

The hamlet of Croft is now owned by the National Trust. In 1797, Croft Castle was owned by Richard Knight (see Appendix G), who also owned Downton Castle in Herefordshire. The castle had previously been owned by the Croft family up until 1746, when family debts forced them to sell to a Mr Yeats, who then sold it to Knight. It has some splendid Georgian ceilings, and much of the furniture dates from the eighteenth century.

Not long after their arrival at the parsonage in Croft, Edward wrote, 'I never saw any person happier than she appeared to be in our new abode.' Their honeymoon idyll was no secret to the Duke and Duchess, as two days later Charlotte received a letter from the Duke, informing her that he 'meant to allow Charlotte £400 per annum payable every quarter day at his bankers'. It was the Duke's steward Charles Turner who stated that His Grace had ordered him to pay her £400 a year but that she was never to enter Blenheim's gates again. They also received the sad news of Mary Treacher's death in Henley. Edward wrote, 'She was a kind hearted, good woman, had been a good mother, good sister – I was greatly grieved at her premature death.' Apparently Mary had been in the best of health and spirits, so it came as a great shock to the whole Nares family. Perhaps the stresses and strains of the last few weeks had been too much for her, especially as she had been so closely involved with all the events leading up to the day of the wedding at Henley.

In his memoirs Edward states that they were not on their own at Croft, a substantial Georgian mansion, as Charlotte's maid had accompanied them; some of Landon's servants also came in to help on occasions. A few days later, Landon himself came down to see all was well and that they lacked nothing. Not long after his visit they started to receive invitations from nearby neighbours and from family friends. Curiously, their nearest neighbour was John, 2nd Viscount Bateman, a first cousin of the Duke of Marlborough. The other invitations were from the Earl and Countess of Essex, who were first cousins to Duchess Caroline, and the Earl and Countess of Oxford, 'who entreated us to use their London home'. Other aristocratic invitations arrived from Lady Diana Beauclerk, the Duke's oldest sister, asking the couple to stay at Richmond in Surrey, and from Lord Robert Spencer, the Duke's youngest brother, inviting them down to Sussex. They even received invitations from the Duke and Duchess of Devonshire at Chatsworth and the Duke and Duchess of Buccleuch at Dalkeith. It seems that the marriage was the talk of the day, and that much of polite society was eager to assist in whatever way it could.

Their first visitors arrived early in June, when Lord and Lady Bateman visited. The Batemans lived at Shobdon Court, a few miles up the road from Croft. Lord John was a descendant of Lady Anne Spencer, one of the 1st Duke of Marlborough's daughters, who had married William Bateman at Blenheim in 1720. Lord John was the son of Lord William, and in 1797 was aged seventy. He was, as Edward writes, 'just a little older than his wife'. In his memoirs Edward continues:

> Lady Bateman who was nearly as old continually visited Charlotte at the parsonage at Croft; she had a great deal of old fashioned civility and etiquette about her and she made a point of always arriving in her coach and six.

Apparently Lady Bateman did not normally do this, but because of Charlotte's position in society she intended to 'honour Lady Charlotte that way'. The journal entry continues:

> For the whole of that summer of 1797 we were almost constantly at Lord Bateman's, whose mode of life reminded one more of the ancient Barons of feudal times. He was rough in his manner but by no means proud. He passed the day riding around his estate and visiting his tenantry. At Christmas he entertained all the villagers in the Great Hall and all the women who attended had a shilling to carry home and every child a sixpence. He would even go to the stables to ensure that the horses of his guests were being properly looked after by his five grooms.

It was not long before Edward and Charlotte were allocated 'a suite of apartments at Shobdon Court', although officially they were in residence at the parsonage at Croft until August 1797.

Lady Anne Bateman kept a diary of their visits to Croft, which still exists today as part of the Herefordshire Archives in the public library at Hereford. The diary starts on 2 March 1788 and ceases on 2 March 1802, the day her husband John died, and is written in ink on parchment paper. It reflects the terrified state of English society during the French Revolution, with riots in the city of Bristol, but the first entry of interest with regard to Edward and Charlotte states that 'Lady Charlotte Spencer was married at Henley on Monday April 17, 1797', despite the church register giving the date as 16 April. Later in her diary Lady Bateman reveals that she had been away in London staying with friends at the time of the marriage, returning home on Monday 5 June at two in the afternoon. Two days later, she wrote:

> On Wednesday 7 June went this evening to visit Lady Charlotte Nares and Mr Nares at the Parsonage at Croft. Astonishing to think of visiting a daughter of the Duke of Marlborough at such a place and that she should have a love match with one of the ugliest and meanest looking of men. She might have fallen in love only with his mind and therefore it is hoped it will be lasting.

In the play adaptation of *Mansfield Park*, adapted by Tim Luscombe and first performed on 13 September 2012 at the Theatre Royal, Bury St Edmunds, there is an intriguing moment when Mr Rushworth interrupts Fanny. In a loud voice Rushworth says, 'I cannot admire him. To see such a tiny, mean-looking man set up for a fine actor is very ridiculous.' Perhaps Lady Bateman's first impression of Edward Nares was nearer to the truth regarding his character than she realised, for as Tim Luscombe writes, 'actors are by nature chamelons',[5] which was why Edward adapted so easily into his various acting roles at Blenheim.

A few days later, the young couple went to Shobdon Court to stay, as Lady Bateman's diary confirms:

> On Saturday 10 June Lady Charlotte and Mr Nares dined and slept here. Sunday 11 June: After dinner I took back Lady Charlotte and Mr Nares. Thursday 22 June: Mr Nares and Lady Charlotte came. Tuesday 27 June: I took Lady Charlotte and Mr Nares home to the Parsonage at Croft. Friday 30 June: Lady Charlotte and Mr Nares returned to Shobdon. Thursday 6 July: We dined with Lady Charlotte and Mr Nares at Mr King's. Thursday 27 July: Lady Charlotte Nares, Lord B. and I dined at Mr Davis's while a friend of theirs a Mr Allen stayed at Shobdon with Mr Nares, who was not quite well. Saturday 5 August: Lady Charlotte and Mr Nares returned here. Tuesday 15 August: Went with Lady Charlotte to drink tea at the Wagnells. Tuesday 29 August Lady Charlotte and Mr Nares went away.

However, they were to return to Croft and then to Shobdon to spend their first Christmas together as husband and wife.

After leaving Herefordshire, Edward and Charlotte went to Oxford before going on to Southampton, where they took lodgings for two months. At Southampton they were visited by family and friends including 'Lord and Lady Mendip, the Archbishop of Cashel and his wife, Lady Somerton of Tipperary in Ireland, the Dowager Lady Clifden [Lady Caroline Spencer], the Duchess of Bolton and Lord and Lady Palmerstone'. They stayed in Southampton until November 1798, by which time Charlotte was pregnant. In his journal Edward writes that 'due to some illness we were prevented from visiting friends during the whole time we were there'; Charlotte was possibly suffering from severe morning sickness.

The next we hear of the couple's whereabouts is from the diary of Lady Bateman – 'Tuesday 19 December 1797: Mr Nares preached in this church a very excellent sermon.' Edward also preached at Shobdon on Christmas Day 1797, and on Sunday 31 December. Lady Bateman also describes 'the good news of the Archbishop of Canterbury giving a living of three hundred a year in Kent to Mr Nares', Lord John Bateman having previously written to the Archbishop regarding a living for Edward. In the meantime the Archbishop had told Lord Mendip (see Appendix G), one of the couple's visitors at Southampton, that 'he proposed to provide for Lady Charlotte's husband'. Edward had received the Archbishop's letter offering the living of Biddenden in Kent while they were having their supper, much to everyone's delight. Lady Bateman even attempted a family reconciliation with Charlotte's parents but without effect.

On 17 January 1798, Edward went to London to receive the orders for the induction of his Biddenden living. As the rectory at Biddenden in Kent was unfurnished, he decided to rent a house near his brother-in-law Captain Preston (Sophia's husband) in Hampshire for five months; Edward felt that an unfurnished rectory would not be at all advisable given that his wife was then heavily pregnant. The final entry in Lady Bateman's diary concerning her guests is dated 1 March 1798 and simply states, 'Mr Nares and Lady Charlotte left us.'

Today the old house of Shobdon Court where the Batemans lived does not exist, except for the arches which were once a part of it. Parts of the original house have been incorporated into the house now called Shobdon Court, which is still privately owned. The year before the old house was demolished in 1933 there was a sale of the contents, which included portraits of Charles Spencer, 3rd Earl of Sunderland, John Churchill by Vanderbank, and Duchess Sarah by Kneller.

Lord John Bateman was one of the first aristocratic patrons of Thomas Gainsborough. In 1770, Gainsborough is known to have presented a group of drawings to him, which may have included a portrait of the painter's mistress, Miss Elizabeth Tyler, a fiery young woman who was the daughter of the vicar of Shobdon. Certainly, Gainsborough's well-known *Landscape with Travellers Returning from Market*, *c.* 1770, was painted in Bath for Lord Bateman. At the time, Gainsborough was living at number 24 Royal Crescent in the city. Gainsborough's first biographer, Philip Thicknesse, was also a friend of Lord Bateman. There is a charming portrait of Lady Anne, which at one time was attributed to Gainsborough, showing her wearing a grey dress with a white fichu (neckerchief) and a black lace scarf, a grey bow on the front and a small black band round her neck, with pearls in her powdered hair. Another wonderful painting, by Nicolas de Largillière (see Appendix G), shows her husband as a boy, dressed as a young cupid, wearing a red robe and holding a flaming torch. On Lord Bateman's death the peerage became extinct and the estate passed to his cousin William Hanbury (see Appendix G) of Kelmarsh Hall, Northamptonshire, which is still in the ownership of the Hanbury family.

Having the Batemans nearby appears to have been a blessing to Edward, as it gave him a golden opportunity to hone his skills at writing sermons and preaching to the faithful. The Batemans and the honeymoon at Croft are portrayed in his memoirs in the most favourable terms, but sadly these idyllic times were soon over. The harsh realities of earning a living and raising a family were to dominate Edward and Charlotte's married life at Biddenden in Kent.

Scene III:
The Curtain Descends

After Edward and Charlotte left Shobdon on 1 March 1798, they arrived at Catisfield, near Fareham in Hampshire, on the 5th and stayed with his youngest sister Sophia and her husband D'Arcy Preston. It was while they were with the Prestons that they received more invitations, this time from Lord Robert Spencer and from Charles Lennox, 3rd Duke of Richmond (see Appendix G) to visit Goodwood. However, these offers were refused, as Edward thought that they might 'give umbrage at Blenheim', although he does not explain why they would cause offence.

On 25 April, Edward visited Biddenden for the first time in order to meet his parishioners. The following day he went to Tenterden where he met the Archbishop's preceptor, the Revd W. P. Warburton, the outgoing incumbent, returning to Biddenden two days later for his induction. On 29 April, he read the articles and gave directions for 'the fitting up my house', and returned to Catisfield on 1 May. Just three weeks later, at three o'clock on the afternoon of 22 May, Charlotte was 'safely delivered of a daughter', Elizabeth Martha. Edward wrote to all members of the family, including the Duke and Lord Blandford. In time he received a letter from Lord Blandford, which enclosed a note saying that 'the Duke and Duchess of Marlborough are glad to hear their daughter is well'. The child was baptised at Biddenden on 8 July, her sponsors being Viscountess Bateman, the Countess of St Vincent (first cousin to Edward's mother) and his uncle, W. Strange, the christening ceremony being conducted by his old Oxford friend Dr Landon. Not long after the birth of Elizabeth Martha, Charlotte was sent an invitation to visit Blenheim, but as it did not include her husband she declined the offer and as a result Charlotte was never again to enter her childhood home.

On 25 August 1798, the Nares family finally took possession of The Rectory in Biddenden. This Georgian house, now named Wykeham House and privately owned, stands close to the parish church of All Saints; it is of a brick construction, with its Georgian façade virtually unchanged. Internally on the ground floor there are three main rooms off a large hallway with an elegant turned staircase. One of these rooms was Edward's study, probably the room at the side of the house overlooking the church, with its Georgian fireplace and hearth still *in situ*. Another staircase leads to a substantial cellar with its original brick floor. However, first impressions of the area were not good. Edward wrote in his memoirs that 'coming out of a most populous neighbourhood nothing could appear more dismal to us at first than the Weald of Kent and Biddenden in particular'.

It was not an easy time for Edward, who 'lamented the angry manner in which some of his parishioners were disposed to receive their new rector'. Apparently they had reacted badly to his taking of the church tithes and had said that they would make him 'wipe the waggon wheels before they entered their fields'. Biddenden was in an agricultural area and had its own spring and autumn cattle and horse fairs, as well as other annual local events including the baking of special Biddenden cakes at Easter, which celebrated the medieval origins of the place. These cakes bear the figures of two women, reputed to be conjoined twins, Mary and Eliza Chulkhurst, who lived at Biddenden in medieval times, although some historians claim that the cakes derive from a later charity that distributed food to the poor from the local so-called 'Bread and Cheese' lands (see Appendix L).

As winter approached, Edward and Charlotte received solicitations urging them to leave Biddenden, which lay in the flood-plain of the River Beult and was thought to be an unhealthy place for a baby. On 7 December, following this advice, they moved to lodgings in Tunbridge Wells, although 'Charlotte had become attached to Biddenden and the house and she did not willingly move to Tunbridge', according to Edward's memoirs.

In March 1799, Edward's uncle died, leaving a library of 80,000 books, pictures, bronzes and fossils. He had been a distinguished book collector when he was the British ambassador to the Venetian Republic, and over a period of thirty years had built up a vast library. A catalogue of the books to be auctioned, drawn up by a Mr Patterson, was published in two volumes under the title of *Bibliotheca Strangeiana*. The auction itself was held at the European Museum in London, but as that was not large enough to display many of the pictures, some were moved back to his uncle's house in Portland Place. Among these family pictures were drawings of The Abelis of Switzerland, which had been drawn for his uncle's friend, the late Earl of Bute.

In his memoirs Edward does not specify exactly when in 1799 they returned to Biddenden though he does say that he 'resided the whole summer at my living'. On 18 July, Charlotte was delivered of their second child, a boy, christened Henry Richard Bateman at Biddenden church on 13 August – 'Henry' after Charlotte's favourite brother, and 'Bateman' after their honeymoon friends at Shobdon.

As winter approached, the Nares family again received invitations urging them once more to leave Biddenden, as Charlotte's health was causing concern. It was while they were residing at Tunbridge Wells during the winter of 1799, that Edward and Charlotte went up to London to take medical advice, as Charlotte was now suffering from 'spasmodic rheumatism'. Sadly, Charlotte 'received no benefit from the advice of those we consulted in London' and in the middle of March 1800 they returned to Biddenden. Worse was to follow, for on 1 April their little son Henry died. Edward wrote, 'He had long been weakly, and we had tried many expedients to rear him, but in vain; he was just 8 months old.'

Better news was to follow on 30 July 1800, when Charlotte was safely delivered of her second daughter, who was christened Charlotte Maria on 27 August. One of the sponsors was Lady Mary Osborne, sister of the Duke of Leeds and later Countess of Chichester, who had been one of the bridesmaids at the royal wedding in 1795. The other godparent was Lord Francis Almeric Spencer, Charlotte's younger brother, whose portrait by Sir William Orpen today hangs in the undercroft entrance to the private apartments of the family at Blenheim. In the latter part of his life, the 4th Duke relied heavily on his youngest son Lord Francis, 1st Baron Churchill of Wychwood. But of far greater worry to Edward was Charlotte's health, which was causing such serious concern that they decided to move to Brighton – 'the sea air being recommended for her' – for the whole of the winter of 1800/01.

It was in 1800 that Edward started writing his book *One God, One Mediator*, which he intended to publish anonymously (see Appendix M). In his memoirs he wrote that 'no person living but Lady Charlotte knew what I was about', and it seems that Edward and Charlotte discussed the various theological arguments presented in the book and that some of Charlotte's own beliefs and ideas were included as well. Charlotte even sketched out a frontispiece for the book, but the expense of having it engraved was too great. It cost Edward £170 to publish and in return he received £18! He did in fact allow his name to appear as the author and dedicated the book to the Archbishop of Canterbury. Edward also seems to have been a born writer of sermons, for in 1803 he published his book *Sermons Composed for Country Congregations*, which included many of the sermons that he had preached every Sunday to his Biddenden parishioners.

A more pressing concern that occupied Edward while at Brighton during that winter was the question of a family reconciliation, especially as Charlotte's health was still causing much anxiety. But sadly nothing more was forthcoming with regard to either a family reconciliation or an improvement in her health, and so they returned to Biddenden from Brighton in the spring of 1801. But hardly had they settled in than Charlotte's health deteriorated further: 'Her spasms became violent, she almost lost the use of her limbs and besides had a bad cough.' So once again they returned to the house at Sandgate, Brighton. Throughout all this, 'Charlotte never uttered a complaint and was constantly cheerful, her children being a constant source of delight'.

Part of his wife's health problems, according to Edward's journal, 'stemmed from one of her "lying-ins", and there was some reason to think that she had received an injury during that time'. In the autumn of 1801, the couple moved to Bath, where it was hoped that 'the thermal waters might prove beneficial to her rheumatism', arriving there on 2 November. They stayed in a house next to her sister Lady Anne Ashley-Cooper, who was there with her own family; in fact, Lady Anne had engaged the house for them.

It was while they were in Bath that Lady Anne, with the best of intentions, pursued the possibility of a family reconciliation, but without having any success. However, as Edward writes, 'it was ill timed as Charlotte was in no fit state to worry about it all' and that although they lived next to the Ashley-Coopers, he did not communicate with or visit them. He also states that 'the only real encouragement that Charlotte received from her parents was that the D[uke] and D[uches]s would be glad to see Her, if they should be in town when she returned from Bath'. Edward continues, 'Alas her return from Bath was never to take place.' It seems that 'each hour Charlotte's condition worsened and that she was too ill to admit company'. The worst part of it was:

When the children were allowed in to see their mother, their playfulness and unconcern and the delight their poor mother seemed to have in their company pierced me to the soul. Nor can time ever obliterate from my mind the remembrance of that moment, when I knew, by all appearances, that I was bidding them wish her good night for the last time.

It was on 14 January 1802 'that I plainly discovered that she could not survive the night. Charlotte retired to her bed at her usual hour and I laid myself down beside her.' In the next room was the physician Dr Haygarth and Charlotte's faithful maid. The doctor prescribed laudanum, after which Charlotte 'complained of a deadly faintness beyond all she had ever felt before'. During the night she drank strong coffee, and at seven o'clock on the morning of 15 January 'she breathed her last' with Edward holding her hand. In his memoirs Edward wrote:

> Thus ended the short life of as good, as amiable, and virtuous a woman as, I think, ever existed. Her attainments were manifold, her understanding sound and strong, her temper so serene that I do not recollect a single instance of its being ruffl'd, and above all, her religious feelings were deep and ardent.

Edward states that 'the exact cause of her death was never decisively known'.

Fortunately, Edward's old Oxford friend and travelling companion Mr Greenhill was in Bath with another friend, the Revd George Burrard. Greenhill came straight round to the house to give comfort to Edward who by now was at his wits' end, which explains why he wrote, 'My sufferings were most acute and with reason. For no man ever I think sustained a more severe loss of that nature.'

So ended the life of Lady Charlotte Spencer. She was not only beautiful, clever and good but a gifted pianist and talented artist (see Appendix S), as were her two older sisters Lady Elizabeth and Lady Caroline. It was through Charlotte's younger sister, Lady Anne, that an application was sent for Charlotte's remains to be deposited in the Spencer family vault at Ardley, Oxfordshire, by the side of her brother Lord Henry, whom she had loved so affectionately. The Duke readily agreed to this application, sending people to make the necessary arrangements and paying the cost of it all, including the mourning expenses of the family servants. His Grace also agreed to continue to pay the £400 allowance, made in the lifetime of his daughter, for the education of Edward and Charlotte's children.

Thus writes Edward:

> On Monday, the 15th, the dismal procession set out for Oxfordshire. Those who have feeling hearts will know what I suffer'd when I had to reply to the enquiries of my eldest child after her Mama, while all the bells in the City of Bath were tolling in my ears.

On 21 January 1802, *The Bath Chronicle* reported: 'Friday died in Duke Street in her 32nd year Lady Charlotte Nares wife of the Rev. Mr. Nares and third daughter of the Duke of Marlborough.' At the end of Duke Street lies the church of St John with its tall spire. It is no wonder that Edward wrote about the bells tolling in his ears as the funeral cortège with his wife's body left the house on that sad day.

Edward continues as follows:

The misfortunes that had befallen me excited, I was told afterwards, a considerable sensation at Bath. I was inform'd that anonymous letters were sent from thence to the Duke and Duchess, not written in the most respectful terms. If this was really the case I deeply lament it, and can only feel myself the more bound to acknowledge that I received from every branch of the family, their Graces not excepted, all the consolation I could expect. The letters I received in reply to those which Mr. Greenhill wrote for me, as well as to the few I was able to write myself, were most considerate and obliging. One of those letters from her eldest brother, Lord Blandford, began as follows: 'The unmerited attention which you have paid to my poor sister during her melancholy illness, calls for my warmest acknowledgements, and I heartily give them ...' Lady Blandford wrote to me as kindly, and both expressed an earnest solicitude about my children. I had similar letters from Lady Diana Beauclerk and the Countess Dowager of Pembroke [daughters of the 3rd Duke of Marlborough], from Lady Elizabeth Spencer [Charlotte's sister], the Archbishop of Canterbury and many others. I must not omit our kind friends Lord and Lady Bateman, who were greatly grieved at my loss.

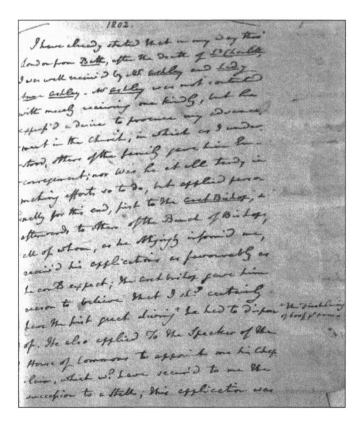

Fig. 6 A facsimile copy from Edward Nares' journals at Merton College, Oxford, dated 1802, the same year that Lady Charlotte died in Bath.

Sometime between Lord Henry's death in 1795 and Lady Charlotte's in 1802, Duchess Caroline had paid for alterations to the church of St Mary at Ardley, involving the rebuilding of the nave and its windows, the five originals being replaced with the four windows that exist today, all of which face due south.

After the funeral at St Mary's church on 28 January 1802, Edward went up to London with his children and stayed with his brother John. It was while he was in the capital that he called on the Ashley-Coopers, even though 'I had never spoken to them since my marriage'. The 6th Earl of Shaftesbury told Edward that other members of the family wished to meet him and his children, but he declined all invitations, saying that 'Charlotte had expressed a wish that her children should not live in London'. Having no desire to return to Biddenden, Edward left London for Brighton to visit a special friend of Charlotte's, although he does not say who this is. While in Brighton, he 'took care to be with his young children whenever possible, especially at meal times, so that he could continue to endeavour Charlotte's way of bringing up the children'. They raised their children in accordance with the progressive child rearing practices advocated by Jean-Jacques Rousseau.

In his journal Edward copied down a poem he had written about the trials and tribulations following Charlotte's death, which includes these lines:

> The fairest pattern that the world e'er saw
> The best example of the purest life
> The fondest mother, and the chastest wife
> The mildest mistress, and the warmest friend.

At the end of his first journal Edward writes, 'With these lines I shall conclude this first volume of my strange life.'

In 1813, Edward was appointed Regius Professor of Modern History at Oxford University, the year of Napoleon Bonaparte's defeat at the Battle of Leipzig, which was followed in April 1814 by Napoleon's abdication when a new political understanding was established between Britain and Russia, resulting in the Congress of Vienna (1814–15). It was during this period that the British Government invited the Tsar of Russia, Alexander I, known as 'The Blessed', to visit London and to receive an honorary degree at the University of Oxford.

Tsar Alexander arrived in England on 8 June and on the following day was created Knight of the Garter at the Prince Regent's London home, Carlton House. Accompanying Alexander was his favourite sister Ekaterina Pavlovna, the Duchess of Oldenburg. On 14 June, the Russian entourage arrived at Oxford at one o'clock and were accommodated at Merton College. Edward recorded in the second journal of his memoirs that the college authorities had decided that the Tsar would be lodged in the Queen's Room, which had been occupied by Charles I's wife, Henrietta Maria, during the Civil War. It seems that the Tsar preferred to sleep on a mattress on the floor in preference to a bed offered him by the college, Edward adding that four of Alexander's entourage slept in their clothes on the landing place of the staircase and did no small damage by their foreign habits and disregard of the value of the furniture. The following day all those involved with the proceedings processed through Oxford to the Sheldonian Theatre for the degree ceremony, wearing long wigs, academic caps and furred academic robes. During the ceremony the Tsar sat on the right of the Prince Regent, while to Prince George's left sat the King of Prussia, Frederick William III, who was there with Marshal Blücher to receive honorary degrees.

To commemorate this royal occasion Peter Vaughan, the Warden of Merton College (1810–1826), installed at his own expense in the Queen's Room two stained-glass windows with the emblem of the Russian double-headed eagle. In the main hall at Merton, Vaughan also erected a monumental tablet with a Latin inscription to commemorate the Tsar's visit.

In *The Works of Samuel Parr* are letters written by Vaughan to Parr concerning the visit of the Tsar and about a Silesian jasper vase, nearly five feet high, which Alexander had sent as a thank-you present to Merton College. Parr, as a classicist, was chosen to compose an inscription on an iron plaque to be placed alongside a similar inscription in Russian by Count Lieven, the Russian Ambassador. This vase is said to be the most important Russian object ever to be donated to the University of Oxford.

In Edward's second journal he also relates his attendance at the 4th Duke of Marlborough's funeral in 1817:

> Tho' conducted very privately the sight was very awful and grand – the body was convey'd from the Front door to the chapel very slowly. The service was read in the vault which was lighted up for the purpose and all the family descended into it, exhibiting a very striking appearance.

By 'the family' Edward meant only the men and the executors, including Lord Ashley-Cooper, the 6th Earl of Shaftesbury, Lord Robert Spencer and the Duke's steward, James Blackstone.

Between 1817 and 1820, Edward, as Regius Professor of Modern History, read a course of twelve lectures on political economy in Merton Hall, Oxford, at seven in the evening on Mondays, Wednesdays and Fridays. He wrote up these lectures in eleven notebooks, which are held in the Bodleian Library.

Whether Edward kept individual diaries of each year of his life is not known, but he did however keep a Commonplace Book covering the years 1791 to 1805, which was sold at Sotheby's on 17 March 1961. In it he recorded various things of interest to him, many of which he had copied from books and newspapers of the time. Some pages are full of classical quotes in Latin and French, others relate to scientific, medical and religious ideas, and there is even a short description of Captain James Cook's voyage:

> Captain Cook with a company of 110 men performed a voyage of 3 years and 18 days throughout all ye climates from 52° north to 71° south latitude with ye loss of a single man only from disease. A curious instance of efficiency of regime in preserving health under all varieties of climate.

Sadly for Edward, his marriage to Lady Charlotte had only been of the same duration as Cook's third and last voyage – five years. No wonder Edward had written at the start of his first journal about life's precariousness.

Cook's remarkable first voyage on his ship *The Endeavour* is memorable for his discovery of Australasia in 1770, his voyages helping to contribute towards Britain's increase in power and influence, which led in time to it ruling large parts of the world. In the 1770s, Britain was at war with its own subjects in America, which in turn resulted in France declaring war on Britain and America's Declaration of Independence. Edward and Charlotte had lived through these politically dangerous years in the reign of George III and the turbulent times of the French Revolution of 1789, the year that saw the last of Blenheim's private theatricals.

ACT V

All the World's a Stage

Two aristocratic families connected to Blenheim who were instrumental in forming their own private theatres were the Lennoxes and the Berkeleys. The Lennox family, who were the Dukes of Richmond, lived in London's Whitehall and at Goodwood near Chichester in Sussex, while the Earls of Berkeley had lived at Berkeley Castle in Gloucestershire for nearly nine centuries.

In 1750, the 4th Earl of Berkeley's daughter Elizabeth was born. Lady Elizabeth (see Appendix O), who loved acting and was deeply romantic, married at the early age of seventeen Lord William Craven, who succeeded to a baronetcy just after their marriage. As young thespians and wealthy aristocrats, Elizabeth and William were invited to certain aristocratic homes including Blenheim. There, on 7 January 1773, Lady Elizabeth recited an extempore epilogue, dressed in a greatcoat and jockey-cap, with a whip in her hand, at the conclusion of the Blenheim production of James Townley's *High Life Below Stairs*. In this, Elizabeth played the part of Rag, Harriet Wrothesley was Tag, whilst Bobtail's part was played by Tibby, a little boy fiddler to the Duchess of Marlborough. Where exactly at Blenheim this took place is not known, but it is feasible that either the Bow-Window Room, used during the 1st Duke of Marlborough's time, or the Duchess's Sitting Room, in the private east wing at Blenheim, were utilised on this theatrical occasion in 1773. It is not known whether the three large murals in the Sitting Room had been completed by then. These pastoral scenes were done in the manner of Hubert Robert, as architectural capriccios, so that Duchess Caroline's decision to use them as a stage backdrop is possible, especially as this room has suitable entrances and exits for the actors to use. However, Elizabeth, writing to her friend Joseph Cradock (see Appendix G), reported that 'there is no stage at Blenheim nor are there any plays to be acted there, that I know of, and if there were I believe I should certainly be informed of them'.[1]

In March 1774, Elizabeth sent a copy of some verses of poetry written by the Revd Charles Jenner (see Appendix G) to the Duchess of Marlborough. It included a prose dedication in French, *À Moi-Meme*, signed on 28 November 1773. At Claybrooke in Leicestershire there is an epitaph on a monument to Jenner's memory, written by Elizabeth Craven after his death in 1774 (see Appendix K). As Lady Craven, Elizabeth had previously organised private theatricals at the family seat of Coombe Abbey in Warwickshire, with the assistance of Jenner and Cradock.

Fig. 7 Courtyard scene at Berkeley Castle, childhood home of Lady Elizabeth Berkeley.

Fig. 8 Berkeley Castle, the home of the Earls of Berkeley, Gloucestershire, for over 800 years.

It is probable that Charles Jenner is from the same family as Edward Jenner (see Appendix G), the father of immunology. Edward was born in the vicarage at Berkeley, right next to the castle where Elizabeth grew up. As children, Edward and Elizabeth would have known each other, Edward being one year younger than her. Today he is remembered for his discovery that inoculation with cowpox gave immunity to the disfiguring disease of smallpox.

Elizabeth kept a diary, which included not just theatrical performances but the people she knew and visited, including the Spencer family at Blenheim, according to A. M. Broadley:

> In London, the duke and duchess of Marlborough shewed their partiality to me, and Mr. Walpole, afterwards Lord Orford, Dr. Johnson, Garrick, and his friend Colman, were among my numerous admirers; and Sir Joshua Reynolds did not conceal his high opinion of me. Charles Fox almost quarrelled with me, because I was unwilling to interfere with politics – a thing which I always said I detested, and considered as being out of the province of a woman.
>
> Blenheim was on the road between Benham [Newbury] and Coombe Abbey [Coventry], and I was constantly in the habit of calling there, and on one occasion stayed there ten days. I there learned from some of the intimates of the Duchess, what it was that induced her to give me such a preference as she appeared to do. It was the perfect conviction that her Grace had, that I had not the slightest desire to attempt to please or govern; as she was particularly apprehensive that any one but herself should have any influence on the Duke. It was here again that my negative virtue came to my assistance.
>
> One day, a little child of the Duchess's, only two years old, threw herself screaming on the carpet on my entrance, and terrified the Duchess. I threw myself instantly on the carpet and imitated the child's cries; which soon pacified the child, and the Duchess was diverted beyond measure.

On another occasion the following amusing event occurred while Elizabeth was staying at Blenheim:

> The first thing occurred at Blenheim, when the Duke of Marlborough desired Lord and Lady Pembroke and me to bring the Duc de Guînes [Adrien-Louis de Bonnières, 1735–1806] to Blenheim. The Duc, one day after dinner, had some common syllabub made of warm milk from the cow, which was brought in for him to taste, as a national country dainty; – he did not like it, and putting down the cup, he turned to the Duchess, and said, '*Pardonnez, Madame la Duchesse, mais je n'aime point votre sillybum.*' The Duke ran out of the room laughing, and the Duchess, who was sitting on a sofa with me, was unable to speak; and as he questioned every body, they all left him but the Duchess and myself: when he, finding he could get nothing out of us, went in quest of Lord Herbert, the present Earl of Pembroke, who, instead of explaining, ran away from him laughing most heartily.[2]

Elizabeth and her husband were at that time living at Benham House, Stockcross, near Newbury, Berkshire. Benham House was rebuilt in 1775 to a design by Henry Holland

and his father-in-law 'Capability' Brown. Two pairs of gate piers were brought from Lord Craven's family seat to adorn the entrance to the carriage drive, and are still visible today from the A4 London–Bristol road.

In 1773, 'Capability' Brown landscaped the park at Benham for Lord Craven, enhancing the estate beside the River Kennet by building a Chinese bridge across the river. Brown had already been working for Lord Craven at Coombe Abbey, the magnificent monastery and deer park that had been in the Craven family for generations, with its collection of portraits including Queen Elizabeth I, Lady Jane Grey, Charles I and Prince Rupert. However, his patron's real interest lay in racing, not in the landscaping of his estates. In her memoirs of 1826, Elizabeth Craven wrote that they had been plundered 'over the costs' by 'the famous man called Capability Brown.'[3] Perhaps some of her hostility was due more to the fact that her marriage to Lord Craven was foundering and that his money was fast disappearing. According to Elizabeth, her husband spent £12,000 on Benham, although Brown's account books show £7,000.

It was at Benham that Elizabeth translated the French playwright Pont de Ville's comedy *La Somnambule*, which was performed at Newbury's Town Hall on 11 and 12 May 1778. Elizabeth then wrote a comedy called *The Miniature Picture*, which was produced at Drury Lane. In 1780, this play was performed at Richmond House in front of various aristocrats, including the Duchess of Richmond, Lady Harcourt, Lady Edgcumbe, Lord Ailesbury, the Hon. Mrs Damer, General Conway and Elizabeth's husband Lord Craven. Her growing success in the world of private theatricals led her to produce a play with the immensely wealthy aristocrat and bibliophile William Beckford of Fonthill in Wiltshire. This was a five-act magical piece entitled *The Arcadian Pastoral*, the cast including not only her own children but also those from three other aristocratic families.

The success of this led Elizabeth and her husband to utilise their London home, Queensberry House, to write and produce musical operettas to be performed solely by children of the aristocracy, but it was this venture that led to Elizabeth's downfall from society following reports of scandalous behaviour at Queensberry House. As a result of this dubious reputation, the children of these aristocratic families were forbidden by their mothers to participate in any further productions there.

It was in 1780 that Elizabeth and her husband separated and she left England. For nearly five years, she travelled around Europe, even going as far as Constantinople in Turkey and later publishing a popular account of her travels entitled *A Journey through the Crimea to Constantinople*. Eventually she settled at the Court of the Margrave of Anspach in Germany in 1787, as the Margrave's adopted sister. Elizabeth had first met the immensely wealthy nobleman in Paris, when he was married to a princess of Saxe-Coburg and kept a French actress as his mistress, but it did not take Elizabeth long to dispatch both of them. In 1791, only sixteen days after she had heard of the death of her husband, Elizabeth married the Margrave in Lisbon. He then sold his principality to the King of Prussia and purchased Benham and its estate from Elizabeth's son, the 7th Baron Craven, later the 1st Earl Craven.

Once they were married she persuaded her stolid German husband to retire to England and purchase a large and fashionable country villa on the banks of the River Thames at

Hammersmith, then a village near London. It was at Brandenburg House that an old riding school was converted into a theatre to enable the Margravine to entertain her husband and at the same time indulge in her favourite pastime of taking centre stage. However, on her return to England, Elizabeth found herself cold-shouldered by the court and high society.

At Brandenburg House she employed a manager, Le Texier, who had previously acted with her at Newbury when she was married to Lord Craven. However, according to A. M. Broadley in *The Beautiful Lady Craven*, the genesis of the dramatic performances at Brandenburg House came from Blenheim, and possibly the music for the Blenheim theatricals was arranged by Dr Philip Hayes (see Appendix G), Professor of Music at Oxford University. A manuscript album belonging to Lady Elizabeth and Lady Caroline Spencer was in Broadley's possession.[4] One of the plays performed at Brandenburg House was the popular *High Life Below Stairs* in which the Margravine played a pert chambermaid. As we have seen, this had been performed at Blenheim in 1773, when Elizabeth Craven had recited an epilogue dressed as a jockey.

On 7 November 1792, *The Times* reported:

> A Theatre building by The Margravine of Anspach, will be very pretty when finished. It is already in great forwardness. The outward appearance of it, however, has nothing to commend it, for one should rather suppose it to be a Bastille, than a temple dedicated to the Muses.

This referred to the fact that the house was built in the castellated Gothic revival style, which had been initiated at Strawberry Hill, Twickenham, by Horace Walpole. Painted on the walls of Walpole's parlour at Strawberry Hill were the decorative motifs of Lady Diana Beauclerk's *Gypsies*. Walpole was the second cousin and godfather of the sculptress Anne Damer, the daughter of Field-Marshal Conway and Lady Ailesbury who lived near Henley at Park Place. Walpole admired his god-daughter's work and had bought her terracotta sculpture of two dogs, one a poodle and the other a spaniel, modelled in 1782. Today the sculpture is at Knowsley Hall, having been bought by the 13th Earl of Derby, who was a collector of fine arts and was no doubt attracted by the amusing and affectionate portrayal of the two animals. The 13th Earl, who succeeded to the title at the age of fifty-nine in 1834, built an extensive aviary and menagerie at Knowsley. Today he is remembered for being the patron of the artist Edward Lear (see Appendix G) who lived and worked at Knowsley from 1831 to 1837, after which he moved to Italy. Anne Damer's marble sculpture of two dogs, which she gave to her brother-in-law the Duke of Richmond, can be seen at Goodwood.

In 1793, the Prince of Wales was invited to Brandenburg House to see the Margravine act. Part of the entertainment for this royal theatrical occasion included a prologue, written by Elizabeth, in which she praises famous men including John Churchill, the 1st Duke of Marlborough. On another royal occasion, she sang in both French and Italian and played various musical instruments in the presence of the Duke of Clarence. In 1805, a new publication about provincial theatre called *The Theatric Tourist* by James Winston was dedicated to 'The Patronage of Her Serene Highness the Margravine of Anspach' and included drawings of many of England's major provincial theatres.

After her second husband's death in 1806, Elizabeth had no heart to continue with her private theatre and decided to move abroad. She died in Naples in 1828. The last tenant of Brandenburg House was the unfortunate Queen Caroline of Brunswick, who died in 1821. The following year, Brandenburg House and its theatre was demolished.

The other famous late eighteenth-century private theatre in London with connections to royalty and to Blenheim was at Richmond House. Owned by the Lennox family, Richmond House stood on what is now Richmond Terrace off Whitehall and overlooked Westminster Bridge. Goodwood House is the country seat of this great family dynasty, whose history starts with the reign of Charles II. Today at Goodwood, the 10th Duke of Richmond's oldest son Lord March has continued to enhance the Lennox reputation in the fields of horse-racing and motor sport. Every year, as part of the festivities, a re-enactment takes place of the Duchess of Richmond's Ball, which first took place on the eve of the Battle of Waterloo at which Napoleon was defeated. In the Small Library, Napoleon's campaign chair is still used.

The Lennox family's love for private theatricals goes back to the year 1732, during the time of the 2nd Duke. It was then that Dryden's play *The Indian Emperour* was performed in front of a select audience that included members of the royal family as well as the Duke and Duchess of Richmond. This royal patronage continued right into the 3rd Duke's life, when Richmond House was patronised by the cream of Georgian society and its theatre had become the most fashionable and exclusive of all private theatres. However, unlike Brandenburg House, Richmond House had no specially designed building, instead utilising rooms specially adapted for the purpose by James Wyatt.

For the first season, in 1787, Wyatt converted two first-floor rooms on the south side of the building into a playhouse, with a large saloon as an ante-chamber. Double doors were thrown open in the ante-chamber when the play was about to start. The royal box with its gilded columns was in a recess on one side of the playhouse, with a gallery in the bow window opposite that could seat fourteen people. The interior decoration was designed by Anne Damer, who was responsible for the theatre's full-length portrait figures by John Downman that were painted on the walls of the theatre. These four portraits were of fashionable ladies who were close friends of the Lennox family: Georgiana, Duchess of Devonshire, her friend Lady Elizabeth Foster, Lady Melbourne and Anne Damer herself. Thomas Greenwood of Drury Lane painted the scenery for the plays, including *The Guardian*, performed at Richmond House in 1787 and 1788. He also painted the scenery at Blenheim in 1788. The actors were either friends or relatives of the Lennox family and included the 12th Earl of Derby, who played the role of Lovemore in *The Guardian*, Anne Damer playing the female lead of Mrs Lovemore.

In the 1788 productions at Richmond House, the celebrated actress Sarah Siddons (see Appendix G) gave advice to the ladies on their costumes, which were always of the highest quality. Owing to the unexpected success of the venture, there were seven performances in the first season, with special friends being allowed to attend an open rehearsal. Tickets were of a different colour for each night and were distributed in small batches to actors or friends. The recipients had to write the name of their guest on each ticket, seal it with their arms and send in the names of their guests the day before. Each performance would start at 8 p.m. On 19 April, the Prince of Wales was the guest of honour and came with his mistress, Mrs Fitzherbert, the Prince sitting between the Duchesses of Richmond and Devonshire. Other guests were the Duke and Duchess of Cumberland, the Sheridans, Mrs Garrick, and the political foes William Pitt and Charles James Fox. On the last night, 17 May, the King and Queen attended with four of their daughters to watch Arthur Murphy's play *The Way to Keep Him*. Rehearsals for the next season of theatricals at Richmond House began just before Christmas, with the dashing Lord Henry Fitzgerald, a nephew of the Duke of Richmond, as one of the principal actors, with his brother Lord Edward and his stepfather William Ogilvie also playing parts.

By 1788, the theatre was in a new location as the Duke had bought the adjoining house on the west side (formerly the home of the Earls of Loudoun and Mar) for Lord George and his son Charles Lennox. In this house Wyatt designed a new theatre with the stage on the first floor and the orchestra and pit sunk below. There was a large central box high up opposite for the Duke and Duchess of Richmond and their guests, with a regal canopy for the King in the centre. There were also side-boxes lined in pea green in which all the seats had backs. The Prince of Wales attended the first night on 7 February, together with the Dukes of York and Gloucester. Apart from royalty and the Lennox family, the audience included Fitzgeralds, Ogilvies and Keppels. Another regular attender, Horace Walpole, wrote reports on it to his friend the Countess of Upper Ossory, who had also started giving theatricals at her own home, Ampthill Park in Bedfordshire. Others who attended included the actor John Philip Kemble and the intellectual blue-stocking writers Hester Piozzi and Hannah More. On one occasion the performance was interrupted by the late arrival of Charles James Fox, Lord North and General Burgoyne.

The beautifully arranged dramatic performances at Richmond House owed their success entirely to the Duke. Cast lists for each production were announced in *The Times,* with a review usually appearing a few days after the opening night. Each performance had a very personal air, with special prologues and epilogues for royal visitors in the first season. Ices and other refreshments were presented at suitable intervals, and supper was served for selected guests afterwards, accompanied by songs and toasts which could last until 4 a.m. The Duke was always trying to improve the detail, managing to create a glittering fantasy world for his guests, where family and the fashionable could mingle at ease. These were not merely social events but were also a forum for intelligent discussion. Richmond House Theatre showed the 3rd Duke of Richmond at his best while working on a project, such as the production of the popular play *The Guardian*, which was also a great favourite at Blenheim and was produced three times there. The Richmond House production included the actor Richard Edgcumbe who replayed the part of Young Clackit he had previously performed at Blenheim. All of this was commented on by Frederick Reynolds, who had just returned to London from Switzerland. In his memoirs he wrote:

> I found the whole town infected with another mania – Private Theatricals. Drury Lane and Covent Garden, were almost forgotten in the performances at Richmond House, and the Earl

of Derby, Lord Henry Fitzgerald, Mrs Hobart [later Countess of Buckingham and step-sister of the Duke's wife] and Mrs Damer in *The Way to Keep Him*, and *False Appearances* were considered, by crowded and fashionable audiences, equal, if not superior, to Kemble, Lewis, Mrs Siddons and the present Countess of Derby, Elizabeth Farren.

The Duke and Duchess of Marlborough, imitating and emulating the example of the Duke of Richmond, erected a splendid theatre at Blenheim, with the intention of there producing a theatrical representation, which should totally eclipse all previous attempts.'[5]

Reynolds does not make reference to Richard Edgcumbe by name, even though he had played a part in Murphy's play *The Way to Keep Him*. Nor does Reynolds mention that the cast of actors included Lady Mary Bruce, the daughter of Charles, 3rd Earl of Ailesbury and the 3rd Duke of Richmond's third wife, or that the Duchess of Richmond's stepfather was General Conway, who dedicated the play *False Appearances* to the beautiful actress Elizabeth Farren (see Appendix G), who directed the plays at Richmond House. It was common knowledge at the time that Elizabeth owed her appointment to the Earl of Derby. Her portrait was included in the set of fashionables painted by Downman for the scenery of the first play *The Way to Keep Him*. Neither does Reynolds mention that General Conway wrote the prologue to that play, nor that the epilogue was written by General Burgoyne, who had retired from his military career after the defeat of the British at Saratoga in the American War of Independence. It was then that Burgoyne withdrew his support of Lord North's government and joined the Whig opposition led by Charles James Fox. At the same time, the 12th Earl of Derby, Edward Stanley, who was the brother-in-law of Burgoyne, also withdrew his political support of the government. It was with Burgoyne's encouragement that the 12th Earl developed a great love of the theatre and for amateur dramatics, which in turn led to his love of the actress Elizabeth Farren, whom he later married.

Elizabeth Farren's patron was the Duchess of Leinster, who was the sister of the immensely wealthy Duke of Richmond and was on the fringes of the free-living Devonshire House set. Elizabeth was employed by the Duke to supervise his theatre during 1787 and 1788, but the Earl of Derby, who was in an unhappy marriage but was not prepared to divorce his wife, had been Elizabeth's protector since 1785. It was Lord Derby who persuaded the Duke to employ her. Lord Derby's first wife was Lady Elizabeth Hamilton, who in 1778 had started an affair with John Sackville, 3rd Duke of Dorset (see Appendix G) after meeting him at a cricket match at 'The Oaks', the Stanley family's country home near Epsom where the famous horse race The Derby was established in 1780. As a result of this affair, Elizabeth Hamilton was ostracised by society and her husband, the 12th Earl, endeavoured to erase all traces of her life. He is reported to have burnt her portrait by Reynolds.

In 1797, the Earl of Derby married his beloved actress, six weeks after the death of his wife. Elizabeth Farren made her final farewell appearance as Lady Teazle in Sheridan's famous play *The School for Scandal* to a packed Drury Lane on 8 April 1797. After her marriage, she never referred to her acting days but was known as the gracious hostess of the Earl's seat at Knowsley. Much of this was reported not only by Frederick Reynolds but also by Caroline Powys in her diary.

1. The Spencer family portrait, painted by Sir Joshua Reynolds in 1778. Lady Georgiana Charlotte Spencer, aged nine, is holding a theatrical mask and stands next to her youngest sister, Lady Anne Spencer, aged five.

2. George Spencer, 4th Duke of Marlborough, wearing the Order of the Garter, painted by George Romney in 1779.

3. *The Young Fortune-Teller*, J. Jones, 1790, after J. Reynolds, *c.* 1774–75, depicts Lord Henry Spencer and Lady Charlotte Spencer, as children.

4. The Orangery at Blenheim Palace was converted into a private theatre for the Spencer family in 1787.

5. Lady Charlotte Spencer in *False Delicacy*, act IV, scene 2, as Miss Rivers, with Lord Charles Spencer as Colonel Rivers, painted by J. Roberts of Oxford, on 8 December 1788.

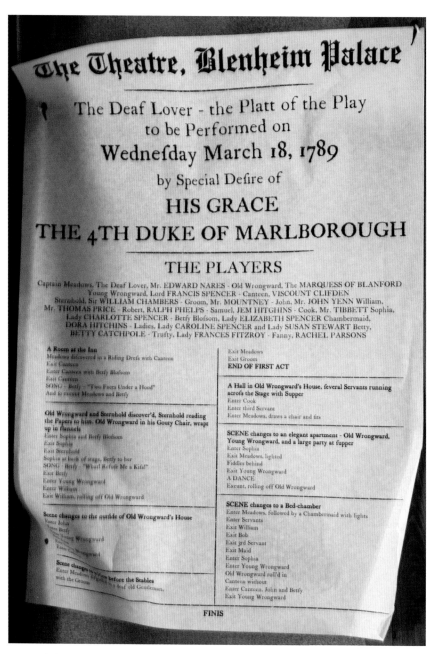

6. Headed *The Theatre*, Blenheim Palace, this poster can be seen by today's visitors to Blenheim Palace, in the exhibition named *The Untold Story*. In the play *The Deaf Lover*, performed on 18 March 1789, Edward Nares played the part of Captain Wrongward and Lady Charlotte Spencer performed the part of Betsy Blossom. The cast included the architect John Venn, who in 1789 designed The Temple of Health at Blenheim to celebrate the recovery of King George III.

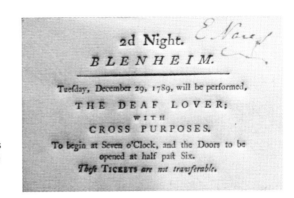

7. Ticket, with the titles of two plays performed at Blenheim Palace on 29 December 1789, inscribed with the name E. Nares.

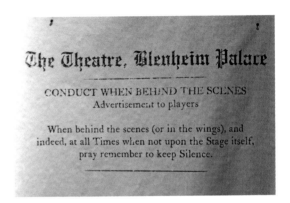

8. Instructions for the actors at *The Theatre*, Blenheim Palace, entreating them to be quiet when not on stage.

9. Ivory theatre box key fobs, dated 1780–91, belonged to Duchess Caroline Spencer, for her private theatre box at The King's Theatre in the Haymarket. The Bridgemans were friends of the Spencer family and lived at Weston Park, in Shropshire, where these theatre fobs were discovered.

10. & 11. These two silhouettes were drawn by Lady Charlotte Spencer, at the time of the private theatricals at Blenheim Palace and are of her brother Lord Francis and her sister Lady Caroline.

12. *Above left:* The caricaturist James Gillray was famous not just for political satire but also for social satire of Georgian society. In this 1791 Gillray cartoon, it is George Spencer, eldest son of the 3rd Duke of Marlborough, a wealthy, eligible young bachelor, who is the target of both the mother and daughter of the ambitious Gunning family.

13. *Above right:* In 2011, Magdalen College School, Oxford, staged in The Orangery at Blenheim Palace, a production of Sheridan's *The Critic*, which had last been performed at Blenheim in 1786.

14. Edward Nares with his older brother George, *c.* 1775, wearing their Westminster School uniform, standing by the gateway, leading to their home, Warbrook House, Eversley, Hampshire. Painted by J. Hamilton Mortimer.

15. Warbrook House was built by John James in 1724 which became the home of the Nares family. Today Warbrook House is an upmarket country hotel.

16. In 1779 Edward Nares was up at Christ Church College, Oxford, as a graduate commoner. At the age of seventeen Edward would have had to travel to Oxford from Eversley, Hampshire, on a stage coach similar to that of *The Blenheim*.

17. As an Oxford University undergraduate, Edward Nares would have enjoyed this view of Oxford from its riverside meadows, while hearing the bells of Oxford's many churches, including the bells of the Cathedral of Christ Church hanging in Tom Tower.

18. Hart Street, Henley on Thames, Oxfordshire leads from Henley's eighteenth century river bridge, up past the Red Lion Hotel and the Church of St Mary into the centre of this attractive town.

19. The Red Lion, is where Lady Charlotte Spencer arrived in a near state of collapse, late in the afternoon of the 21 March 1797, after secretly fleeing from Blenheim Palace to join Edward Nares.

20. The Church of St Mary, Henley on Thames, is where Dr Landon, Provost of Worcester College, Oxford, married the Revd Edward Nares and Lady Charlotte Spencer on 16 April 1797.

21. The Georgian Rectory at Biddenden lies next to the parish church, where the Revd Edward Nares lived with his wife, Lady Charlotte Spencer, from 1798 till her premature death in 1802.

22. The Revd Edward Nares was the Rector of Biddenden for forty three years.

23. The Revd Edward Nares, 1762–1841, Fellow of Merton College, Oxford, 1788–97. In 1827 Edward Nares portrait was painted by Anna Dovetin. The portrait was given to Merton College by his kinswoman, Miss Agatha White.

24. Some of Edward Nares memorabilia in Merton College library, Oxford, includes Edward's hand written journals of his life, letters and four silhouettes drawn by Lady Charlotte Spencer

25. In Whitehall, London, at the 2nd Duke of Richmond's house, the Lennox family put on for the Christmas season festivities, Dryden's *The Indian Emperour*. The Duke of Richmond can be seen watching the performance, leaning over his wife's chair.

26. Berkeley family portrait by O. Humphry, 1780. The inscription reads. *Earl of Berkeley R.N. Countess of Granard. Lady Craven. Lord Craven. The Hon. Berkeley Craven. The Hon. Keppel Craven.*

27. Edward Stanley, the 12th Earl of Derby's great passions were for horse racing, the theatre and the beautiful actress, Elizabeth Farren, whose portrait by Lawrence, hangs in the National Portrait Gallery.

28. The Earls of Derby have lived at Knowsley Hall, near Liverpool, with its beautiful front façade built in the 1720s.

29. In the 1797 Gillray cartoon of Cupid and Pysche, it is the 12th Earl of Derby's marriage to his tall actress bride, Elizabeth Farren that is being satirized. Lord Derby married his beloved actress, who he had courted for many years, after the death of his first wife, Lady Elizabeth Hamilton, née Gunning.

30. Witts family portrait by John Hamilton Mortimer, *c.* 1769. From left to right: John Witts [1750–1816] Richard Witts [1747–1815] Edward Witts [1746–1816] and Apphia Witts, later Lady Lyttleton [1743–1840]. This portrait now hangs in the Cheltenham Art Gallery and Museum.

31. Agnes Witts, wife of Edward Witts, a Cotswold woolstapler of Chipping Norton, Oxfordshire. Painted by Joseph Wright of Derby, painted in Bath *c.* 1776.

Painted by Howard A.R.A.   Published by Longman & Co March 1816.   Engraved by C. Heath

32. *Lover's Vows* owed some of its popularity in that the actors could be observed publicly touching one another.

On 7 December 1787, *The World* reported that the second play to be performed, *False Appearances*, had been translated by Conway from Boissy's *Les Dehors Trompeurs*. Conway may well have heard about Boissy's play being performed almost half a century earlier by the Lennox family. In 1740, when the 3rd Duke of Richmond Charles Lennox was five, he took part in this play at his childhood home of Goodwood, which would have been performed in French. Nearly fifty years later Conway's translation of this play was performed at Blenheim in August 1789, when Edward Nares was the newest addition to the cast.

There were to be no more performances at Richmond House after June 1788, as the King's mental breakdown had cast a great gloom over the court. It was decided to dismantle the theatre, which was subsequently converted into a private house for Lennox and his wife Lady Charlotte. In 1791, Richmond House was destroyed in a fire and never rebuilt. As the building was on an uninsured leasehold and the Duke's income was declining, he was persuaded, partly by his architect James Wyatt, to extend his house at Goodwood. It was there, on the Sussex Downs, that Charles Lennox made room for those works of art that had survived the fire at Richmond House, adding two wings to Goodwood to house what remained of his art collection of nearly 400 oil paintings.

Later in his life the Duke of Richmond supervised the building of a theatre at Chichester, near his Goodwood estate. Holding up to fifty people, it was generously furnished by the Duke and included some beautiful scenery that had previously been at the Richmond House theatre in London. In 1801, on the first evening of the races at Goodwood, many fashionable patrons attended Chichester's new theatre in South Street.

The reason for the closure of the Duke of Richmond's theatre in 1788 is understandable, and it is interesting that in 1790 Blenheim also closed its private theatre. A possible explanation for Blenheim's closure is the scandalous state of affairs that had occurred at the Adlestrop House theatricals in 1788. Duchess Caroline may well have been aware of this and of the elopement concerning the Saye and Sele family in January 1790. The proud Duchess would have been deeply concerned about the possibility of improper pursuits occurring at her home, especially with the onset of family marriages. It was this theme concerning the dangerous intimacy of private theatricals that Jane Austen was to develop in her novel *Mansfield Park*, particularly with the inclusion of the play *Lovers' Vows*, in which the actors reveal through close physical proximity their sexual desires in the roles they played.

ACT VI

Scene I:
The Dangerous Intimacy of Private Theatricals

Private theatricals lie at the heart of Jane Austen's famous novel *Mansfield Park*. Jane was to make much of some of the prejudices of the time concerning these performances, in particular that they led to immorality among the actors. In Georgian society the reward for virtue was a stable marriage and a happy home, and men tended to marry when they were in their late twenties, by which time they had the means and property to provide for their partner. For a member of a family to marry below their social station was a disaster.

Jane was an impressionable young woman, and it is probable that she would have read in the newspapers all about Lady Charlotte Spencer and Edward Nares. Jane's father enjoyed reading the newspapers to his family, and newspapers were only too happy to divulge gossip, especially where private theatricals were concerned.

Jane would have been aware not just from the newspaper reports of the Spencer family and their life at Blenehim Palace, but also through her favourite brother Henry. In 1788 Henry with his brother James and his cousin Eliza de Feuillide visited Blenheim during the time of its private theatricals. Five years later Henry joined the Oxfordshire Militia as a lieutenant, whose colonel in chief was Lord Charles Spencer, brother of the 4th Duke of Marlborough. Lord Charles assisted Henry's promotion to that of regimental paymaster. After Henry's resignation from the militia, he was appointed as Deputy Receiver of Taxes for Oxfordshire, under the auspices of Lord Charles' son, John, who was the Receiver of Taxes for Oxfordshire. John had become romantically involved with Lady Elizabeth Spencer, while acting at Blenheim and in 1790 they married. Since the start of Blenheim's theatricals Lord Charles had been a member of the cast and John had joined the cast in 1788. Henry Austen as a keen amateur actor may have discussed the Spencer family involvement with private theatricals with his family. While Henry was working with John Spencer, he was on occasions invited to the family home of Wheatfield, near Thame. Henry would have been only too well aware that aristocratic lives were under constant scrutiny and that high life scandal was a staple of the newspapers. This was also of considerable concern to the Austen family connections, who were cousins of the Twisleton family of Broughton Castle, Oxfordshire, who at the time had their own family marriage problems.

To fully appreciate this, it is necessary to investigate the family ties of the Leighs, the Twisletons and the Austen family, all of whom were an intriguing mix of gentry, clergy and in part aristocracy. On the aristocratic side, Jane could trace her maternal family origins back into the seventeenth century to James Brydges, 1st Duke of Chandos (see Appendix G). His sister was Lady Mary Brydges, who married Theophilus Leigh (see Appendix A) and had three sons, William, Theophilus and Thomas, known as 'Chick' as the youngest son. Thomas took holy orders and as a fellow of All Souls College, Oxford, was appointed to the college livings of Whaddon and Sonning in Berkshire. When the Revd Thomas Leigh died in 1763, he was the rector of Harpsden. One of his daughters, Cassandra, married Jane Austen's father, the Revd George Austen. His other daughter, Jane, married the Revd Dr Edward Cooper (1728–92).

One of Jane's cousins was James Henry Leigh, who married Julia Judith Twisleton, Lord Saye and Sele's daughter. This branch of the Leigh family lived at Adlestrop, near Stow-on-the-Wold in Gloucestershire. Also living in Adlestrop was Thomas Leigh, who held the family living of the church there for over fifty years. It was this cousin who Jane, at the young age of ten, was to refer to in her pocket book, when she wrote that in October 1785, he had visited Jane and her sister Cassandra at their school near Reading and gave them half a guinea each. A year later, Jane wrote in her pocket book that on Friday 8 December 1786, James Henry Leigh of Adlestrop and Longborough had married Julia Judith Twisleton, his cousin, daughter of the 7th Baron Saye and Sele.

Julia's mother Elizabeth was a gifted actress and musician. She may have played on the English Gothic harp made of maple and spruce that today's visitors to Broughton can admire. It is unusual as it has eight pedals and forty-seven strings and is not decorated with angels. At Broughton there is a painting by Angelica Kauffman of Baron Gregory's wife Maria with her harp. In the autumn of 1787, Lady Saye and Sele performed in the theatricals at Adlestrop House, taking the part of Belvidera in *Venice Preserv'd*, first written by Thomas Otway in 1680. She also performed as Andromache in *The Distressed Mother*, written by Ambrose Phillips in 1711, and as Lady Townley in *The Provok'd Husband*. All of this was described by *The World* on 29 October 1787 as 'Lady Saye and Sele's theatricals'. Among the audience in the autumn of 1787 were the Duke and Duchess of Richmond, Mrs Damer and Lord Henry Fitzgerald, but there is no mention of the Spencer family of Blenheim attending.

One of Julia's brothers was Thomas James Twisleton who, like his mother, was a born actor. He was a pupil at Westminster School, where he excelled both at classics and acting, and there is a painting by Hopner in the Long Gallery at Broughton of him as Phaedra in one of the school's classical plays, *Eunuchus* by the Roman playwright Terence. When this painting was restored it showed Thomas in chains. This probably signifies the family ties of family loyalty and money, although it may be that it shows Thomas tied to his profession as an actor. Hopner painted the portrait two days after Thomas's eighteenth birthday.

In 1787, Thomas appeared as Pierre in *Venice Preserv'd* at Adlestrop House with his mother. His first public performance followed in May 1788 at The Freemasons' Hall, Great Queen Street, London, in Robert Jephson's tragedy *Julia*, first performed at Drury Lane in 1787, in which he played the part of the hero Mentevole, the heroine's part being played by a young and beautiful actress Charlotte Anne Wattell (see Appendix G). Among the audience were Lady Saye and Sele's friends, the Duke and Duchess of Richmond, as well as Albinia Hobart, Countess of Buckingham.

Thomas had previously admired Charlotte from afar and now formed an attachment to her, even though he was still at Westminster School. On 28 September 1788, the two young thespians eloped to Gretna Green where they married. However, family pressure was brought to bear and on 4 November they were married again, this time under English law, at St Mary's, Marylebone. A month later, the couple performed at the Christmas theatrical season at Adlestrop House. The plays included the tragedy *Matilda* by Dr Thomas Franklin, a popular play of its time, and another of Jephson's plays, *The Count of Narbonne*. Another fashionable and popular play performed at Adlestrop House was *Bon Ton* by David Garrick. Among the audience was Agnes Witts, who had previously attended the Blenheim theatricals in October 1788, and wrote up an account of the events at Adlestrop in 1789 in her diary:

Friday Jan: 9th Still no change of weather, went early to Dress, dining early to go to the Play at Adlestrop, with which we were far more entertain'd than expected. Matilda the Play, the performers Mr. Leigh, Mr. & Mrs. Twisleton, Miss Twisleton, Mr. Oliphant, Mr. Thickets & Mr. Heynes, Bon Ton the Farce in which none but Mr. Oliphant were near so capital as in the Play the Drawing Room, made a tolerable good Theatre tho the stage was too small: 24 Spectators out of the Neighbourhood, & the refreshments good & plenty not at home till ½ past one rather fatigued.[1]

The final play of that Christmas season at Adlestrop House was Hannah Cowley's *Who's the Dupe?* in which the young couple played the parts of Gradus and Charlotte. Both *Bon Ton* and *Who's the Dupe?* were after-pieces to the other plays, all of which was reported in the *Morning Post* on 22 January 1789. Curiously *Who's the Dupe?* was also part of Blenheim's theatrical season later in 1789, when Edward Nares played the part of Gradus and Miss Peshall played the part of Charlotte.

Agnes Witts included another account of the Adlestrop theatricals in her diary:

Wednesday Jan: 21st Damp & close in the Morning, & at Noon began raining violently, & so continued the whole Day & night. Mr. Naper came home to Dinner from Cirencester & we early went to the Play at Adlestrop Venice Preserved & who is the Dupe, with a Prologue between by Mr. Oliphant in the character of Mother Shipton riding on a Broomstick, Mr. Twisleton was very great in Pierre & Mr. Leigh little less so in Jaffier. Mrs. Twisleton was not equal to Belvederes difficult part, the Theatre was very full & we did not get home till past two; thro' some perils from floods in Stow Lane the Upper Slaughter family were obliged to sleep here, the floods being too strong to make it safe for them to go home. Rec'd a Letter from Ld. Edward Bentinck & wrote to Mr. Hunt.[2]

The Restoration play *Venice Preserv'd* was first performed in 1682, while the first performance of the farce *Who's the Dupe?* took place at Drury Lane in 1779. These private theatricals at Adlestrop House took place in the drawing room of the Leigh family home. As at Blenheim, Agnes would have been invited to the supper party afterwards.

During the summer of 1789, the Leigh family visited Agnes Witts:

Monday Aug. 10th Just such another fine warm Day too hot to walk much in the Morning, worker & chatted very comfortably, Mr. Leigh his Aunt Mrs. E. Leigh & Miss Twisleton, (Mrs. Leigh not well enough to come) dined here & also Mr. Earle an easy chearfull visit after they were gone walket & play'd a rubber at whist rec'd a Letter from my Sister Travell & wrote to Mrs. Tyrwhitt.[3]

Two days later, it was Agnes's turn to visit the Leighs:

Wensday Aug. 12th A most wonderfull hot Day quite overcoming, we were almost broil'd going in the two Post Chaises to Dine at Mr. Leighs at Adlestrop, first making a short visit at the Parsonage, sat down 11 to Dinner, rather formal but Mrs. Leigh is always pleasant & agreeable; not at home till quite late, rec'd a Letter from Lady Hereford & answer'd it, a small shower at night.[4]

On Thursday 13 August, Agnes received a letter from her friend Mrs Savage of Tetbury, who acted in the theatricals at Blenheim. The two ladies wrote frequently to each other throughout their lives, though none of their correspondence seems to have survived.

The Leighs of Adlestrop were good friends not only of the Witts family but with Warren Hastings of nearby Daylesford. This is what Agnes wrote in her diary in 1789:

Wensday Oct. 14th A very thick Fog in the Morning early but clear'd off so well as to be a most delightfull fine Day with warm air & bright sun, the Gentlemen went to a Land Tax meeting at Chip: & I took Mrs. Western to visit both the Houses of Leigh at Adlestrop, going by the way to survey Mr. Hastings's great works & improvements at Dailsford, a fine situation but a great undertaking to go thro it. Found only Lady Say & Sele & Miss Twisleton at home. Mrs. Rollinson & her Daughter Patty came to us at Dinner, & we had a chearfull evening again, play'd at Cribbage rec'd a Letter from Miss Anne Snow.[5]

The Lady Saye and Sele referred to is Elizabeth Turner (1741–1816), the granddaughter of William Leigh of Adlestrop. She married Thomas Twisleton in 1767, becoming Lady Saye and Sele in 1781 when her husband successfully claimed the title via the Committee of Privileges. Jane Austen and her mother met this garrulous peeress when they were at Stoneleigh Abbey in 1806. While Mrs Austen considered her tiresome, Jane found her affected behaviour most amusing.

The Revd Francis Witts, Agnes's son, also describes Daylesford, the home of Warren Hastings at the time he was being tried in the House of Lords for corruption. Hastings, the first Governor-General of British India from 1773 to 1785, had been impeached for corruption but was acquitted in 1795. Having returned to England in 1784 as a very rich man, Hastings had used his wealth to reacquire the family estate at Daylesford. The previous owner, Jacob Knight, had started building a house but had never finished it, leaving it as a rectangular shell. Despite the uncertainty of his pending impeachment, Hastings set about improving the estate (see Appendix U).

Agnes Witts' description of the plays at Adlestrop House in 1789 is of further interest concerning Thomas and Charlotte Twisleton's decision to become professional actors. Their first professional engagement was at Cheltenham and one of their last theatrical engagements together was at Liverpool in 1793. Here they were accompanied by the theatre impresario Joseph Holman. After Liverpool, the couple were engaged by Thomas Harris for Covent Garden, but Thomas's family persuaded him not to accept the offer. Charlotte defied their advice and made her début, as Belvidera, at Covent Garden in February 1794.

Charlotte refused to stop her stage career while having her children, all of which was to add to the stresses and strains of a thespian life. Sadly for Charlotte, all her five young sons died within ten years of each other, only a daughter surviving into adulthood. In June 1794, Thomas applied for a deed of separation. When the divorce was granted in 1798, he stated that his wife had reduced him to poverty, although at the time he was attending Oxford University, where he had decided to study divinity in order to take holy orders. When giving evidence in the divorce case at the House of Lords, rather than focusing on his wife's alleged adultery with a Mr Stein, he concentrated on her seduction by the world of the theatre as the cause of the couple's initial separation. After his divorce, he married Miss Anna Ashe, whose father was an ex-Bengal Army officer. In 1804, Thomas and Anna went to Ceylon (now Sri Lanka) with their young son, Frederick Benjamin, where Thomas was a minister of the British garrison church. Later in his ecclesiastical career he was appointed as the first Archdeacon of Ceylon. He died in 1824, after twenty years' service to the church in Ceylon.

Some of these scandals were still causing problems with the Leigh and the Saye and Sele families in the mid-nineteenth century. In 1848, Francis Witts wrote in his diary all about these family difficulties, when the Witts gave a dinner party for the Bishop of Antigua and their guests included the new Lord Saye and Sele, formerly Frederick Twisleton of Adlestrop:

February 22nd 1848 In the course of the evening Lord S. and S. opened to me the very anxious position in which he has been placed by the necessity of proving his right to his title before a Comm. of the H. of Lords. The matter is still pending nor can he take his seat, till it is determined in his favour. His father, Dr. Twisleton, Archd. of Ceylon, and a younger Brother of the Lord S. and S. of that day, was a very gay and dissipated young man. Even when a pupil at Westminster School he devoted himself to private theatricals, and at a very early age became entangled with a Miss Wattell a Stage heroine, as young and giddy as himself. Her he married, and poverty, dissention, and separation were the result of the ill conditioned union. She bare him no live child, and on their being parted, she went on the stage as a means of support, he prosecuting his studies at Oxford. At Edinburgh, as an actress, she became the mistress of one Stein, a merchant, who kept her till she had borne him a Son, and eventually separated from her. This connection enabled Mr. Twisleton to obtain a divorce; after which he married a Miss Ashe, the mother of the present Lord and his two brothers. – Till Lord S & S. succeeded to the title and estates, which were left to him by his deceased cousin – who had never married, but had lived a dissipated & eccentric life, always of late years recognizing his cousin, the Rector of Adlestrop, as his heir and successor, these not very creditable family histories had been lulled to sleep, and were hardly remembered, except as recorded in one or two memoirs of persons long since deceased, particularly in those of one Reynolds, an Actor & wit, and companion of the early life of the Archdeacon. – Now it became necessary to revive them; and chiefly to prove that the Son of Mrs. Twisleton, born after her separation from her husband, and before their divorce, could not be his Son by reason of non-access. Extraordinary success has attended the researches made by Lord S. & S's Solicitors. They have discovered, still living, an octogenarian, the Mr. Stein who cohabited with Mrs. Twisleton, the Actress, at Edinburgh, who, having survived to this period, seems to have felt it a point of honour and justice to declare the truth; admitting that he lived with Mrs. T. as man and wife, that a Son was the produce of that connection, whom he considered as his own, and whom he educated for many years, intending to place him in a respectable situation. But losses in trade & crippled means prevented the fulfilment of that design, and the Son eventually became a private sailor in the commercial marine. He, therefore, was sought after by Lord S & S's agents, and was, after long and difficult enquiry, discovered at some seaport on the eve of embarking on a distant voyage; a common sailor of fifty two years of age, the person who might put in a claim to the peerage – but the estates were all securely conveyed so as to be without his reach. He readily confirmed the statement made by Stein, whom he considered his father, who had treated him as his son by whom he had been educated &c. – It remained to prove that circumstances precluded access between Twisleton the husband and his unchaste wife, so as to negative his being the Father of the Sailor. And this could be done; for a correspondence which had been preserved shewed that during part of the time of gestation and before it, Mr. T. had been hiding himself from his Creditors in the West of England, – and that during the remainder of the time he had been keeping term at Oxford, which could be proved by the production of the battle books of his college – St. Mary Hall. The decision of the case will not be long deferred; and it is fully expected a decision favourable to the Rector of Adlestrop.[6]

This indeed proved to be the case, and the rector soon became Archdeacon of Hereford as well as Lord Saye and Sele and owner of Broughton Castle. In 1857, he married again, Caroline, daughter of Chandos Leigh, who had been created Lord Leigh of Stoneleigh, and perhaps the girl whom her mother had brought to Stow for confirmation years before. A family story relates how the archdeacon assembled all his household in the chapel at Broughton Castle before their departure to Hereford, but continued reading Isaiah for so long that his wife sent all the servants to catch the train without him.[7]

Further family dramas occurred at Broughton Castle not long after the private theatricals at Adlestrop House ceased, when Thomas's youngest sister, Mary Cassandra, aged sixteen, eloped with Edward Jervis Ricketts, a solicitor, on Friday 29 January 1790. As Mary Cassandra was a minor, she needed her mother's consent before the wedding took place in

Marylebone. Seven years later, Ricketts discovered incriminating letters between Mary and her lover, one Charles Taylor MP of Cavendish Square, London, which led to their divorce in January 1799. In time, she was to benefit from the will of Thomas Leigh of Adlestrop to the tune of £1,500.

Some years later, in May 1801, Jane Austen went to a party at the Assembly Rooms in Bath, knowing that the fairly large family group there would include her adulteress cousin Mary, whom she had never met. Jane wrote to her own sister Cassandra:

> By 9 o'clock [we] entered the rooms ... and I am proud to say I have a very good eye at an Adultress, for tho' repeatedly assured that another in the same party was *She*, fixed upon the right one from the first! She was not so pretty as I had expected, her face has the same defect of baldness as her sister's, and her features not so handsome. She was highly rouged and looked rather quietly and contentedly silly.[8]

Jane's surviving letters also provide evidence of earlier visits with her sister Cassandra to their other cousins at Adlestrop. In her private account book on 2 July 1794, Jane wrote that Thomas Leigh had passed over £1 16s 6d to his wife Elizabeth to give to Cassandra. It was also during this visit that the Revd Leigh's neighbour and cousin, Mrs Chamberlayne of Maugersbury House near Adlestrop, met the two Austen girls and thought that 'they were charming young women'.

Both Bath and Adlestrop were important to Jane, as they provided not only useful background material for her novels but considerable credence with regard to the Austen family relatives. In particular it was through the Leigh family connections to the Brydges family, Dukes of Chandos, that Jane would have learnt of the 1st Duke of Marlborough's connections with James Brydges, who was paymaster to Marlborough during the War of the Spanish Succession. She might also have found out about James Brydges' investments of land and property in Bath during the 1720s.

Jane was fully aware of the strict code of conduct concerning courtship and marriage, and of the problems that it could cause families. During the Christmas season of 1795–96, she became involved with a handsome and blond family friend named Tom Lefroy. Jane enjoyed flirting with Tom, although it seems that Tom was keener on her than she on him. Tom never forgot Jane, even though he married Mary Paul in March 1799, and in time rose to become Chief Justice of Ireland. Another member of the Lefroy family, a nephew of Tom's, was Captain Anthony Thomas Lefroy, whose son, also named Anthony, became the Chief Constable of Gloucester from 1839 to 1865 (see Appendices G and X).

A few years later, in 1799, after visiting Bath, Jane again visited the Adlestrop cousins. As before, she stayed in the parsonage and worshipped in the church of St Mary Magdalene in Adlestrop, which contains many memorials to the Leigh family, the family vault being under the south transept. However, the most memorable of all Jane's visits to Adlestrop was in July 1806, when she was accompanied by her mother Cassandra. While they were there they received the news that her cousin Thomas Leigh had inherited Stoneleigh Abbey in Warwickshire. This had come about because Mary Leigh of Stoneleigh Abbey had written in 1788 a codicil in her will that her two leasehold estates, one of which was Stoneleigh, were to be held in trust by Thomas Leigh for his nephew, James Henry Leigh of Adlestrop. (After Thomas Leigh's death in 1813, it was James Henry and his wife Julia Twisleton who made further improvements to the landscape and to Stoneleigh's interior decoration.) When Mary Leigh died on 2 July 1806, and because the title to Stoneleigh was likely to be disputed, Thomas Leigh was advised by a local solicitor to take possession as soon as possible. Thus it was that on 5 August, Jane together with her mother and cousin set off for Stoneleigh in the rectory chaise. Accompanying them was Thomas's lawyer, Joseph Hill.

It is possible that Jane was later to use this magnificent house as a model for Sotherton Court in her novel *Mansfield Park*, inherited by Mr Rushworth. After taking possession of Stoneleigh in 1806, James Henry Leigh was to employ the garden designer Humphry Repton to improve the approach to the estate, whose views of the River Avon were blocked by high walls. Repton widened the river in front of the house to form a lake and built a picturesque stone bridge. Prior to this improvement, James Henry had employed Repton at Adlestrop to landscape the park round the manor house. Here he enlarged his parkland by a hundred acres to the west of the house. Legend has it that James Henry personally conducted Jane on a tour of his new park, which was bordered by two artificial lakes on the western end. In order to achieve this, the old road through the village of Adlestrop and nearby Daylesford was closed in 1803. Repton's landscaping improvements at Adlestrop included enclosure of the village green, moving the entrance of the rectory to open up the back of the house and diverting a stream through the gardens to create a picturesque view of the lake. A new stretch of road was then built to replace the old highway, which over the years became a bridleway.

It is said that Jane disapproved of Repton's grandiose landscaping at the expense of the villagers of Adlestrop. This may account for her mildly disrespectful comments about landscaping in *Mansfield Park*, while her description of Thornton Lacey in *Mansfield Park* could well be the village of Adlestrop:

> A retired little village between gently rising hills, finely sprinkled with timber, a small stream, a striking large and handsome church on a sort of knoll to my right, a mansion-like looking house and a parsonage with the air of a gentleman's residence within a stone's throw of the said knoll and church.[9]

In *Mansfield Park* the first group activity before the play sequence is the outing to Sotherton Court. The purpose of the outing ostensibly is to advise its owner, Rushworth, that he is foolish to have already cut down 'two or three fine old trees … that grew too near the house' and now 'talks of cutting down the avenue' of trees at Sotherton, which Jane's character Fanny laments on. Fanny's main concern is, however, with the private theatrical performance of *Lovers' Vows* and the mock marriage ceremony in the Jacobean family chapel and the theatrical tableau of events.

In two of her novels, *Mansfield Park* published in 1814 and *Lady Susan* published posthumously in 1871, Jane Austen was to reveal her love of going to the theatre and of acting in private family theatricals at her parents' home at Steventon, although by the time she was writing *Mansfield Park* private theatricals were no longer the vogue in country houses. In fact, *Mansfield Park* combines several unconnected events in Jane's life, including her great-grandfather Theophilus Leigh's three sisters, Repton's improvements at Adlestrop Park, the Austen theatricals at Steventon Vicarage, and Jane's relationship with her sister-in-law Eliza. The novel is a truly human one, as it portrays both the loss and disappointment that all humans experience.

The choice of the title *Mansfield Park* is also connected to the campaign against slavery. In 1772, Lord Chief Justice Mansfield had started off the process of the abolition of slavery in Britain and freedom for the slaves. In her book *The Real Jane Austen*, Paula Byrne states, 'It is hard to believe it a coincidence that the Austen novel most connected to the slave trade was given the title *Mansfield Park*'.[10] Another of Jane's novels, *The Watsons*, an unfinished manuscript, was sold on 14 July 2011, at Sotheby's in London, for around £1 million. It was bought by the Bodleian Library, Oxford, and is to be displayed there. *The Watsons* is a story about the four daughters of a widowed clergyman and is the earliest surviving manuscript of a novel by Jane Austen.

Scene II:
Jane Austen and Private Theatricals

Amateur theatricals at the time of Jane Austen's birth in 1775 were much in vogue not only amongst the English aristocracy and the gentry but its clergy as well. The Austen family were by no means unique in succumbing to this prevailing craze of late Georgian times. The fashion for private theatricals followed the accession of George III in 1760, a time that witnessed a development of all forms of leisure stimulated by a booming economy that followed the end of the Seven Years War.

The Austen family lived at Steventon in Hampshire. Jane's father, George, was the rector of Steventon and nearby Deane and had married Cassandra Leigh at the church of St Swithin, in the parish of Walcot, Bath, on 26 April 1764. The ceremony was performed by a friend of the bride's family, the Revd Thomas Powys. Jane's mother had grown up at Harpsden in Oxfordshire, where her father, the Revd Thomas Leigh (1696–1764), was the rector and lived in an elegant Queen Anne house. Jane's parents had inherited a fortune of £6,000 and were regarded as better off than many clergy. This enabled them not only to take good care of their children but also to ensure that they received a happy upbringing, as much in terms of their spiritual well-being as of their physical well-being.

Spiritually the season of Christmas and New Year was important, especially when it came to the question of family entertainment at home, which was a sensible and practical way of keeping large families happy and busy. At the same time, these entertainments gave the children an opportunity to broaden their education and to give them confidence in their own abilities. Family entertainment did not just entail acting; it included the broader spectrum of singing, playing an instrument, reciting poetry and dancing. Many families could not afford to educate their children away from home and it was up to the parents to do what they could for their offspring's education before sending them off into the world to earn a living.

Jane had six brothers – James, George, Edward, Henry, Francis and Charles – and one sister, Cassandra, born in 1773, two years earlier than Jane. All the Austen children were born over a fourteen-year span and they all lived on into the nineteenth century. As young girls, Cassandra and Jane were fortunate to be sent to a boarding school near Reading in 1783, Jane's parents having decided that this would be better for them as the house was full of boys. The headmistress of the school, Mrs La Tournelle, was obsessed with the world of the theatre, and play-acting was an integral part of the education provided at the school. In 1786, both Cassandra and Jane left the school and returned home with a love for the theatre and, in Jane's case, a knowledge of certain plays. Even before they had been sent to school in Reading, both sisters had already experienced the joys of family theatricals at home. The Steventon theatricals took place between 1782 and 1790, during the years when some of Jane's earliest literary works, or 'Juvenilia', were written.

In 1782, Jane was only seven when the dining room-cum-parlour was used as a makeshift theatre. The first production, Franklin's play *Matilda*, was produced by Jane's oldest brother James, who was then nearly eighteen years old. It is probable that Jane was only a spectator on this occasion, especially as the play needed a cast of only six players. The following year, no amateur theatricals took place in the Austen household due to the death of a close member of the family, and the same year Jane's brother Edward was adopted by the Revd Thomas Knight of Godmersham Park, Kent, who was extremely wealthy, having been left a fortune on the death of his father. He and his wife Catherine were childless, and in time Edward would inherit the Knight fortune.

By the summer of 1784, the social requirements of mourning were over and Sheridan's comedy *The Rivals* was performed at Steventon Rectory in July of that year. Once again, brother James wrote the prologue and epilogue in verse, and it is feasible that Jane, now aged eight and a half, may have taken the part of a pert maid servant called Lucy. The success of these early performances may have led her father to fit up the old tithe barn 'quite like a theatre', as quoted in a letter by her cousin Philadelphia in 1787. This included a stage, a green baize curtain and oil lamps or candelabra, with the stage scenery done partly by the family with semi-professional help.

For the Christmas season of 1787 at Steventon, Garrick's *Bon Ton* or *High Life Above Stairs*, first performed at Drury Lane in 1775, was proposed. This was to be accompanied by *Which is the Man?* by Hannah Cowley. It is probable that these two plays were chosen due to Jane's first cousin Eliza de Feuillide. Born in Calcutta on 22 December 1761, Eliza was said to be the illegitimate daughter of Philadelphia Hancock and Warren Hastings, and was a pretty and flirtatious girl who enjoyed life to the full in pre-revolutionary France. She had even stayed with French friends who had had a theatre built for acting parties.[1] Eliza married the Comte de Feuillide, who was to be guillotined in 1794 at the height of the French Revolution. In 1787, Eliza and her mother visited England to see their relations and to take the waters at the fashionable spa town of Tunbridge Wells in Kent. It was there, in September 1787, that Eliza saw the two plays *Which is the Man?* and *Bon Ton*. The theme of both is the conflict between the *laissez-faire* French attitude to love and marriage and the more sober and sentimental English one. Eliza may well have fancied herself in one of the leading female roles and was determined that the play should be part of the Austen family Christmas entertainment for 1787. It is probable that Jane's father decided that the plays were not suitable for family entertainment and instead chose Mrs Susanna Centlivre's play *The Wonder: A Woman Keeps a Secret*, first produced in 1744. This was a melodrama set in Portugal. The plays most striking feature is a saucy proposal of marriage by the heroine, who preferred not to listen to her stern father's threats of an arranged marriage or of banishment to a nunnery.

Thus as a young twelve-year-old in 1787, Jane may well have gathered suitable material for her novel *Mansfield Park* written many years later. For the new year of 1788, the play chosen by the Austen family was *The Chances*, a comedy set in sixteenth-century Naples that had been adapted by Garrick from the much older play originally written by John Fletcher. The plot once again dealt with the confusions of disguised ladies and jealous gallants in their search for love. Later that year, Jane wrote a short play called *The Mystery*, which she dedicated to her father. In fact, the year 1788 seems to have been the climax of the Steventon theatricals, with plays being performed every few months. The next production was Henry Fielding's burlesque *The Tragedy of Tragedies or The Life* and *Death of Tom Thumb the Great*. This play, written in 1731, had remained a favourite throughout the eighteenth century.

At Christmas 1788, two more plays were performed at Steventon Rectory: *The Sultan* and *High Life Below Stairs*. *The Sultan* was a two-act farce by Isaac Bickerstaffe, first performed in London in 1775. In this play an English girl, Roxalana, persuades the Turkish Sultan by her teasing wit and charm to disband his harem and make her his one and only Sultana. The other play, *High Life Below Stairs*, written by James Townley in 1759, was a pastiche on etiquette and told the story of a household of idle servants who mimic their masters by drinking, flirting, gambling and quarrelling. This play seems to have inspired Jane, at the age of fourteen, to compose a short vignette herself, entitled *The Visit*, which she dedicated to her brother James in honour of these private theatricals. This winter season of 1788–89 saw the last of the amateur theatricals at Steventon, as Jane's eldest brother James, the family's actor-cum-manager, now had other more serious literary interests in mind. Furthermore, Jane's father may well have been aware that his son Henry had become infatuated with his married cousin Eliza de Feuillide and that it would be injudicious to encourage further amateur theatricals at the rectory.

When the Austen family moved to Bath in 1801, the theatrical scenery was disposed of at the Steventon auction of Austen possessions. This auction took place on Tuesday 5 May 1802 at Steventon and was conducted by an auctioneer named Stroud. In the sale catalogue the scenery was described as a set of theatrical scenes.

It was during the period between 1782 and 1790, when the Austen family's Steventon theatricals took place, that Jane Austen wrote her earliest literary works. Later, memories of these theatricals were to serve Jane well in her adult life as a novelist, especially when it came to the writing of *Mansfield Park*.

Scene III:
Jane Austen and the Theatre

Jane Austen lived through one of the great ages of English stage comedy. Especially popular were the comedies written by Richard Sheridan and Hannah Cowley. In her letters, Jane reveals that she was so steeped in the world of theatre that she particularly enjoyed reading aloud from her favourite plays. The first surviving documented reference to her theatre-going relates to a visit to Astley's Theatre in Lambeth, London, in August 1796: 'We are to be at Astley's tonight, which I am glad of.'[1] Astley's provided entertainment such as pantomime, acrobatics, sword-fighting and musicals. It was this theatrical love that Jane Austen capitalised on as a novelist.

Three years later, in 1799, she visited the theatre in Bath with her mother. Here Jane hoped to see the famous actress Sarah Siddons at the city's Little Theatre, close by the Theatre Royal in Orchard Street. Built in 1749, it was licensed as a Royal Theatre in 1767 and it was considered to be the most successful playhouse outside London. It was also used as a place for actors to 'cut their teeth' prior to performing in London. The original Theatre Royal in Bath is now the Masonic Hall. When the present theatre in Beaufort Square opened in 1805, it was nearly twice the size of the old theatre. Today, a portrait of David Garrick by Jean-Baptiste van Loo *c.* 1740 hangs at the Theatre Royal. It is part of the Somerset Maugham Collection now housed there and at the Holburne Museum in Bath.

Going to the theatre was an integral part of life in Bath, almost as necessary as taking the waters or going to the Assembly Rooms. This is precisely what Jane Austen did on Saturday 22 June 1799 at Bath's Orchard Street Theatre. Here Jane watched Charles Dibdin's play *Birthday*, with *Bluebeard* as the after-piece. This was her second visit to Bath, when she stayed in Queen Square, which was a more central position than Paragon Buildings, close to the River Avon, where she had stayed on her first visit to the city.

The many attractions Bath had to offer may have accounted in part for the Austen family's decision to move there in 1801, although the idea might have been prompted by the Saye and Sele family, who were doing just that at the time. Bath was also where Jane's maternal grandfather had retired in the 1760s and where her parents were married. However, the move from Steventon to Bath would not have been easy for Jane's father, who was suffering from ill health. When the Revd George Austen arrived in the city for the sake of his health he was under the care of a Dr Fellowes, who was Physician Extraordinary to the Prince of Wales. Jane's mother appears to have known this family, as Jane mentions her going to the theatre with Mrs Fellowes.

Jane lived opposite Sydney Gardens, which she thought 'very pleasant'. She noted that 'we might go into the labyrinth every day, as well as the fashionable public breakfasts: so we shall not be wholly starved'.[2] Although Jane at times was dismissive of Bath, she seems to have enjoyed the concerts and fireworks held on Tuesday evenings. Indeed, she was fortunate to be living in the city at a time when the Theatre Royal was at the peak of its popularity. Perhaps it helped take her mind off her father's ill health. Sadly for Jane, her father's health remained of great concern until his death in 1805, the same year as the Battle of Trafalgar and the death of Lord Nelson. Jane cut off a lock of her father's hair as a keepsake. After her husband's death, Mrs Austen and her two daughters decided to move to Southampton in order to be near Jane's brother James and his wife Mary. However, before they finally settled in Southampton the Austens made a round of family visits, including to their Leigh relations at Adlestrop.

In 1808, Jane's brother Edward, having been adopted by the wealthy Knight family of Godmersham, gave his mother and sisters the option of settling in the Kentish village of Wye, near Godmersham, or moving to a cottage in the Hampshire village of Chawton, not far from a palatial property called The Great House that was owned by Edward. Jane had visited her brother and his family at Godmersham on several occasions before 1808, and a portrait exists of Edward by Ozias Humphry (see Appendix G) showing in all probability Godmersham House in the background. At Godmersham it seems that everyone enjoyed taking part in the family entertainments and theatricals, especially as Edward's large family were keen on acting. In the summer of 1805, Jane participated in a performance of Bickerstaffe's *The Spoilt Child and Innocence Rewarded* at Godmersham. Edward's oldest daughter Fanny recorded in her diary acting out a 'game of school' with her aunts, including Jane, her grandmother and her governess.[3] Eventually the Austen ladies decided on Chawton, as it was only twelve miles from her brother James, who lived at Steventon. Chawton was to be Jane's last family home.

During her life it is known that Jane visited the theatre in London on several occasions. Usually she stayed at Brompton with her brother Henry, who had married his widowed cousin Eliza de Feuillide. In 1811, Eliza, who was a talented actress and had a keen interest in the theatre, went with Jane to see *The Hypocrite* by Bickerstaffe at the Lyceum. This play was based on the earlier French play *Tartuffe* by Molière. However, Jane was once again disappointed at not seeing Sarah Siddons perform. This famous actress had been immortalised as 'The Tragic Muse' in a portrait by Sir Joshua Reynolds, after her impassioned performances in Shakespeare's *Macbeth*. During the last year of Eliza's life, Jane was busy working on her novel *Mansfield Park*, and it is said that the characters of Lady Susan and Mary Crawford were based on Eliza. Sadly for the Austen family, Eliza died in 1813, the year that *Pride and Prejudice* was published. *Mansfield Park*, published in 1814, was certainly appreciated by the public, the first edition selling out by the end of the year.

In March 1814, Jane went to London, accompanied by her brother Edward and her favourite niece Fanny, to stay with Henry in Henrietta Street, Covent Garden. During this visit they went to Drury Lane to see Edmund Kean playing the role of Shylock in *The Merchant of Venice*, going the following day to Covent Garden to see *The Farmer's Wife*, written by Charles Dibdin junior. Later that year in November, again at Covent Garden, Jane was to see her last play, *Isabella*, by the dramatist Thomas Southerne, written in 1694. In a letter about this theatre visit Jane wrote:

Fig. 9 The 1895 illustration from the Macmillan original publication of *Mansfield Park*, reveals a Georgian family around a pianoforte. Musical entertainments such as these was often included in the staging of private theatricals.

November 29th We were all at the play last night to see Miss O'Neill in *Isabella*. I do not think she was quite equal to my expectations. I fancy I want something more than can be. Acting seldom satisfies me. I took two Pocket Handkerchiefs but had very little occasion for either.[4]

The role of the heroine, previously acted by Sarah Siddons (who had now retired), was played by the celebrated young actress Eliza O'Neill. Her attempt to follow in the footsteps of Siddons apparently failed to impress Jane, who made a joke of this with her niece Anna, who was watching it with her father Edward Austen. On the occasion of this visit, Jane was in London in order to negotiate the publication of *Mansfield Park*.

The year 1814 was also most probably when the portrait of Jane Austen seated in a room overlooking Westminster Abbey was drawn by an unknown artist (see Appendix O). This is now on display at her family home in Chawton. Four years later, Miss O'Neill was seen in Nottingham, in September 1818, by the Revd Francis Witts:

The sight of a placard announcing that Miss O'Neille was about to perform the character of Belvidera in Venice Preserv'd, a treat which I could not have expected on my Journey, hurried me to the Theatre, & I found the piece already commenced, but the enchantress had not yet trodden the stage. With difficulty I obtained a seat, for the boxes were crowded: the house, more spacious than Country Theatres in general, was but a poor structure, but genius and feeling atone for many deficiencies. Venice & her state are themes of interest in more ways than one; I can say with Lord Byron.[5]

Throughout her life Jane took members of the Austen family, including some of her many nephews and nieces, to see the latest theatrical productions, and these theatre visits provided Jane with plenty of material for the famous play-acting sequence of *Lovers' Vows* in her novel *Mansfield Park*, published three years before her death in 1817.

Scene IV:
Lovers' Vows

Jane was to incorporate the world of amateur private theatricals into her novel *Mansfield Park* with the inclusion of a play called *Lovers' Vows*. This play, translated and enlivened by Elizabeth Inchbald, had originally been written by the dramatist August von Kotzebue. A romance, both in its story and in its sentiments, it had first been staged at Drury Lane in 1724 and was performed many times at Bath's Theatre Royal when Jane was resident in that city. One of Jane's favourite actors was Robert Elliston, the star of the Theatre Royal, who played the role of Frederick in *Lovers' Vows* several times. Elliston had refused offers of acting in London because of his wife's academy of dance and deportment in Bath, but later in his career he became manager and lessee of the Drury Lane Theatre in London.

By today's standards, *Lovers' Vows* is not that remarkable. However, it does fit into the framework of that small, tight world of Sir Thomas Bertram's home in *Mansfield Park*. Jane chose the play with deliberate care, as it would have been relatively well known to her readers in 1814. More importantly, the play contained the exact number of characters to fit the principal persons in her novel, and its simplicity of plot and language was well suited to the capabilities of amateur actors. *Lovers' Vows* gave the actors a far greater opportunity for getting away with the enjoyment of illicit behaviour than was possible in real life, for once on stage they could openly touch and caress one another. Like Susanna Centlivre's play *The Wonder: A Woman Keeps a Secret* performed in 1787 in the Austen household at Steventon, *Lovers' Vows* contains a daring proposal of marriage from a young lady.

In *Mansfield Park* Jane explores the enjoyments of private theatricals, the choosing of the play by the actors, the distribution of the parts, the dressing-up, the gossip, the jokes and even the quarrels involved. All of this is revealed at Sir Thomas Bertram's home, Sotherton Court, as a prelude to the actual performance of the play. Jane also writes about the public interest generated in aristocratic private theatricals:

> To be so near happiness, so near fame, so near the long paragraph in praise of the private theatricals at Ecclesford, the seat of the Right Hon. Lord Ravenshaw, in Cornwall, which would have immortalised the whole party for a least a twelvemonth.[1]

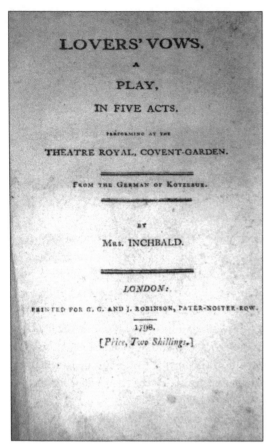

Fig. 10 Jane Austen saw the play *Lover's Vows* when she lived in Bath.

The whole party, which would primarily consist of family and friends, might also have enjoyed the delights of the *pique-nique*, which was much in vogue at the time.

Not long before Jane Austen died, she spent three weeks in Cheltenham, in May 1816, in search of a cure. Some months later, her sister Cassandra also came to take the waters. She stayed in lodgings in the town's High Street at a cost of three guineas a week, which Jane thought expensive. She wrote to her sister, 'How much is Cheltenham to be preferred in May.'[2] A year later, Jane died in College Street, Winchester, on Friday 18 July 1817 at the age of forty-one, and was laid to rest in Winchester Cathedral.

Though Jane never married, her own search for romance and love was of great importance. Even in her impressionable teens she wrote a burlesque on the question of *Love and Freindship* (*sic*), which was based on Samuel Richardson's earlier poetic thoughts. Later, as an adult, Jane was to become the first novelist to explore fully the human relationships of English middle-class society. Her novels were to confirm the popular prejudice that private theatricals led to immorality and to a general lowering of standards of behaviour in Georgian England, which was of such concern to both the clergy and the new burgeoning middle-class of late Georgian society.

Epilogue

In June 1803, at Cranbrook in Kent, Edward Nares remarried. His second wife was Cordelia Adams, daughter of Thomas Adams, a local landowner. Edward and Cordelia had four children, two sons and two daughters, all of whom survived into adulthood and grew up with Edward's only surviving daughter, Elizabeth Martha, from his first marriage to Lady Charlotte Spencer. Elizabeth Martha had been alone at Blenheim at the time of the 4th Duke of Marlborough's death in 1817. Seven years later, she married Lord Henry Spencer-Churchill, son of the 5th Duke. Lord Henry died in 1828, aged thirty-two, and on 18 August 1834, Elizabeth Martha remarried at Biddenden. Her second husband was William Whately, a lawyer, who represented the Nares family at the funeral of the 5th Duke of Marlborough at Blenheim on 5 March 1840. The following year, Duchess Susan, the 5th Duke's wife, died and her funeral was held at Blenheim. A gifted artist, she had befriended Elizabeth Martha, becoming a surrogate mother to her after her mother's death. In her will, Duchess Susan left Elizabeth Martha £200 and a Japanese cabinet from her apartment at Hampton Court, as well as a bookcase with its contents from her London home, and also bequeathed a picture to William Whately.

In March 1860, George Scharf's Blenheim Catalogue was published, which included every painting both at Blenheim and the Spencer-Churchill's London home at 10 St James's Square. The introduction to Scharf's catalogue was written by William Whately QC. In 1857, William and John Whately signed the Residuary Accounts of the Blenheim estate of the 6th Duke of Marlborough and these accounts were passed to the auditors in 1858. William died in February 1866, only eight years before the birth of Winston Churchill at Blenheim in November 1874.

One of Elizabeth Martha's step-sisters was Caroline Louisa, who in 1830 stayed at Blenheim and drew the east front of the palace. It was Caroline Louisa who married the Revd Samuel White, the vicar of Stanstead in Kent and the domestic chaplain to the 7th Duke of Marlborough from 1871 to 1879. Following his death, the post was taken by his son, the Revd George Cecil White until 1889. In 1903, George published *A Versatile Professor*, which was all about his grandfather, Edward Nares. George died in 1936, and it was his daughter Agatha who in her will left Edward's memoirs and some Nares family silver and other memorabilia pertaining to the private theatricals at Blenheim to Merton College, Oxford, in 1961.

Edward Nares was no doubt delighted to have been a part of Blenheim's private theatricals in the 1780s, especially as his own theatrical interests lay in the world of script-writing. Blenheim's theatrical tradition could be traced back to the time of the 1st Duchess of Marlborough, Sarah Churchill, and to her daughters, Mary, Duchess of Montagu and Henrietta, Lady Godolphin, although both Mary and Henrietta had fallen out with their mother over the years. Henrietta had lost her reputation by her relationship with the poet and playwright William Congreve, who was said to be the father of her daughter, Lady Mary Godolphin. All these aristocratic ladies patronised the fashionable world of the theatre, as had Duchess Caroline during the Georgian era's golden age of private theatricals.

Today Blenheim's theatrical tradition continues. In 2011, Magdalen College School, Oxford, put on a production of *The Critic* by Richard Sheridan in The Orangery, the play having first been performed at Blenheim in 1786. Over the years, Blenheim has provided the backdrop for many film productions, including *Young Victoria* and *Harry Potter*, no doubt all of which would have pleased Vanbrugh, who as a playwright and architect visualised Blenheim as a baroque theatrical backdrop for the aristocratic Marlborough family.

Appendices

Appendix A: Select Family Trees

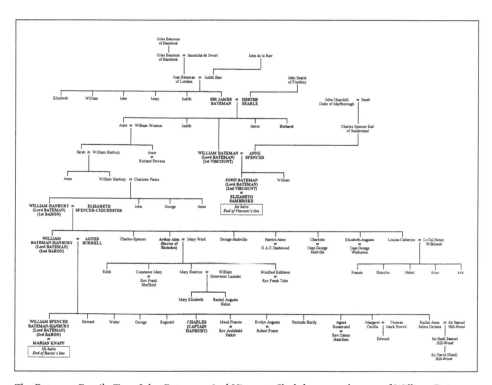

The Bateman Family Tree. John Bateman, 2nd Viscount Shobdon, was the son of William Bateman, who married Lady Anne Spencer at Blenheim in 1720. Lady Anne was a daughter of the 1st Duke of Marlborough, John Churchill.

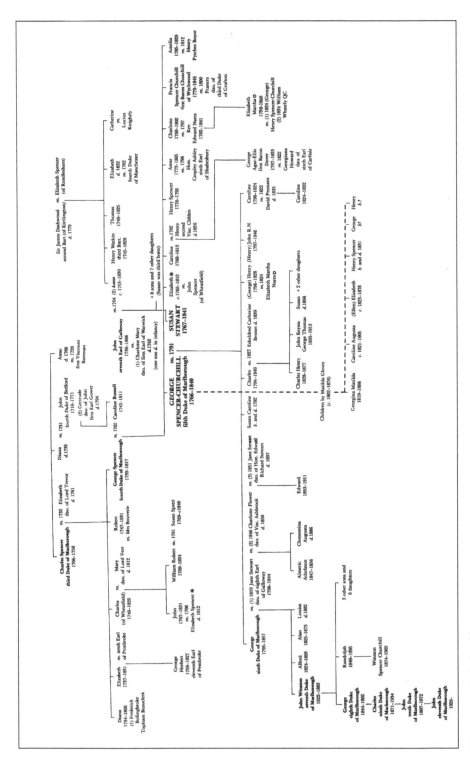

Select Genealogical Table.

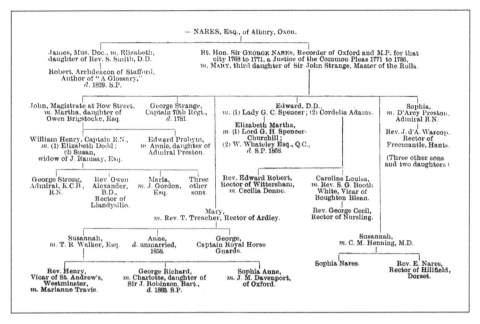

The Nares Family Tree.

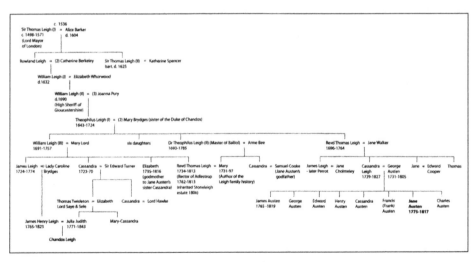

The Leigh and Austen Family Tree.

Appendix B: Chronology 1762–1841

1762	Edward Nares born
1769	Lady Charlotte Spencer born
1775	Jane Austen born on 16 December
1776	American Declaration of Independence from Britain on 4 July
1778	War between France and England over the colonies
1779	Lord Francis Spencer born
1781	Astronomer William Herschel discovers Uranus
1783	William Pitt becomes Prime Minister at the age of twenty-four
1784	War over the American colonies
1785	Hot air balloon makes the first crossing of the English Channel
1787	New private theatre is created in The Orangery at Blenheim
1788	George III shows first signs of madness
1789	French Revolution begins with the storming of the Bastille on 14 July
1790	Lord John Spencer of Wheatfield marries his cousin Lady Elizabeth Spencer
1791	George Spencer-Churchill, 5th Duke of Marlborough, marries Lady Susan Stewart, daughter of the 7th Earl of Gallaway
1791	Radical journalist Thomas Paine publishes *The Rights of Man*
1792	Lady Caroline Spencer marries Henry Welbore Ellis, 2nd Viscount Clifden
1793	Revolutionary France declares war on Britain after executing Louis XVI
1795	The Prince of Wales marries Princess Caroline
1795	Lord Henry Spencer dies abroad
1796	Lady Anne Spencer marries Cropley Ashley-Cooper, 6th Earl of Shaftesbury
1797	Edward Nares marries Lady Charlotte Spencer
1798	Elizabeth Martha Nares born
1799	William Pitt introduces income tax
1800	Lord Francis Spencer marries Frances, daughter of the 3rd Duke of Grafton
1802	Lady Charlotte Nares dies
1805	Lord Nelson dies victorious at the Battle of Trafalgar
1811	The Prince of Wales becomes Regent
1814	Napoleon is exiled to Elba
1814	Jane Austen's novel *Mansfield Park* is published
1815	Wellington is victorious at the Battle of Waterloo and Napoleon is exiled to St Helena
1817	Jane Austen dies on 18 July
1820	George III dies
1841	Edward Nares dies and a memorial tablet is placed in the church of the All Saints, Biddenden

Appendix C: Nares memorabilia at Merton College, Oxford

Apart from Edward Nares' two journals, written after Lady Charlotte's death, other memorabilia belonging to Edward have also been presented to Merton, including some eighteenth-century family silhouettes (considered in those times to be the poor man's portraiture). Among other items are two play tickets, one for 20 October 1788 and the other for 29 December 1789, with 'E. Nares' inscribed at the top right corner. There are also various play programmes, including *The Deaf Lover* and *Cross Purposes*; *False Appearances* and *Who's the Dupe? False Delicacy*, *The Guardian* and *The Liar*.

In addition, the college has five items of silver belonging to Edward: a William IV pair of coasters, R. Garrard *c.* 1836; another pair of coasters with a presentation inscription in memory of Edward Nares, R. Garrard *c.* 1845 (presented by Mrs Ruth Fisher in 1968, another of Edward's granddaughters); and a George III hot-water jug, Richard Sitley 1802, engraved with a crest, with a fluted spout and ivory handle and an inscribed pedestal foot, 10 inches high. The inscription reads, 'In memory of Edward Nares, M.C. 1813–41'. It was presented by his granddaughter Agatha White. Lastly, there is the portrait of Edward Nares, aged sixty-five, painted by Anna Dovetin in 1827.

Appendix D: Plays performed at Blenheim Palace, 1718–89

1718   *All for Love* by John Dryden
1773   *High Life Below Stairs* by James Townley
1786   *She Stoops to Conquer* by Oliver Goldsmith
1786   *The Guardian* by Philip Massinger
1786   *The Critic or A Tragedy Rehearsed* by Richard Sheridan
1787   *The Guardian* by Philip Massinger (produced by David Garrick in 1759 at the Theatre Royal, Drury Lane)
1787   *The Liar* by Carlo Goldoni (inspired by Pierre Corneille's *The Lyar* of 1644)
1787   *False Delicacy* by Hugh Kelly (produced in 1782 at Drury Lane with the actress Mrs Harley)
1787   *Who's the Dupe?* by Hannah Cowley
1788   *The Musical Lady* by George Colman the Elder
1788   *The Maid of the Oaks* by John Burgoyne
1788   *The Provok'd Husband* by John Vanbrugh and Colley Cibber
1789   *Cross Purposes* by William O'Brien
1789   *The Deaf Lover* by Frederick Pilon
1789   *False Appearances* by Henry Seymour Conway (adapted from Boissy's play and dedicated to the actress Elizabeth Farren, produced at Drury Lane, Richmond House and Blenheim)
1789   *Who's the Dupe?* by Hannah Cowley

Between 1786 and 1790, there were nineteen private theatrical productions at Blenheim. *The Guardian* was produced three times and the following were produced twice: *The Liar, Who's the Dupe?, The Musical Lady, The Maid of the Oaks* and *False Appearances*.

Appendix E: Dramatis personae – the cast of principal actors at the private theatricals at Blenheim Palace, 1786–89

Men

Lord Charles Spencer 1740–1820

Brother of the 4th Duke of Marlborough, he was MP for Oxfordshire mainly between 1754 and 1790. His home, Park House at Wheatfield, was destroyed in a fire, today only the church and the stable block remaining. He married Mary Beauclerk in 1762. (See also Henry Austen, Appendix G.)

John Spencer 1767–1831

Son of Lord Charles Spencer, he married his cousin Lady Elizabeth Spencer in 1790. John was an enthusiastic musician and actor and was the Receiver of Taxes for Oxfordshire at the time when Jane Austen's favourite brother, Henry, was deputy Receiver of Taxes for Oxfordshire.

George Spencer, Lord Blandford 1766–1840

Oldest son of the 4th Duke of Marlborough, he married Lady Susan Stewart in 1791. He lived at Whiteknights near Reading, now owned by Reading University, and succeeded to the title of 5th Duke of Marlborough in 1817.

Lord Henry Spencer 1770–1795

Second son of the 4th Duke of Marlborough. At Christ Church College, Oxford, he was a friend of George Canning. After Oxford, Lord Henry was employed at the British embassies in Holland, Sweden and Prussia. In July 1792, in Dresden, while on his way to Vienna on a special mission on behalf of the British Government to compliment the new Emperor on his succession, he met Lady Elizabeth Webster (see Appendix G). His great-grandfather, John Churchill, the 1st Duke of Marlborough, was the only Englishman ever to be awarded the title Prince of the Holy Roman Empire, for saving the city of Vienna from the armies of Louis XIV during the War of the Spanish Succession. Henry, who was shy but charming, succumbed to the charms of Lady Elizabeth. In her diary she wrote that 'he was very witty and possessed a superabundant stock of irony' and 'in short, he became ardently in love with me ... he was the first man who had ever produced the slightest emotion in my heart'.[1] Elizabeth followed in Henry's footsteps, but on arrival in Vienna she found that he had gone to Pressburg (now Bratislava). She followed him there and made a note in her diary that they had parted not later than 25 or 26 September, and it must have been at this time that Henry gave her a Blenheim spaniel, 'Pierrot'. This dog can be seen in the portrait of Elizabeth painted in Naples by Robert Fagan, governor of the Ionian Isles, probably in May 1793. By August 1793, Elizabeth was in Brussels, heading home to England, but her mind was still preoccupied with Henry. When she arrived in Belgium she received a packet of letters from him, who 'talks of coming to meet me, but it was not to be easy as he can be absent from The Hague [where he was Secretary to Lord Auckland] only by stealth'. Alas, they failed to meet as Henry was sent to Stockholm. Two years later, Henry died in Berlin, aged twenty-four, where he was Envoy Extraordinary to the Court.

Frederick Robinson 1746–1792
See Appendix G.

Lord William Russell 1767–1840
His grandfather was John Russell, 4th Duke of Bedford, who was married to Gertrude Leveson-Gower. It was their son Francis, Marquess of Tavistock, who married Lady Elizabeth Keppel. Their third son married Lady Charlotte Anne Villiers, eldest daughter of the 4th Earl of Jersey, in 1789. His oldest brother became the 7th Duke of Bedford and his other brother, John, was twice Prime Minister. Lord William was murdered by his valet, François Benjamin Courvoisier, in May 1840. In the correspondence of Harriet, Countess Granville, she writes about this shocking murder:

> On 12th May, Lady Holland writes agitatedly to Henry Fox about the murder of Lord William Russell, Lord John's uncle: '... I have been so much overwhelmed with horror ... nothing is proved ... case very strong against the Valet ...'

Three days later, Charles Greville also reported the case, which, 'has excited a prodigious interest, and frightened all London out of its wits'. Courvoisier was tried, convicted and hanged.

The following male members of the cast were not members of the Spencer family:

Richard Edgcumbe 1764–1839
The only child of George, 1st Earl of Mount Edgcumbe in Cornwall, he went to Christ Church, Oxford, matriculating in 1781. On 21 February 1789, he married Lady Sophia, one of the daughters of the 2nd Earl of Buckinghamshire. Edgcumbe was Tory MP for Fowey from 1786 to 1795, the year he inherited the earldom. An enthusiastic amateur actor and musician, he wrote an opera, *Zenobia*, which was performed at the King's Theatre in the Haymarket in 1800. He was the author of *Musical Reminiscences of an Old Amateur*, concerning the Italian opera in England from 1793 to 1823.

In May 1787, Edgcumbe played the part of Sir Brilliant Fashion in *The Way to Keep Him* at Richmond House, wearing a richly embroidered crimson velvet jacket with quantities of rings, seals and diamond pins. It appears that he wore a virtually identical costume at Blenheim, as can be seen in James Roberts' picture of him in the cast of *The Guardian*.

Lord Henry Fitzgerald 1761–1829

The fourth son of Emily, Duchess of Leinster, he grew up at Leinster House in Dublin, which was designed by Richard Cassels in 1745 for the Earl of Kildare (later the 1st Duke of Leinster). This house, said to be the prototype for the White House in Washington DC, is now the seat of the Irish Parliament. Henry's father also owned Carton, Co. Kildare, well known for its private theatricals. After a short military career, Henry joined the social round in London and in Dublin. A born actor, he was invited in 1787 by his cousin, the Duke of Richmond, to join the cast of *False Appearances* and given the role of the Marquess to perform, Lord Derby playing the part of the Baron, and Mrs Damer the part of the Countess. Henry became the company's star performer, the Earl of Ailesbury writing in his diary, 'Lord Henry's acting was incomparable.' He was even said to rival that other great amateur actor Lord Derby, who was enamoured by the beautiful actress Elizabeth Farren. It was under Elizabeth's direction at Richmond House in 1788 that Henry took the role of Don Felix (made famous by David Garrick, who played the part sixty-five times in twenty years), a Spanish nobleman in Susanna Centlivre's play *The Wonder: A Woman Keeps a Secret*. This was his first attempt at comedy. In November 1789, Henry left the Duke of Richmond's company and opted for the Duchess of Marlborough's theatre at Blenheim. Not long after, he married Charlotte Boyle of Boyle Farm, near Thames Ditton, Surrey.

Henry was the 3rd Duke of Richmond's nephew and a cousin of the politician Charles James Fox. His brother, Lord Edward, one of Ireland's leading radical revolutionaries, was at one time the lover of Mrs Elizabeth Sheridan before his marriage in 1792 to Pamela Egalité, the illegitimate daughter of Philippe, Duke of Orléans.

Robert Banks Jenkinson, Lord Liverpool 1770–1828

Eldest son of Lord Hawkesbury, 1st Earl of Liverpool, Robert was educated at Charterhouse and Christ Church College, Oxford, where he was known as 'Jenky'. Having entered parliament in 1791 as MP for Rye, in 1801 he was Foreign Secretary and on Pitt's return to office joined the Home Office. During his time as Prime Minister from 1812 to 1827 he became known for taking strong measures to maintain order during the difficult years that followed the Napoleonic Wars.

Thomas Parker 1763–1850

Parker was the 5th Earl of Macclesfield, brother of the 4th Earl, and lived at Shirburn Castle, near Tetsworth, Oxfordshire.

Ladies

Lady Caroline Spencer 1763–1813

Oldest daughter of the 4th Duke of Marlborough, Lady Caroline was baptised at the church of St Martin in the Fields, London. In March 1792, she married Henry Welbore Ellis, 2nd Viscount Clifden of Gowran, at Syon House in Middlesex. Lady Caroline's married name was Agar until her husband changed his surname by licence to Ellis in 1804. MP for Co. Kilkenny in Ireland and a Fellow of the Society of Antiquaries, he died at Twickenham in 1836. The couple had two children, Caroline and George.

Lady Elizabeth Spencer 1764–1812
Elizabeth married her cousin John Spencer of Wheatfield in 1790.
Her epitaph at St. Mary's, Ardley, states what a great loss Lady Elizabeth's death was to her family.

Lady Charlotte Spencer 1769–1802
On 16 April 1797, Lady Charlotte married Edward Nares in Henley-on-Thames. When she fled Blenheim to join Edward at Henley, she took letters from her brother Henry that may have alluded either to his affair with Lady Elizabeth Webster or to Charlotte's thoughts and views on her relationship to Edward prior to Lord Henry's death in 1795. Lady Charlotte gave gifts of her drawings to Queen Charlotte, her godmother, after whom she was named. She was also named Georgiana after her godfather, George III. Queen Charlotte's miniaturist painter was Samuel Finney, who painted a miniature of Lady Charlotte Spencer, before her marriage to Edward Nares.

Lady Susan Stewart 1767–1841
Daughter of John Stewart, 7th Earl of Galloway, she loved dancing and had a reel named after her. In 1791, she married the oldest son of the 4th Duke of Marlborough, George Spencer, later the 5th Duke. Their son George became the 6th Duke and married his cousin Lady Jane Stewart. Duchess Susan was a gifted artist; her floral art is still much admired by visitors to Blenheim today.

Unfortunately, it has not been possible to ascertain the complete dates of two of the principal lady actors who were not members of the Spencer family:

Isabella Pigot 1750–?
Born in Westminster on 5 November 1750, she never married and procured one of the few jobs open to gentlewomen when she became companion to the Prince of Wales's mistress Maria Fitzherbert, being invaluable to them as a go-between, note carrier and social secretary. The Prince became very attached to Isabella, naming her 'Piggy'. In Lady Forrester's autograph book she was described as 'Belle Pigot' and 'a most singular person'.

Isabella knew all the court gossip and was a welcome guest on the many regular visits she made to the great houses of Staffordshire and Shropshire. Her relatives were Lord George Pigot who acquired Patshull Hall in Staffordshire in 1765. It was designed by James Gibbs *c.* 1730. Lord George, the 1st Baron, never married and after his death the estate passed to his brother Robert. In 1785, Isabella wrote to Duchess Caroline from Althorp (see Appendix I) and the following year she acted at Blenheim in Goldsmith's comedy *She Stoops to Conquer*.

Elizabeth Maria (Mary) Peshall
Said to be the daughter of Sir John Peshall of Horsley in Staffordshire, she married Sir Busick Harwood, Professor of Anatomy at Cambridge University, in July 1798. They had no children.

Catherine Savage
Friend of Duchess Caroline and of Agnes Witts, the diarist. (See Appendix W.)

Lady Frances Fitzroy 1780–1866
Family friend of Duchess Caroline. (See Appendix Y.)

Appendix F: A brief synopsis of five of the private theatricals performed at Blenheim

Hugh Kelly's *False Delicacy*

This comedy, first performed on 23 January 1768, starts with Lady Betty Lampton's refusal of Lord Winkworth's offer of marriage, which was 'infinitely more the result of an extraordinary delicacy, than the want of affection for your lordship'. However, the plot is further complicated by showing that Miss Marchmont is in love with Sidney, but will marry out of a mistaken sense of obligation to Lady Betty. Sidney is expected to marry Miss Rivers, but she secretly prefers Sir Harry Newburgh.

John Burgoyne's *The Maid of the Oaks*

This comic opera revolves around the theme of love. Oldsworthy prepares a *fête-champêtre* to celebrate the marriage of Maria to Sir Harry Groveby; she is a paragon, and proves to be Oldsworthy's daughter and a great heiress, but Oldsworthy has concealed these facts lest pride and flattery corrupt her. In the underplot Lady Bab Lardoon rumbles the lady-killer Dupeley by pretending to be a shepherdess. The piece is enlivened with much music and song, and at the end a druid makes an appearance, as a fashionable touch. The play was first performed at Drury Lane in November 1774.

George Colman the Elder's *The Musical Lady*

In this play, first performed on 6 March 1762, a penniless wooer persuades Sophy, an heiress, to marry him by pretending to share her taste for Italian music. However, once he has secured Sophy and her fortune, he mocks her out of her enthusiasm, to the delight of her father, who declares that 'this passion for music is but one of the irregular appetites of virginity!'

Hannah Cowley's *Who's the Dupe?*

In this comedy the nimble-witted aristocrat Granger is shown making a fool of the *nouveau riche* merchant Doiley. Though his daughter Elizabeth is in love with Granger, Doiley is determined that she should marry the scholar and pedant Gradus. Elizabeth, who dislikes solemnity, employs the help of her cousin and friend Charlotte to be rid of Gradus, leaving her free to marry Granger. Meanwhile, to her astonishment, Charlotte accepts a proposal of marriage from her rejected suitor. The play was first performed in 1779.

Richard Sheridan's *The Critic*

The play was first performed at Drury Lane in 1779 and follows a day in the life of a theatre critic, Mr Dangle, whose advice is sought after by numerous caricatured theatrical persons, from worthless playwrights to arrogant actors. Dangle glorifies the theatre, and in his self-appointed role as London's pre-eminent critic, he believes that it will bring him fame and power. In Act I, Dangle is joined by his fellow critic, the aptly named Mr Sneer, who introduces the first subject for Sheridan's wit to attack the pious moralising and melodramatic use of the theatre as a 'school for public morality', as Sneer would say.

Appendix G: Supporting cast of dramatists and other persons connected with Blenheim, primarily in the eighteenth century

Miles Peter Andrews.1742–1814

Andrews was a dramatist who enjoyed the society of actors and authors and had a reputation for wit and good humour. As well as being a producer at Drury Lane from 1774 to 1790, he wrote plays and operas, and was assisted by Frederick Reynolds at Covent Garden. He wrote an epilogue for *The Agreeable Surprise* at Brandenburg House for the Margravine of Anspach in which the Margravine appeared as Cowslip; it achieved fame after James Gillray's cartoon of her as Cowslip was published. Several of his plays were performed at The Haymarket, including a five-act comedy, *Dissipation*, in 1781. In the epilogue to his play, Andrews wrote about the fashionable world of the Ton: 'Ladies, for us exert this darling passion; Do, ton it here, and make the play the fashion.' At his house in Green Street, Mayfair, he entertained the rich and famous of Georgian Society. There is a memorial to him in St James's church, Piccadilly.

Henry Austen 1771–1850

Henry was not only Jane Austen's favourite brother but her first official biographer. After graduating at St John's College, Oxford, in 1788, the year that he visited Blenheim Palace with his brother James and his cousin Eliza de Feuillide, he eventually decided on a military career. In 1793, he joined the Oxford Militia as a lieutenant before finally rising to a captaincy. The Oxford Militia had been formed under the auspices of the 4th Duke of Marlborough and was fully recognised once George Spencer had signed for its official formation at Marlborough House in London on 9 April 1778. Amongst other signatories was Lord Charles Spencer, the Duke's brother, who was appointed its Colonel-in-Chief.

Following his marriage to Eliza, Henry took her to Ipswich and rejoined his regiment. While at Ipswich, Eliza had many admirers, including Lord Charles Spencer, which was to assist Henry in his promotion in the militia, in time becoming the regimental paymaster. It is probable that this financial experience encouraged him to resign from the militia in 1801 and go into banking. In 1804 and 1807 respectively, Henry was joined by two fellow ex-officers, Henry Maunde and James Tilson, to found the bank of Austen, Maunde and Tilson in London's Covent Garden.

His friendship with Lord Charles Spencer continued throughout his banking career and led to his appointment as Deputy Receiver of Taxes for Oxfordshire, following a loan of £2,500 to Lord Charles. Henry was also invited to Lord Charles's home at Wheatfield, when he was on official taxation business with John Spencer, the actual Receiver of Taxes. John, Lord Charles Spencer's son, had married his cousin Lady Elizabeth Spencer in 1790. In 1813, the year that Henry's wife Eliza died, Henry was appointed to take over from John Spencer, who had fled to the continent in order to escape his creditors. One of the creditors was Henry's bank, which had loaned John £6,500. In 1816, when Henry's bank went into liquidation and he was declared bankrupt, his career took a completely new direction. He took holy orders and became the curate at Chawton in Hampshire. The following year, he attended his sister Jane's funeral in Winchester and following her death became the rector of Steventon. Henry's second wife was Eleanor Jackson, whom he married in 1820. In 1824, Henry was appointed perpetual curate at Bentley near Farnham, not far from Chawton. He died at Tunbridge Wells and is buried there.

Richard Barry, 7th Earl of Barrymore 1769–1794

Barry was an infamous rake, gambler, womaniser and friend and companion to the dissolute Prince of Wales (later George IV). Nicknamed 'Hellgate', he is said to have squandered £300,000 in his career. At his home at Wargrave, Berkshire, he built a private theatre in the 1780s at a cost of £60,000. Later the 7th Earl enlarged it to include a special box with its own drawing room and private staircase for the Prince of Wales. He bought the Marionette Theatre in Savile Row and renamed it the London Theatre. Owing to his extravagance he had to sell the theatre at Wargrave and have it demolished. He accidentally shot himself while serving in the Royal Berkshire Militia and died of his wounds. One of Barry's associates was the well-known actor Major Arabin, who was involved in a high-profile divorce case in 1786.

John Bateman, 2nd Viscount Shobdon 1721–1802

The son of William Bateman and Lady Anne Spencer, his services to the Spencer family may have led to him obtaining posts within the royal household, first as Treasurer (1756–57) and then as Master of the Buckhounds. It is known that 'in 1762 the Duke of Marlborough's hounds hunted buck every morning in the recent races' at the Burford and Bibury courses.[2] From 1776 to 1790, there was an annual three-day meeting, the Dukes of Marlborough being amongst the noblemen whose names appeared as owners of various horses that raced. The very last Burford race meeting was held in 1802.

On the death of his father in 1744, he had inherited Shobdon Court in Herefordshire, and four years later he married Elizabeth Sambrooke. Between 1747 and 1768, Bateman was MP for Woodstock. As a Tory, he supported Lord North's government, and when that collapsed he retired from politics in 1782. Bateman was one of the first aristocratic patrons of Thomas Gainsborough, and it was at Shobdon that Gainsborough painted his landscape *Going to Market* between 1768 and 1771. The artist is known to have presented a group of drawings to Bateman in September 1770. The peerage became extinct on his death, and the estate passed to his cousin, William Hanbury of Kelmarsh, Northamptonshire.

Sir George Beaumont 1753–1877
The 7th Baronet was a politician, amateur painter and patron of British art. He played a crucial role in the creation of the National Gallery in London by making the first bequest of paintings to the nation.

John Bell 1745–1831
Bell was a pioneer publisher and bookseller, who was responsible for Bell's British Theatre, a comprehensive selection of sixty plays, each prefaced by an interesting character portrait. In 1773, his acting edition of Shakespeare was based on the prompt books of the Theatre Royal, showing which of Shakespeare's plays were popular at that time. Helped by the playwright Miles Peter Andrews, he published *The World, or Fashionable Gazette* at the British Library in the Strand in 1778.

Gavin Hamilton Augustus Berkeley, 4th Earl of Berkeley 1715–1755
He married Elizabeth Drax, who was noted for her needlework, which is still admired by visitors to Berkeley Castle in Gloucestershire. Their daughter Elizabeth married Lord William Craven; her second husband was Christian, Margrave of Anspach, Bayreuth and Brandenburg. The father of musician and composer Lennox Berkeley, born in 1903, was the illegitimate son of the 7th Earl of Berkeley.

Monck Berkeley 1764–1793
The son of the Revd George Berkeley, Prebendary of Canterbury Cathedral, and the grandson of Bishop Berkeley, he went to Magdalen College, Oxford, and then joined the Inner Temple as a law student. He was a poet as well as a writer and is best remembered as the author of *Literary Relics* and *An Inquiry into the Life of Dean Swift*. He died a bachelor in 1793, his death 'an unspeakable grief to his parents' as reported by his friend Frederick Reynolds.

Louis de Boissy 1694–1758
A French dramatist and writer, he was elected to the Académie Française in 1784. His best known comedy is *Les Dehors Trompeurs*, which was the hit of the 1740 Parisian season.

Charles Oldfield Bowles 1729–1780
Bowles was a man of culture, the owner of an extensive library as well as an amateur musician, artist and botanist. The *Oxford Journal* reported that on 6 February 1773, Arthur Murphy's two-act farce *The Upholsterer* had been performed at North Aston. Perhaps Bowles had been inspired by the performances at Blenheim in January 1773 to fit up his own theatre. The poet laureate William Whitehead wrote a prologue for the opening of the theatre, which was later published in *The Universal Magazine*. The next theatricals took place on 23 December 1774, when *Every Man in his Humour* by Ben Jonson and *The Mayor of Garratt* by Samuel Foote were performed. Members of Oxford University as well as the neighbouring gentry were sent tickets, but whether this invitation extended to the Spencers at Blenheim is unknown.

In 1776, Bowles converted a barn into an even larger theatre, which opened in November with a local production written by Edward Taylor called *The Siege of Scutari*. Taylor lived nearby at Steeple Aston and was a man of many talents. Following Bowles' death it was not until 1782 that the theatre reopened, when Mary, his widow, played the part of Belvidera in *Venice Preserv'd*.

The success of the Blenheim theatricals stimulated Bowles' son to new theatrical endeavours, a rumour even circulating that the two companies would join forces and that Lord Charles Spencer from the Blenheim troupe would take the part of Sir John Oldham in Samuel Foote's *The Nabob*. However, the illness of George III put an end to the festivities and the theatre was closed down in 1791.

Sir Henry Bridgeman 1725–1800

His mother was Lady Anne Bridgeman (née Newport), who was the granddaughter of Lady Elizabeth Wilbraham. In 1762, Sir Henry succeeded to the estate at Weston Park, Shropshire, on the death of his uncle, the 4th Earl of Bradford, and became the 5th Baronet. He was MP for Ludlow and Wenlock for many years. Weston Park was built in 1671, Lady Elizabeth Wilbraham using Palladio's *First Book of Architecture* to design the house we see today. Her daughter Mary married the 2nd Earl of Bradford. The present holder of the title, Richard Bridgeman, the 7th Earl, donated the house to the nation in 1986 through a charitable foundation. The park includes a Roman bridge and a Temple of Diana built by James Paine, *c.* 1760.

Lancelot 'Capability' Brown 1716–1783

Brown was a landscape architect who had a major influence on the gardens of royal palaces and stately homes in the eighteenth century. He was famous for his serpentine shapes, as evidenced by the vast lake he designed for the 4th Duke of Marlborough at Blenheim.

James Brydges, 1st Duke of Chandos 1673–1744

In 1719, he became the 1st Duke of Chandos of Canons Park, Middlesex, Earl of Caernarvon and Baron Chandos of Sudeley Castle, Winchcombe, Gloucestershire. He made his fortune as paymaster to the 1st Duke of Marlborough during the War of the Spanish Succession, a post that is reputed to have brought him £600,000 and the sobriquet 'Princely Chandos'. Handel composed the Chandos Anthems in his honour. In 1726, the Duke and Duchess spotted an investment opportunity on a visit to Bath at a time when the city was a unique place of health and pleasure. The following year, the Duke signed a contract with the architect John Wood, investing £14,426 on buying land, and building and equipping houses in Bath.

The Brydges are related to Jane Austen's family. James's sister Mary married Theophilus Leigh of Adlestrop. Mary had twelve children and died at the age of thirty-seven. One of her sons was Dr Theophilus Leigh, Master of Balliol College, Oxford. Another was the Revd Thomas Leigh, who in 1760 retired as rector of Harpsden in Oxfordshire and settled with his wife and two unmarried daughters, Jane and Cassandra, in Bath. It was Cassandra who, on a visit to her uncle Theophilus, met the handsome proctor of St John's College, Oxford, the Revd George Austen. Cassandra was witty and shrewd, while George was scholarly and serene. They were married at the church of St Swithin, Bath, in 1764.

John Burgoyne 1722–1792

Burgoyne was a soldier and dramatist, who at Westminster School had made friends with Lord Strange, the eldest son of the 11th Earl of Derby. Stationed as a young officer at Preston, Lancashire, he went to see his old school fellow at Knowsley, the Derby family home near Liverpool. This resulted in his elopement with Lord Strange's sister Lady Charlotte Stanley in 1743. After the couple's return from France, Burgoyne was reconciled with his father-in-law and in 1768 he became MP for Preston. He was a friend of Sir Joshua Reynolds and was known for being a reckless gambler and also for his amateur acting. In 1774, he wrote *The Maid of the Oaks* at a house called 'The Oaks', on the occasion of the marriage of his wife's nephew, Lord Stanley, to Lady Betty Hamilton. The following year Garrick brought the play to Drury Lane.

Burgoyne was sent to America to fight in the American War of Independence, against his wishes, as his wife Charlotte was seriously ill. She died in the year of the Battle of Bunker Hill, at which her husband was present, surrendering to superior forces at Saratoga in 1777. On retirement, Burgoyne turned his mind to dramatic writing. His comedy *The Heiress*, written at Knowsley in 1786, was dedicated to the 12th Earl of Derby, who married the famous actress Elizabeth Farren. Burgoyne later formed a relationship with a popular singer, by whom he had four children. His London home at 10 Hertford Street, off Park Lane, was bought by the playwright Sheridan after Burgoyne's death.

Frances (Fanny) Burney 1752–1840

Born at King's Lynn in Norfolk, she moved with her family to London in 1760. Her father Charles had been made a Doctor of Music by the University of Oxford in 1769, and in 1776 he published his first volume of *A General History of Music*. He also collected playbills, notices and press cuttings relating to private theatricals. Fanny had no regular education and remained at home until 1786, when she was appointed Mistress of the Robes to Queen Charlotte, a post she held for five years. Her literary career began with the publication of *Evelina* in 1778, the year her diary was begun. In it she describes acting as 'a nerve-wracking ordeal' in which she was subjected to the scrutiny of male members of her family and their friends. Fanny's other published works included *Cecilia*, *Camilla* and *The Wanderer*. However, it is her diary that gives Fanny her best claim to fame, although the early diary was not published until 1889. *Camilla*, her third novel, was finished and prepared for publication during the years 1794–95. The list of subscribers for the book is long and impressive, among the more humble names being that of Jane Austen.

Fanny and her husband Alexandre named their cottage near Westhumble in Surrey 'Camilla', as it was built from the proceeds of the novel. Fanny had met General Alexandre D'Arblay in 1792, when she visited her married sister Susanna Phillips at her home at Mickleham, near Dorking. Close by was an eighteenth-century house, Juniper Hall, owned by the Lock family and leased by aristocrats fleeing from the French Revolution. Fanny's lessons in French pronunciation with General D'Arblay led to romance, and they were married at Mickleham in July 1793. There is in the author's family an original painting of Juniper Hall, executed by Thomas Dibdin in 1844. This was passed to the Lloyd-Jacob family and to the present owner, my sister-in-law Jenny.

Sir William Chambers 1722–1796
Famous as an architect of garden buildings for the aristocracy, his best known are at Wilton House and at Kew. He designed fifty-two buildings during his lifetime. John Yenn worked as an assistant to Chambers in his private office in London. Both were employed by the 4th Duke of Marlborough at Blenheim, and were responsible for the oval floral garden design situated south-west of the palace.

George Colman the Elder 1732–1794
Colman was a playwright and theatre manager, born in Florence, possibly the son of the English envoy to that city, William Pulteney, Earl of Bath, who brought the boy up. Having been educated at Westminster School and Oxford University, in 1755 he was called to the Bar. He founded a magazine, *The Connoisseur*, and in 1760 wrote his first theatrical piece, *Polly Honeycombe*, which was produced at Drury Lane with David Garrick, Colman being the performance director. In 1766, he collaborated again with Garrick on *The Clandestine Marriage*. With Garrick he succeeded in establishing strong theatrical management in mid-eighteenth-century London theatre. He bought the Covent Garden Theatre and was its manager from 1767 to 1774, and in 1777 he purchased the Haymarket Theatre and was responsible for the first staging of *She Stoops to Conquer* at Covent Garden with Garrick. *The Musical Lady* performed at Blenheim in 1788 was one of his more popular dramas, as was *The Jealous Wife*. He was paralysed by a stroke in 1785.

George Colman the Younger 1762–1836
He was educated at Westminster School, 1772–79, and at Christ Church, Oxford, 1780–81. As a young man he worked for three years at Wynnstay for the Wynn family, which seems to have fostered his taste for the stage, although his father hoped he would not follow him in a theatrical career. However, following his father's stroke, George acted as manager at the Haymarket Theatre. He also married an actress, which he kept secret from his father. On his father's death in 1794 the patent for the Haymarket Theatre was transferred to him. Most of the plays he wrote were comedies with musical backing, including *The Heir at Law* in 1797, which enjoyed over a hundred years of success.

Henry Seymour Conway 1719–1795
Educated at Eton College, Henry was the second son of Francis Seymour Conway, 1st Marquess of Hertford. He fought in the battles of Dettingen, Fontenoy and Culloden, and during the 1745 rebellion was aide-de-camp to the Duke of Cumberland. In 1747, he married Lady Caroline Campbell, the widow of Charles, Earl of Ailesbury, and they had one daughter, Anne, who married John Damer, Earl of Dorchester.

Conway was MP for Higham Ferrers and Secretary of State in the Rockingham government of 1765–68. Towards the end of a noteworthy military career he became embroiled in the John Wilkes affair, attacking the attempts by the Government and Crown to use 'general warrants' to remove Wilkes from parliament. In the end, the King was forced to concede and accept the administration of the Marquess of Rockingham. In 1768, Conway returned to military life, which was much more to his taste. Further promotions to General and Field-Marshal followed, and in 1785 he was appointed Governor of Jersey. Conway took great interest in his estate at Park Place, near Henley.

The Revd Francis Witts writes in his nineteenth-century diary about Conway's estate, although by then it had been sold to James Harris, the 1st Earl of Malmesbury:

> Near Park Place, a magnificent Seat of Lord Malmesbury within a mile of Henley, a very severe hill has some years ago been broken by an ingenious manner, by which immense quantities of Soil cut from the Top was conveyed to the bottom where the ascent was most abrupt by means of carts, the full one bringing up an empty one the weight turning a windlass. At the foot of this Hill is a large plantation of Lavender & manufactory of Lavender Water established by the late Gen Conway, to whom Park Place formerly belonged.[3]

Near to this, Conway created an ancient Druid temple site out of forty-five granite stones from Jersey, which were part of a burial mound and had been presented by the people of Jersey to their Governor as a mark of their gratitude. Conway had patented a furnace for brewers and distillers, and it is clearly this furnace that helped him to develop his commercial lavender business. In 1787, he wrote the prologue to the play *The Way to Keep Him* for the Duke of Richmond's theatre, which was performed by amateur actors there in 1787 and 1788. In 1789, the play *False Appearances* was also first performed at the Richmond House Theatre with Conway's dedication to the actress Elizabeth Farren. The play was later produced at Drury Lane. Conway died in 1795 at Park Place, the house he had bought in 1752.

Hannah Cowley 1743–1809

A dramatist and poet, Hannah Cowley (née Parkhouse) was the daughter of a Tiverton bookseller. She was a prolific writer for the London stage after her first success with *The Runaway* at Drury Lane in 1776, followed by *The Belle's Stratagem* in 1780 and *A Bold Stroke for a Husband* in 1783. She also wrote sentimental verses under the pseudonym Anna Matilda. Her play *Who's the Dupe?* was even performed aboard ships of the Royal Navy, including the crew of HMS *Bedford* in 1791, the sailors also playing the female leads. Garrick was responsible for producing some of her plays at Drury Lane. Hannah married Thomas Cowley, a captain in the East India Company, and after his death abroad in 1797, she retired to the West Country and died at Tiverton, where she is buried.

Joseph Cradock 1742–1826

Cradock was a man of letters, having attended Cambridge University, and he acquired a taste for the stage and for London society. In 1765, he married Anna Francesca and during his honeymoon the Duke of Newcastle confirmed upon him the MA degree. He lived in Dean Street, Soho, and was known for his wit and as an enthusiastic play-goer, later moving to Gumley in Leicestershire, where he was High Sheriff of the county in 1766 and 1781. He gave private theatricals at Gumley, where Garrick offered to play the Ghost to Cradock's Hamlet. In 1771, he wrote a tragedy based on Voltaire's *Les Scythes*, which was performed at Covent Garden. His musical skill took him to Lord Sandwich's seat at Hinchingbrooke, where he sang in oratorios, and in 1774 an ode written by Cradock was set to music by William Boyce. From 1783 to 1786 he travelled through France and Holland with his wife. In 1823, he sold his Leicestershire estate and moved to London. He was described as a 'twin brother' of Garrick, both in mind and body. He died at the age of eighty-four.

Lady Elizabeth Craven 1750–1828
Elizabeth was the third child of the 4th Earl of Berkeley. She married William Craven in 1769, but they separated in 1783 after numerous scandals on both sides. Elizabeth travelled widely in Europe and Turkey, her major literary work being *A Journey through the Crimea to Constantinople*. Later in her life she remarried to become the Margravine of Anspach. Following a dispute about a footpath across her land at Benham, Elizabeth moved to Naples, where she died and is buried.

Lord William Craven 1738–1791
William was the nephew of the 5th Lord Craven and succeeded as Baron Craven in 1769. In 1771, he married Elizabeth Berkeley of Berkeley Castle. Four years later, he built Benham House near Speen in Berkshire. William also built Craven Cottage beside the River Thames near London, where Fulham Football Club's stadium is now situated. It is also the scene of the famous annual Oxford and Cambridge University Boat Race, which has taken place since the 1850s.

William's family connections to Jane Austen are well known. Jane knew of William Craven's son, the 1st Earl, also named William, through Tom Fowle, her sister Cassandra's fiancé, who was a cousin of William. Tom, a former pupil of Jane's father, was presented with the ecclesiastical living of Allington, near Amesbury, in 1793, and served as the 1st Earl's private chaplain in the West Indies in 1795. Tom died at Santo Domingo in 1796 – a great tragedy for both Cassandra and her younger sister Jane. When Lord Craven heard the news, he said that had he known of Tom's engagement to Cassandra, he 'would not have let him go'. It was the 1st Earl of Craven who sold his estate at Benham to the Margrave of Anspach.

Anne Seymour Damer 1748–1828
The only child of Henry Seymour Conway, Anne was the half-sister of Lady Mary Bruce, wife of the 3rd Duke of Richmond, and was an important part of the extended Goodwood family. Anne studied sculpture under Ceracchi and Bacon and anatomy under Cruikshank. In 1767, she married John Damer, eldest son of Lord Milton, afterwards Earl of Dorchester. However, the marriage turned out to be an unhappy one, as her husband was a drunkard and a gamester who, with his brothers, contracted a debt of £70,000. On

their father's refusal to pay off the debt, Damer shot himself through the head in 1776 at the 'Bedford Arms' in Covent Garden after a riotous supper. He was only thirty-two and heir to £22,000 a year. Left with a jointure of £2,500, Anne devoted herself to the art of sculpture, creating *Two Sleeping Dogs* in terracotta with such success that it was repeated for the Duke of Richmond. Anne also owned a copy of Daniel Gardner's painting *The Three Witches* (1775), showing Anne and her two friends Elizabeth Lamb (Lady Melbourne) and Georgiana (Duchess of Devonshire). It is not known where this painting was executed, or if was it done for a specific performance, but it is mentioned in Lady Mary Coke's journal in 1775 and may have been a result of Horace Walpole's tract *The Dear Witches*, which was a metaphor for female involvement in politics. David Garrick staged a revival of the play's original script.

In 1779, she was taken prisoner on a privateer on her way to Jersey to see her father General Conway, then Governor of the island, but was eventually allowed to join him. She was commissioned to sculpt two busts for the bridge at Henley-on-Thames in 1785, and later sculpted a dog for which she was highly honoured by the Academy of Florence. She executed three busts of Napoleon, one of which is at Windsor Castle, having been presented to George IV, another being in the Guildhall in London. She gave a bust of her friend Charles James Fox to Napoleon, who in return gave her a snuff box with his portrait set in diamonds.

In 1800, she staged the comedy *Fashionable Friends* written by her friend Mary Berry. Anne was a niece of Horace Walpole, who left his house and its contents at Strawberry Hill to her. She lived there until 1812, and six years later bought York House, Twickenham. On her death, her working tools, apron and the ashes of her favourite dog were buried with her. All her papers were burnt, except for the notebooks containing passages from Mary Berry's letters. Anne's bust of Mary stands in the National Portrait Gallery in London with that of her other great friend, Elizabeth Farren.

Thomas Dibdin 1810–1700
Thomas Robert Dolman Dibdin was the son of a famous London dramatist, also named Thomas. As an artist, Thomas travelled widely in Europe, where he specialised in drawing historic towns and their ancient buildings. His painting of Juniper Hall, Surrey (1844) was used as the frontispiece to Constance Hill's *Juniper Hall*, published in 1903 by John Lane of the Bodley Head.

John Dryden 1631–1700
English poet, dramatist, critic and translator of Virgil, Horace and Ovid, Dryden dominated the literary life of Restoration England. A King's scholar at Westminster School and at Trinity College, Cambridge, in 1663 he married Lady Elizabeth, sister of Sir Robert Howard. His greatest success was *All for Love*, written in 1678. After James II was deposed in 1688, Dryden was succeeded by Thomas Shadwell as poet laureate.

One of Dryden's most famous plays was *The Indian Emperour*, first performed in 1665 at the Theatre Royal, Drury Lane, today the Royal Opera House. In the play Dryden presents the conflict between love and honour when Montezuma refuses a chance to save his kingdom from conquest for personal reasons. In 1668, an amateur production of this play was performed at Court, this royal patronage continuing into the eighteenth century when the play was performed in 1732 at John Conduit's house, formerly the Royal Mint. In the audience were members of the royal family and the Duke and Duchess of Richmond. The first performance, by a group of children, was such a success that the children were asked to repeat it before the King and Queen at St James's Palace on 27 April 1732.

> The scene shows friends and family of the 2nd Duke. On the left the Earl of Pomfret, wearing the red sash of the Order of the Bath, leans past the Duke of Montagu to talk to a man traditionally identified as Thomas Hill, Secretary to the Board of Trade, possibly also the Duke of Richmond's friend and erstwhile tutor. The Duke of Richmond leans on the back of his wife's chair, while beneath the chimneypiece the royal children, William, Duke of Cumberland and his sisters look on. In the foreground their governess, Lady Deloraine, instructs one of her two daughters to pick up a fan lying on the floor. On the stage are, from left to right, Lady Sophia Fermor and her brother Lord Lempster [speaking her lines] and Catherine Conduitt. The hosts, Mr and Mrs Conduitt, are shown only through their portraits. The Countess of Pomfret, who is not shown, was the great-niece of Louise de Keroualle, and therefore a second cousin of the Duke. The bust of the recently deceased Sir Isaac Newton dominates the wall and the leading Freemason Dr. Desaguliers is the prompter in the background.[4]

Welbore Ellis, 1st Baron Mendip 1713–1802

Ellis was a statesman who rose to become a Lord of the Admiralty and served as Secretary for the Colonies during the American War of Independence. He was ennobled in 1794 in recognition of his government service. As he died without issue, the baronetcy went to Henry Welbore Agar, 2nd Viscount Mendip, who assumed the additional name of Ellis.

Elizabeth Farren 1759–1829

The daughter of strolling players, Elizabeth started her acting career as a child. Her first appearance was at the Haymarket in *She Stoops to Conquer* in 1777, the year she met the 3rd Duke of Richmond and was supervisor of his private theatricals at his house in Privy Gardens, Whitehall. Here she met Edward Stanley, 12th Earl of Derby, one of the amateur actors, who offered her his protection in 1785. The following year, Elizabeth acted in the play *The Heiress* at Richmond House before it went to Drury Lane; it was also in 1786 that she moved to Grosvenor Square, Mayfair, near to Derby House. Lord Derby's first wife, Lady Elizabeth Hamilton, had run away with the Duke of Dorset, and Derby formed a platonic friendship with Elizabeth that lasted for many years, being unable to divorce his wife without an Act of Parliament. It was not until his wife died in 1797 that he was able to marry his beloved actress and, as Countess of Derby from 1797 to 1829, Elizabeth lived mainly at Knowsley. Elizabeth bore her husband two daughters and one son, later coaching her young step-grandson Edward Stanley, the 14th Earl, in public speaking. When he became Prime Minister, he used these skills to become one of England's greatest parliamentary orators.

Elizabeth had been painted by Sir Thomas Lawrence in 1789, the same year as she acted in a command performance before the Prince of Wales and the Duke of York at Drury Lane. She was a close friend of Horace Walpole and of General Conway and his wife and daughter. Elizabeth died in 1829 on St George's Day, 23 April, and was buried at the parish church in Ormskirk where there is a memorial to her life. Written as an epitaph were the words 'She kept herself unspotted from the world'. Her only surviving daughter, Mary Smith-Stanley, later married and became the Countess of Wilton, living at the family home, Heaton Hall, until she died in 1860.

Elizabeth Farren's sister Margaret was famous as an English comic actress in the 1770s and 1780s, developing her stage career to much acclaim. In 1787, she married the well-known actor-dramatist Thomas Knight, who had acted at the Duke of Richmond's theatre before he went on to find fame in Bath, dying there in 1820, long after the death of his wife in 1804.

Charles James Fox 1749–1806

Third son of Henry Fox, Lord Holland, he was a descendant of Charles II through his mother, a daughter of Charles Lennox, the 2nd Duke of Richmond. His aunt, Sarah Lennox Bunbury, was the wife of Sir Charles Bunbury, owner of 'Diomed', the winner of the first Epsom Derby. Fox became an MP at nineteen, and at twenty was a Lord of the Admiralty. Following the surrender of Cornwallis at Yorktown and the fall of the Tory Ministry, he was Secretary of State for Foreign Affairs in Rockingham's coalition ministry and took a prominent part in the negotiations of the peace treaty with the American colonies. He was widely and affectionately known simply as Charles. His most statesmanlike contribution was his authorship of a bill to abolish the slave trade, formally passed in the year of his death, 1806.

Thomas Gainsborough 1727–1788

One of England's greatest portrait and landscape painters, he was born in Gainsborough House, Sudbury, Suffolk, which is now a museum of his life and work. *The Blue Boy*, painted in 1770 and now in the Huntington Collection in California, is one of his most famous paintings. *The Pink Boy* is at Waddesdon Manor, Buckinghamshire, built by Baron Ferdinand de Rothschild and now in the care of the National Trust.

Daniel Gardner 1750–1805

Gardner was a successful portrait painter, having been a pupil of Romney, Zoffany, Dance and Bartolozzi. In 1776, he married the sister of the engraver Francis Haward. Among his works are a painting of one of General Burgoyne's daughters, Maria, and also a portrait of Elizabeth Farren. Gardner's painting *The Three Witches*, which shows the cauldron scene from *Macbeth*, has recently been acquired by the National Portrait Gallery.

David Garrick 1717–1779

Born in Herefordshire in 1717, Garrick made his début as Richard III in Shakespeare's play with such success that he was soon drawing crowds to the theatre. In 1747, he became involved in the management of Drury Lane, where the majority of his working life was spent. Two years later, he married Eva-Maria Veigel, a Viennese dancer. His funeral in 1779 was attended by much of London society, and he was buried in Westminster Abbey.

London's famous Garrick Club, opened in 1831 with the Duke of Sussex as its patron, was a gentleman's club restricted to 700 members. The present club, opened in 1864, has a fine collection of theatrical portraits and a working library. Over time its membership has grown into thousands.

James Gillray 1756–1815

Gillray was a caricaturist and print-maker famous for his political and social satires, mainly published between 1792 and 1810. One of his most famous works depicted Prince William, the then Duke of Clarence and third son of George III and his mistress, the actress Dora Jordan. When in 1802, Colonel Granville set up the short-lived Pic Nic Society, made up of stage-struck aristocrats including Lady Buckingham, Gillray lampooned the group in his cartoon *Blowing up the Pic Nics*. This 1803 cartoon included Sheridan, Sarah Siddons, Charles Kemble and even the ghost of Garrick rising from beneath the boards. In another cartoon, *Dilettanti Theatricals*, he satirised the vogue of private theatricals and the exhibitionism of well-connected actors such as the Earl of Derby. Gillray also ridiculed the Earl's friendship with the actress Elizabeth Farren in a cartoon.

Carlo Goldoni 1707–1793

Born in Venice, Goldoni wrote plays for amateur theatrical companies. In 1761, he moved to France and wrote in French and Italian for the Comédie-Italienne in Paris. He was the Italian tutor to the daughter of Louis XV, Princess Adelaide from 1764 to 1765, and to other royal children at Versailles from 1768 to 1780. His best known play, *Il Bugiardo* (*The Liar*), produced in Mantua in 1750, was translated into English in 1753.

Oliver Goldsmith 1728–1774

His most famous play, *She Stoops to Conquer*, which was first produced at Covent Garden in 1773, was an instant success. Goldsmith put much of himself into the play's characters.

Thomas Greenwood the Elder 1752–1797

Greenwood was a scene painter who worked at Drury Lane from 1771 until his death in 1797. In 1775, he painted the scenery for General Burgoyne's play *The Maid of the Oaks* and three years later was working for the Duke of Richmond's theatre. In 1787, he was employed by Duchess Caroline at Blenheim to paint the scenery. He excelled at landscapes, and two of his designs for theatrical scenery are in the Victoria and Albert Museum in London.

William Hanbury 1704–1768

Kelmarsh Hall in Northamptonshire was built for William Hanbury, a wealthy antiquarian, in 1732 to a Palladian design by James Gibbs. The project took much of Hanbury's fortune, which he had acquired by marrying a niece of Viscount Bateman of Shobdon Court, and Hanbury went on to acquire the Shobdon estate as the Batemans died childless. On inheriting the estate, he decided to move his household to Shobdon and let Kelmarsh to William Angerstein of Lloyd's of London fame. In 1779, the press reported on the fact that Hanbury was noted for his thespian activities and for putting on private theatricals at his home. Five years earlier, at a performance at Kelmarsh, the dramatist Richard Cumberland commended the paternalism of private theatricals in a prologue to the performance.

In 1927, Kelmarsh was let on a ten-year lease to Ronald Tree, a local MP, who married Nancy Langhorne, an American interior designer, in 1920. It was she who transformed the interior of Kelmarsh Hall. However, the couple were disappointed that they could not purchase Kelmarsh and surrendered the lease in 1933, buying Ditchley Park, near Blenheim. Ditchley was used by Sir Winston Churchill during the Second World War as a safer alternative to the Prime Minister's official country house at Chequers. After her divorce from Ronald Tree in 1947, Nancy married Colonel Claude 'Jubie' Lancaster, but sadly the marriage was not a success. The Lancaster family remained at Kelmarsh until 1982, when Cecily Lancaster set up the Kelmarsh Hall Trust. Today Kelmarsh Hall is open to the public.

George Harcourt, 2nd Earl Harcourt 1736–1809

He became the 2nd Earl Harcourt in 1777, and as a young man had gone on the Grand Tour during 1754–56. George Harcourt married his cousin Elizabeth, daughter of Simon Harcourt, in 1765, who was appointed a lady-in-waiting to Queen Charlotte in 1783. They lived at Nuneham Park in Oxfordshire, the park and grounds of which were landscaped by Lancelot 'Capability' Brown.

James Harris 1709–1780

Harris was a literary theorist, philosopher of language, musical impresario and politician whose home city was Salisbury. He was secretary to Queen Charlotte, and his uncle was the 3rd Earl of Shaftesbury. Harris moved amongst the great writers and musicians of the day, including Handel, J. C. Bach and Dr Charles Burney, whom he assisted in compiling *A General History of Music*. In 1795, his son James acted as a proxy to the Prince of Wales's marriage with Princess Caroline of Brunswick, for which George IV never forgave him.

Warren Hastings 1732–1818

Hastings was appointed as the first British Governor-General of India in 1773. On relinquishing this position in 1785, he returned to England with his wife and a fortune of £80,000. Two years later, Hastings was impeached by the House of Lords for actions he had taken in India as Governor-General. The impeachment action, led by Edmund Burke on rather malicious grounds, was opened in Westminster Hall in February 1788, with a hearing lasting thirty-five days. It was then adjourned and resumed in April 1789. This complex case lasted a total of 145 days over seven years and was not finally completed until 1795 when the Lords proceeded to debate on their judgment. During the trial innumerable testimonials and addresses were made on Hastings' behalf, many by Indian princes. On 23 April 1795, The Lords finally pronounced Hastings innocent of all charges brought against him. The £70,000 cost of his defence left him without any means of subsistence, but the East India Company generously came to his aid. He received addresses of congratulation on his acquittal from various quarters and was even offered a £2,000 pension per annum by the Nawab of Oudh, which he declined. Hastings died at Daylesford on 22 August 1818 and was buried in the parish church there.

Nicholas Hawksmoor 1661–1736

Hawksmoor worked for Wren on Chelsea Hospital, St Paul's Cathedral, Hampton Court, Greenwich Hospital and the west towers of Westminster Abbey, and with Vanbrugh at Castle Howard in Yorkshire. After Vanbrugh's fall from grace with Duchess Sarah, Hawksmoor took charge at Blenheim; he designed the Woodstock Gate in the form of a triumphal arch. In Oxford he worked on university churches and the colleges of All Souls, Worcester and Queen's.

Philip Hayes 1738–1797

Hayes was a composer, organist, singer and conductor whose early musical education was overseen by his father William, Professor of Music at Oxford. He was awarded his Bachelor of Music in 1763 and a doctorate in 1777. Hayes had sung at the Chapel Royal from 1767, but returned to Oxford to take up his post as organist at New College in order to assist his ailing father, whom he succeeded in 1777. He also replaced his father as organist of Magdalen College, Oxford, and was a fellow of Magdalen. He was organist of the university church and in 1790 organist at St John's. His lectures took the form of odes and oratorios in the Music School, now Holywell Music Rooms, built in 1742 and part of Magdalen College. In 1791, he presided over Haydn's visit to Oxford. He wrote over twenty songs between 1769 and 1794, including *The Muses Delight* in 1786 and *The Muses Tribute to Beauty* in 1789. During the years of Blenheim's private theatricals, Hayes was known for his difficult personality and for his corpulence. He left his manuscripts to the Bodleian Library.

Albinia Hobart 1737–1816

In 1757, Albinia married George Hobart, 3rd Earl of Buckingham, who was both a theatre manager and politician. As Countess of Buckingham she was well known for her lavish assemblies and for dramatic performances staged at Nocton Hall, Lincolnshire, and the Hobart family home on Ham Common in Surrey. She was also famous in the 1790s for gambling at the faro table and for being an enthusiastic thespian.

William Hogarth 1697–1764

Hogarth was a painter and engraver of social and political caricature whose works include four famous series: *A Harlot's Progress, A Rake's Progress, Marriage à-la-Mode* and *The Election*. In 1729, he married the daughter of artist Sir James Thornhill. Hogarth was also a popular portrait painter, and in 1746 he painted David Garrick as Richard III. In the 1750s, Hogarth's cartoons of the election of an Oxfordshire MP were published. On his death, Garrick composed an inscription for his tomb.

Joseph Holman 1764–1817

An actor and dramatist, Holman was the son of an army officer who died when he was two years old. He went to Queen's College, Oxford, but took no degree. In 1784, he made his first appearance on the stage as Romeo at Covent Garden, but after three seasons he left to act in Dublin and the provinces. However, he later returned to Covent Garden, but in 1799 was held responsible for further managerial problems and was either dismissed or resigned and took up farming. In 1812, Holman went to America and achieved considerable acting success in New York and Philadelphia. Five years later, he married a singer but died the same year on Long Island, New York. Several of his theatrical works were performed, including the comic opera *Abroad and at Home*. His reputation as an actor remained high throughout his lifetime.

Ozias Humphry 1742–1810

Born at Honiton in Devon, Humphry studied at Shipley's Academy of Art in London, owned by the 3rd Duke of Richmond, and was also attracted to the Sculpture Gallery of Casts in Richmond House, set up by the Duke to encourage young artists. His works include a portrait of Charles Lennox. After his Shipley studies he left for Bath where he lodged with the Linley family and became a good friend of Linley's daughter, later Mrs Sheridan. In 1773, with his friend George Romney, Humphry went to Knowle in Kent to paint a portrait of his patron, the Duke of Dorset, which still hangs in the house. While there, he probably visited or stayed with his brother William, who was vicar of Seal, near Sevenoaks. At the time, Humphry was *en route* to Italy, where he studied under Bertotti Scamozzi. On his return in 1776, he was encouraged by Sir Joshua Reynolds, and the following year painted a portrait of his friend George Stubbs. That Stubbs stayed at Goodwood for some time is known from Humphry's memoir:

> The first commission of importance Stubbs received came from the Duke of Richmond, and it obliged him to take up residence at Goodwood. In nine months he painted many portraits and pictures among them a hunting piece, 9 feet by 6 feet.[5]

The Duke of Richmond may have been told about Stubbs in London by the 12th Earl of Derby, Edward Stanley. In 1780, Humphry painted his famous portrait of the Ladies Waldegrave. That same year he also painted a portrait of the Berkeley family of Berkeley Castle, a copy of which when restored was said to include a young Jane Austen, aged four or five. In 1782, he painted a portrait of Georgiana, Duchess of Devonshire. From 1785 to 1788 he painted miniatures in India, although later in life he abandoned miniature painting for crayon drawing. In 1788, he painted a portrait of Jane Austen's brother Edward in the grounds of Godmersham Park. He also painted portraits of Cassandra Austen and possibly of a young Jane Austen (see Appendix O). In 1791, he was elected a member of the Royal Academy and the following year was appointed Portrait Painter in Crayons to the King, George III. In 1797, his eyesight failed, and in 1810 he died at Hampstead in London. In time, the British Museum acquired a large number of his papers. Some of his miniature paintings are in the Royal Collection, the Holburne Museum in Bath, the Pierpont Morgan Collection in New York, and at Woburn.

John James 1672–1746

James was an architect and surveyor who started his working life as a storekeeper and assistant Clerk of Works of Greenwich Hospital. He published his own architectural works, and in 1710 rebuilt Orleans House at Twickenham from his own designs. He became assistant surveyor at St Paul's Cathedral in 1716, succeeding James Gibbs as one of the two surveyors of the fifty newly built London churches. In 1724, he built Warbrook House at Eversley in Hampshire (now a hotel) for himself. James was Master of the Carpenters Company in 1734, and succeeded Nicholas Hawksmoor as Principal Surveyor of His Majesty's Works in 1736. Between 1736 and 1745 he completed the west towers of Westminster Abbey to Hawksmoor's design. He was buried at Eversley and after his death Sir George Nares bought Warbrook House.

Revd Charles Jenner 1736–1774

Jenner was an accomplished musician, novelist and poet, his stories and poems being published mainly during the 1760s. He was the vicar of Claybrooke, Leicestershire, from 1769 to 1774.

Edward Jenner 1749–1823

Born at Berkeley, where his father was the vicar, Jenner went to London to train as a doctor under the famous Scottish surgeon John Hunter. In 1773, he settled at Berkeley and acquired a large practice. Jenner was intrigued by the country lore that milkmaids who caught mild cowpox could not catch smallpox, which at the time killed up to 20 per cent of the population. He devised an experiment involving a milkmaid, a young boy and a cow named 'Blossom' and published his results in 1798. In 1980, the World Health Organization announced that smallpox had been eradicated from the globe. The little hut where Jenner vaccinated the poor, without charge, can still be seen today at his home, The Chantry, next to Berkeley Castle and the parish church.

Hugh Kelly 1739–1777

A newspaper critic and playwright, Kelly was born in Killarney and moved to London in 1760 in order to make his reputation as a newspaper hack. His first comedy, *False Delicacy*, written in 1768, is his best known play, 'delicacy' being another name for sensitivity or even quixotry. Although Johnson attacked the play for being too sentimental, it was one of the most successful comedies written at that time. Kelly prepared his play for Garrick's perusal, and it was Garrick who invested heavily in its production at Drury Lane, where it became a great favourite of the London theatre world. Among Kelly's other plays are *A Word to the Wise* (1770) and *The School for Wives* (1773).

John Kemble 1757–1823
Kemble was an actor and manager of Drury Lane. In 1803, he became manager of the Royal Covent Garden Theatre. He and his eldest sister Sarah Siddons together achieved fame for their Shakespearian roles.

Richard Knight 1659–1749
Knight was a wealthy iron master, the owner of the Croft Estate in Herefordshire. On his death it passed to his grandson, Richard Payne Knight (1751–1824), who created a new Gothic revival house at his other estate of Downton Castle, five miles from Ludlow. In 1824, his daughter Charlotte married Sir William Rouse-Boughton of nearby Downton Hall, at Stanton Lacy. It has been in this family's ownership since 1860 and is not open to the public.

Nicolas de Largillière 1656–1746
De Largillière was a friend of Peter Lely, who worked at Windsor in the reign of Charles II. In 1743, he was appointed Chancellor of the French Academy. He was best known for his portraits of the family of Louis XIV and other famous Frenchmen, including Voltaire.

Thomas Lawrence 1769–1830
Born in Bristol, Lawrence was a portrait painter whose first royal commission was a portrait of Queen Charlotte in 1790. He was President of the Royal Academy from 1820 to 1830, and is remembered for his romantic portraits in the days of the Regency. His well-known portrait of Elizabeth Farren was exhibited in 1790 at the Royal Academy, where it hung next to his portrait of Queen Charlotte. At his death he was said to be the most fashionable painter in Europe.

Edward Lear 1812–1888
Lear was the youngest of twenty children and was educated at home, mainly by his sister Anne. He was employed by the Zoological Society of London as an illustrator, and by the 13th Earl of Derby from 1832 to 1836, to make coloured drawings of the rare birds and animals in the menagerie at Knowsley Hall. Under the Earl's patronage, Lear travelled widely in Italy and Greece and published several books of his paintings, as well as his own sketches. His poem *The Owl and the Pussycat* was written for the 13th Earl's children, and in 1846 he published *A Book of Nonsense*. The closest Lear came to marriage was to a lady who was forty-six years younger than him, but his proposal was rejected. After a long decline in health, he died at his villa in San Remo of heart disease in 1888.

Anthony Thomas Lefroy 1802–1890

In 1851, Lefroy married Mary Amelia Jane Elliott, daughter of George Lettsome Elliott of the Bombay Civil Service. Lefroy joined the Irish Constabulary *c.* 1823, and became the Head of Police in Wicklow. He was selected to organise and train the nascent Gloucestershire Constabulary in 1839, and for twenty-five years was its Chief Constable at a difficult period owing to Chartist agitation. When he retired in 1865 his offer to commute his pension at six years' purchase was disallowed and he continued to draw it for twenty-five years. He died on 23 March 1890 in Pittville, Cheltenham, and was buried in the Old Cemetery there. He is reputed to have always slept with a cutlass under his pillow.

Charles Lennox, 3rd Duke of Richmond 1735–1806

Lennox inherited the title at the age of fifteen, when he was still at Westminster School. Whilst on the Grand Tour he went to Leiden University and studied medical science, and on his return was painted by Reynolds in 1758. At Richmond House he had a sculpture gallery constructed and encouraged young artists to work there, including Ozias Humphry. He fought at the Battle of Minden in the Seven Years War and was promoted to Major-General at the age of twenty-six. In 1765–66, the Duke was Ambassador Extraordinary to the Court of Louis XV at Versailles. As a radical in politics he supported the independent American colonies. In 1782, he was Master of the Ordnance for William Pitt's government, and became a Field Marshal in 1796. The Duke was at the forefront of Enlightenment thinking, commissioning a wide spectrum of paintings by prominent artists such as George Stubbs, who went to the family's country home at Goodwood for nine months in 1759. George Romney also painted a number of Lennox family portraits. The Duke married Lady Mary Bruce, daughter of the 3rd Earl of Ailesbury, but the marriage did not produce an heir, although he did father three illegitimate children. He died heavily in debt and was succeeded by his nephew Charles, son of Lord George Lennox.

George Granville Leveson-Gower, 1st Earl Granville 1773–1846

After going up to Christ Church College, Oxford, in 1789, he went on the Grand Tour, during which time he met Lord Henry Spencer, son of the 4th Duke of Marlborough. At the time, Lord Henry was working abroad for the government. In 1809, George married Lady Harriet Cavendish, whose father was the 5th Duke of Devonshire, but prior to his marriage he was the lover of Harriet's maternal aunt, Henrietta Ponsonby, Countess of Bessborough, with whom he fathered two illegitimate children. He was also romantically involved with Lady Hester Stanhope, the first woman traveller to cross the Syrian Desert. He was created Viscount Granville in 1815 and Earl Granville in 1833. Some of his private correspondence concerning the years 1781–1821 was published by John Murray in 1916.

Philip Massinger 1583–1640

Massinger wrote more than fifty plays and worked at the Globe Theatre in London as its chief writer. His most famous play, *A New Way to Pay Old Debts*, was revived by Garrick in

1748. Another of Massinger's plays, *The Guardian*, was performed by the King's Men at the Blackfriars Theatre in 1633 and revived by Garrick in 1758.

William Mavor 1758–1837
An assistant at Burford Grammar School, Mavor later took holy orders, in 1781, and became rector of Woodstock, Stonesfield and Bladon under the patronage of the 4th Duke of Marlborough. In 1787, he published his *Guide to Blenheim*, republishing it two years later as a *New Description of Blenheim*. In 1808, he became Mayor of Woodstock, and Headmaster of Woodstock School in 1810.

John Montagu, 4th Earl of Sandwich 1718–1792
Montagu was the originator in 1762 of this item of food. As First Lord of the Admiralty he was unpopular due to incompetence and corruption, retiring to his country house at Hinchingbrooke, near Huntingdon, in 1782. Captain James Cook named the Sandwich Islands (now the Hawaiian Islands) after him.

J. Hamilton Mortimer 1740–1789
A Neo-classical painter known primarily for his romantic paintings and for pieces set in Italy, Mortimer studied under Thomas Hudson, whose portrait of the 3rd Duke of Marlborough's family hangs at Blenheim. His portrait of Edward Nares as a boy, with his older brother George, was painted *c.* 1775 when they were both at Westminster School. In 1769, he painted the Witts family group. Mortimer was a friend of the potter Joseph Wright of Derby, who painted a portrait of Agnes Witts in 1776.

Robert Nares 1753–1829
Edward Nares' cousin Robert was a scholar and philologist, a member of the Natural History Society and a Fellow of the Society of Antiquaries. From 1779 to 1783 he was tutor to the Wynn family in London and at Wynnstay in Denbighshire. For two years from 1786 he was Usher at Westminster School, still as tutor to the Wynn family. Later in life he was assistant librarian at the British Museum and also keeper of the manuscripts. He published a glossary for readers of Elizabethan literature in 1822, which became the vade-mecum on Shakespearian studies.

William O'Brien c. 1738–1815
An actor and dramatist of Irish origin, in 1758 he was engaged by Garrick to act in *The Recruiting Officer* by George Farquhar. In the same year he also took the role of Young Clackit in Garrick's play *The Guardian*. He acted until 1764, when retired from the stage and eloped with Lady Susan Fox-Strangways, marrying her without her father's consent. Lady Susan was the daughter of Stephen Fox, the 1st Earl of Ilchester. It seems that his father-in-law forgave him, and O'Brien was gazetted Secretary and Provost-Master-General of the Bermudas in 1768. Four years later, he wrote *Cross Purposes* for Covent Garden, which was an adaptation of Joseph de la Font's play *Les Trois Frères Rivaux* and a play called *The Duel*

by Sedaine. Later in life he was Receiver-General of Dorset and died at Stinsford House, near Dorchester, in 1815.

Pierre Patte 1723–1814

A French architect and designer, Patte worked as an assistant to the great architectural professor Jacques-François Blondel. He was famous as a designer for improving stage lighting in Paris at the time of Louis XV.

Frederick Pilon 1750–1788

An author and dramatist, as a young man Pilon joined a group of theatrical strolling players at the Edinburgh Theatre and then drifted to London, where he was employed on the *Morning Post*. In 1779, he wrote a play called *The Deaf Doctor*, which was reworked as *The Deaf Lover* in 1780 and achieved some success. After deserting Covent Garden for Drury Lane, he produced a comic opera, *The Fair American*. His last play, *He Would be a Soldier*, was produced at Covent Garden in 1786.

William Pitt, 1st Earl of Chatham 1759–1806

Pitt the Younger, as he was known, was a Whig statesman who was Prime Minister from 1783 to 1801, and again led the country between 1804 and 1806. Pitt's strength was his extraordinary parliamentary skill which enabled him to dominate the House of Commons, and his single-minded devotion to victory over France secured Britain's dominant position in world affairs.

Beilby Porteus 1731–1808

Porteus's parents were Virginian colonists who had moved back to York. In 1757, he was ordained and by 1762 he had been appointed domestic chaplain to Archbishop Secker of Canterbury. In 1769, he was appointed George III's chaplain, and seven years later became Bishop of Chester. In 1787, he was appointed to the Diocese of London and was known for organising missions to India and the West Indies.

Caroline Powys 1738–1817

The only daughter of John Girle, Caroline married the oldest son, Philip, of the Powys family of Hardwick House in Oxfordshire, who were related to the Austens. She visited many of the best families of the time in Oxfordshire and London, including Richmond House in 1789, writing up these visits in her diary. Thomas Powys, the rector of Fawley, near Henley, was her brother-in-law and was always styled 'brother' in her diary.

Frederick Reynolds 1764–1841

Reynolds was born in London where his father was a solicitor. After leaving Westminster School he worked in his father's office and in 1782 was admitted as a student of the Middle Temple. At school he knew George Colman the Younger, and it was here that his interest in the theatre developed; his first play, *Werter*, was staged in Bath in 1785. Four years later, he wrote *The Dramatist or Stop Him Who Can!*, probably his best known play, which was followed in 1790 by *Better Late than Never*, written in collaboration with Miles Peter Andrews. In the 1790s, he became involved with Becky Wells, a celebrated actress, but married another actress, Elizabeth Mansel, in 1799. He wrote about one hundred pieces over some forty years, his most notorious play being *The Caravan or the Driver and his Dog*, which saved Drury Lane from financial disaster. The appeal of the play was that it involved a dog that dived into a tank of water to rescue a child from drowning. He is remembered for his two-volume autobiography, *The Life and Times of Frederick Reynolds*, published in 1826, and for being a passionate cricketer and an early member of the MCC.

Sir Joshua Reynolds 1723–1792
Born at Plympton in Devon, Reynolds was apprenticed to Thomas Hudson and later became the first president of the Royal Academy of Arts. Knighted in 1769, he was the principal portrait painter to George III.

John Inigo Richards 1731–1810
Richards was a landscape painter and stage designer with a lifelong interest in theatre design. A founding member of the Royal Academy in 1768, he was its secretary from 1788 until his death.

Hubert Robert 1733–1808
A French artist and landscape architect trained in Classicism and influenced by the Rococo Movement, he was responsible for some of the garden design at Versailles and was Keeper of the Museum and Keeper of the King's Pictures for Louis XIV. As a Councillor to the French Academy he was closely connected to Marie Antoinette, Voltaire, Elisabeth le Brun and the Duc de Choiseul. In the private east wing of Blenheim Palace there are three pastoral scenes painted in Robert's pastoral style.

James Roberts 1753–1809
Roberts was an artist, engraver and scene painter who entered the Royal Academy Schools in 1771. He excelled in theatrical portraits that displayed famous dramatic moments performed by well-known actors such as in Sheridan's famous play *The School for Scandal*. In 1809, he published *Introductory Lessons in Water Colours*. He created over sixty watercolours of actors for *Bell's British Theatre* publications and designed the plates for one hundred of the 1781 edition of *Bell's British Theatre*. From 1784, he worked in Oxford as a drawing master, moving to London in 1794, where he held the post of portrait painter to the Duke of Clarence. For the 4th Duke of Marlborough, Roberts painted three scenes from the private theatricals performed at Blenheim. These three oil paintings, now hang in the private east wing of Blenheim Palace.

Frederick Robinson 1746–1792
The second son of Thomas Robinson, 1st Baron Grantham, his oldest brother Thomas became 2nd Baron Grantham. Frederick, known as Fritz, accompanied his brother to Spain

as his secretary, but ill health forced him to return to England in 1777. He was MP for Ripon from 1781. In 1785, he married Katherine Gertrude Harris, the eldest surviving daughter of the musician and publisher James Harris. In December 1787, he resigned his seat as an MP and accepted a pension. The following year, he purchased No. 8 Whitehall Gardens, today known as Malmesbury House. After his death, his widow lived on there until she died in 1834. There is a painting of Thomas *c.* 1785 on display at Saltram House, near Plymouth, which now belongs to the National Trust. Also at Saltram are the family papers of both Frederick and Katherine Robinson. Frederick probably took part in the private theatricals at Blenheim in 1788.

Thomas Robinson, 2nd Baron Grantham 1738–1786

The eldest son of Thomas Robinson, he was born in Austria where his father was the British Ambassador. Educated at Westminster School and Christ's College, Cambridge, he went on the Grand Tour from 1758 to 1761. In Rome, in 1760, he had a portrait painted by Nathaniel Dance with his friends James Grant, John Mytton and Thomas Wynn, *The Conversation Piece*, which is now in the Philadelphia Museum of Art.

As a young man he was a close friend of Francis Russell, Marquess of Tavistock. In 1770, he succeeded to the peerage and was the Ambassador to Spain from 1771 to 1779. He married Lady Mary Jemima Yorke in 1780, and served as Foreign Secretary in Lord Shelburne's administration from 1782 to 1783. There is a portrait of Robinson at Newby Hall, North Yorkshire, in the collection of the Earl of Seafield. On his death in 1786, he was succeeded by his oldest son Thomas, who became the 6th Baronet of Newby in Yorkshire.

Sir Thomas Robinson 1703–1777

Robinson was an architect and politician, who was created 1st Baronet of Rokeby in 1730. Rokeby Hall was built for him in the 1720s, but he was forced to sell the estate in 1769. He was Governor of Barbados between 1742 and 1747, and was one of the stand-in dukes at the coronation of George III on 22 September 1761. After his death, he was succeeded by his brother William.

Michael Angelo Rooker 1743–1801

Rooker studied under Paul Sandby as a watercolourist and engraver. He was the principal scene painter at the King's Theatre in London from 1778 to 1798. At Blenheim Rooker was responsible for the scenery designs for the private theatricals of 1787. As a professional engraver, he did most of the landscapes for Kemsley's *Copper Plate Magazine* between 1775 and 1777. Rooker was responsible for the headings of the *Oxford Almanac*, receiving £50 for each one. As a skilled watercolourist he did autumnal tours of Norfolk, Suffolk, Somerset and Worcestershire, making drawings of architectural remains which appeared in William Watts' *The Seats of Nobility and Gentry* in 1786. This publication included eighty-four copperplate drawings by Rooker, Sandby and other artists. In 2013, there was an exhibition at the Royal Academy entitled 'Makings of a Landscape' which included Rooker's work.

Lord Francis Russell, Marquess of Tavistock 1739–1767

Lord Francis was the eldest son of the 4th Duke of Bedford. In 1764, he proposed to Lady Elizabeth Keppel at Blenheim and they were married on 8 June that year. They started their married life at Houghton Hall, near Woburn, from where they made numerous journeys to see his sister Caroline, 4th Duchess of Marlborough. It was a period of idyllic happiness until the dreadful day in March 1767 when Francis was thrown from his horse while hunting and fractured his skull. He died two weeks later.

Following his death, Elizabeth fell into a decline and always carried a small miniature by Ozias Humphry of Francis either in her hand or round her neck. Her father-in-law arranged for her to travel abroad, as he thought it would be beneficial for her health, but Elizabeth pined away and died of a broken heart in Lisbon in November 1768. The miniature shows Francis dressed in a scarlet coat with powdered hair and is displayed in the miniature case marked with a black star in the Gold Vaults at Woburn.

John Russell, 4th Duke of Bedford 1710–1771

The 4th Duke was a famous statesman and leader of the Bedford Whigs, who lived at Woburn Abbey with its parkland of over 3,000 acres, surrounded by eleven and a half miles of walls. In 1731, he married Diana Spencer, daughter of Charles Spencer, the 3rd Earl of Sunderland. Sadly, Diana died in 1735, and two years later Russell married Gertrude Leveson-Gower. Their daughter Caroline married George Spencer, 4th Duke of Marlborough.

Lady Caroline Russell, 4th Duchess of Marlborough 1743–1811

As a young girl, Caroline was a gifted artist in the making. In 1753, her Italian singing teacher Caterina Galli, a noted soprano, was paid £13 13s 0d. Caroline drew a sketch of her teacher, *c.* 1754. In 1758, when Caroline was fifteen, her mother presented her at Court. In a letter to Caroline's father, her mother wrote:

> I got Miss presented to the Prince of Wales yesterday and she behaved as well to him as she did per contra to his grandfather. When she saw the latter coming to her, she opened her eyes to stare at tremendous Majesty, but never attempted a curtsey, or stooped to receive his kiss. But when she found he persisted, she almost knocked him down with her chin. I assure you it was so bad that I expect to hear he did not like her, though I think he could not help it. She looked so very pretty, and the whole drawing room was of my opinion.

To her mother's letter, Caroline added a postscript:

> Mama desires me to add to this that Mr. Denoyer has just been with me and says that the Prince of Wales thinks me very pretty and that I've exactly Mama's smile. I was against writing you this, for fear you should think me a saucy, vain Puss. But Mama insisted upon it.[6]

Denoyer was her dancing master and was connected to the royal family.

At the age of eighteen she was a bridesmaid at the wedding on 8 September 1761 of George III – not yet crowned – to Princess Charlotte of Mecklenburg-Strelitz. The coronation took place two weeks later, on 22 September. The Russell family, who were at Bedford House in London, had once more to be in gala attire. Lady Caroline, like her mother, wore a hooped skirt embroidered in silver. Her tight bodice, with stays, was made of what was described as a very rich embroidered material.

In her correspondence dated 27 April 1762, Caroline wrote of a Mr Robinson who had been corresponding with her brother Francis, Marquess of Tavistock, who at the time was on the Grand Tour and was at Bologna in Italy. She also wrote about a visit to Bath in a letter to her mother, which she signed 'your most dutiful and affectionate daughter'.[7] When Francis wrote home about his sister's betrothal to George Spencer, 4th Duke of Marlborough, he stated that 'it was a love match'.[8]

On 23 August 1762, Lady Caroline was married to George Spencer, in the little cedar-lined chapel at Bedford House and the following month her husband brought her to Blenheim. On 14 September, now as Duchess Caroline, she wrote a letter to her father:

I came here last Friday. I am much pleased with the place, which will some time or other be much finer, when the Duke of Marlborough has made all the improvements he talks of.

My brother is gone from hence to Northampton this morning, and means to go over to Woburn, where Mama now is. I am to meet her in town in about ten days' time.

I won't say how strongly I feel your absence. It is only putting us both in mind of disagreeable things. But I will flatter myself with the hopes of visiting you at Paris, and please myself with that thought. You have been too good to me all my life for me not to feel always something wanting to my happiness when I am not with you and Mama.

But I must say that the Duke of Marlborough's kindness and attention to me increases every day, and leaves me hardly anything to wish. My brother and he seem as well disposed to like one another, too, as I can desire, and as long as he stays in England I hope we shall see a good deal of him.

I have been over to see Blandford Park, which is, I think, a very pretty place, and seems a comfortable living house. Lord and Lady Charles Spencer are coming down there as soon as they are married.

I don't think it reasonable to take up any more of your time, which must be now so precious, than to add the Duke of Marlborough's best respects to you and to assure you, my dear Father, how much I am,

Your dutiful and affectionate daughter,

C. MARLBOROUGH[9]

In a further letter to her father, dated 14 September 1762, Caroline wrote about her husband 'carrying the Sword of State at the coronation of George III' and stating that 'the order had come through the Duke of Devon for Marlborough to do this'.[10]

Their first child, Lady Caroline Spencer, was born in 1763, and their second child, Lady Elizabeth, was born on 2 December 1764. When Duchess Caroline gave birth, her husband wrote:

There never was a quicker or safer labour, she was not half an hour from the time her pains grew at all considerable. She had not even time to take her clothes off and she is now lying on her bed in the same clothes she had on this morning. The little girl's face is as round as an apple but she is not handsome as her eldest sister, though I do not think she is ugly neither.[11]

John Frederick Sackville, 3rd Duke of Dorset 1745–1799

Originally a Whig MP, Sackville later became a Tory and supported Pitt. He saw service in America in 1779 as a colonel in His Majesty's forces and was ambassador to France from 1787 to 1789. He was a notorious womaniser and is also remembered for his passion for cricket, being an expert bowler. In the summer of 1777, Lord and Lady Derby entertained a company of friends at their house near Epsom and Sackville was among those invited. The cricket match at 'The Oaks' resulted in an easy victory for the visiting team, of which Sackville had been the star performer. What followed after the match is described by Horace Bleackley in *The Beautiful Duchess*:

> On the second day, when the match was finished, some frolicsome soul suggested that the ladies should play cricket too, and as the notion appealed to Lady Betty's sense of fun, she agreed to take part in the experiment. So after sides had been chosen the members of the female coterie sallied onto the lawn, clad in summer gowns of sprigged muslin or coloured lutestring, unimpeded by hoop or pannier, with mob-caps aslant their lofty coiffures, and soon a lively match was in full progress, in which these dames of fashion, encouraged by the laughter and applause of the spectators, struggled for notches as eagerly as the men of Chertsey or Coulsdon. Among the players were the Countesses of Essex, Carlisle, and Eglinton and a dozen other ladies of the first rank all of whom took part in the game, while the hostess [Lady Betty], who was as agile as a kitten, batted and bowled as dexterously as the best of them. Oddly enough, the incident escaped the notice of the newspapers, but the Duke of Dorset described the match in a letter to a friend, and depicted the contest in a watercolour drawing, which after various adventures found a permanent home in the pavilion at Lord's. History does not relate what was said by the Duchess of Argyll when she learned that her daughter had become the first of lady cricketers.

This cricket match was to be the undoing of the marriage of Lord Derby and Lady Elizabeth, who had always had a soft spot for Sackville, well before her marriage in June 1744.

Marie-Thérèse Louise de Savoie-Carignan 1749–1792

A French aristocrat, born in Turin of the House of Savoy, she was known as the Princess de Lamballe. Beautiful and charming, she was appointed superintendent to the household of Marie Antoinette in 1744 and became the Queen's intimate companion. In 1767, she married Louis de Bourbon, but he died the following year. She escaped during The Revolution to England in 1791, but later returned to share the Queen's imprisonment. She refused to take the oath of detestation of the monarchy, and immediately after leaving the courtroom she was violently killed by the Paris mob.

Richard Brinsley Sheridan 1751–1816

The famous playwright and theatre manager purchased Garrick's share of the Drury Lane Theatre in June 1776 and became its manager. Among his works are *The Rivals* and *The Critic or A Tragedy Rehearsed*, which was first produced at the Theatre Royal, Drury Lane, in October 1779. In *The Critic* he deftly mocked the follies of everyone connected with the theatre, from playwrights to spectators. The biggest issue of the time was the American War of Independence, which Sheridan compared with the sixteenth-century Spanish threat and incorporated into *The Critic*. Sheridan was a radical Whig, a strong believer in the laws of libel, and a defender of the principles of the French Revolution. He retained his Whig values until his death.

Sarah Siddons 1755–1831

Famous for playing tragic roles, especially Lady Macbeth, Sarah Siddons worked in the provinces, mainly in York and Bath, for six seasons before achieving true success at Drury Lane, where she became the queen of the theatre for twenty years. There were problems with her marriage to William Siddons and they later separated.

Henry Singleton 1766–1839

Singleton was a painter and miniaturist noted for his work on contemporary historical events. Examples of his work can be seen in the Royal Collection at Buckingham Palace.

Edward Stanley, 12th Earl of Derby 1752–1834

The 12th Earl's passions were the theatre and horse-racing, and he founded The Derby at Epsom in 1780, his horse 'Sir Peter Teazle' winning the race in 1787. His main racing activities were centred on Newmarket where the Jockey Club had established its headquarters and the Earls of Derby have traditionally maintained a stud for the breeding and foaling of their racing stock. This is where the 2000 Guineas in April is run as part of the Triple Crown of racing, the other two races being The Derby at Epsom, usually in May or June, and the St Leger at Doncaster in September. This famous race takes its name from Lieutenant General Anthony St Leger who founded it on 24 September 1776. The Earl of Derby also established the racecourse at Aintree, where the Grand National is run.

He married his second wife, Elizabeth Farren, in 1797, and the couple lived at their London home, Derby House in Grosvenor Square, or at the Stanley family home of Knowsley, where they led a busy country life with their children and grandchildren and entertained on a grand scale. When his second wife died in 1829, Lord Derby was cared for by his daughter Mary for the last five years of his life. Knowsley stood in an extensive park with two lakes, one of which was three miles wide.

Edward Stanley was not only one of the richest peers of the realm but reputedly the ugliest. He and Elizabeth were caricatured by James Gillray as Cupid and Psyche, which was based on the Roman intaglio collected by the 4th Duke of Marlborough and known as the Marlborough gem. When Pitt died in 1806, Lord Derby finally got into power as Foreign Secretary in the short-lived Ministry of All the Talents, with Sheridan, Grey and

Fitzpatrick. He managed to set in motion the abolition of the slave trade, but died of cirrhosis of the liver in 1834 before he could achieve his second goal – peace with France. At his request, his body was laid to rest beside Elizabeth Farren at the parish church in Ormskirk, Lancashire.

In 1868, William Pollard in his history of *The Stanleys of Knowsley* had this to say about his funeral, which took place ten days after his death:

> The vehicles which joined the mournful cortège as it emerged from the Stanley gate entrance to Knowsley were upwards of 60 in number. The church was filled some hours before the funeral procession arrived and several hundred were unable to obtain admission. The funeral cortège left the hall at nine o'clock in the morning headed by four mutes on horseback with pages one each side. These were followed by tenants of the Knowsley estate, two hundred and eighty in number, riding on black horses and wearing hat bands and scarfs. To these succeeded the house-hold servants walking two abreast. Four mourning coaches followed containing respectively the deceased Earl's physicians, clergymen and pallbearers with four pages on each side of the coaches. Two mutes on horseback again succeeded followed by his lordship's coronet and cushion on a state horse. Next came the body, borne in a hearse drawn by six horses with heraldic insignia. Four mourning coaches, drawn by four horses each followed. These were followed by the deceased Earl's carriage drawn by six horses, the Earl of Derby's carriage and Lord Stanley's carriage each drawn by four horses and all closed. On the cortège arriving at Stanley gate about 2 miles and a half from Ormskirk, it was joined by the general procession consisting of 36 private carriages containing the members of the leading families and other gentlemen, among them, the Mayor of Liverpool and the Reverend Jonathan Brooks and the Reverend Augustus Campbell, Rectors of Liverpool. Upon the procession arriving at the church about 11 o'clock in the forenoon the body was met by the Reverend Joshua Thomas Horton, vicar of Ormskirk, who performed the funeral service. The coffin was covered with rich crimson silk velvet, ornamented with massive silver handles chased like coronets.
>
> On the lid there was a fine chased ornament with a large silver plate bearing the following inscription: Edward Smith Stanley, twelfth Earl of Derby, born September 12, 1752, died October 21, 1834.
>
> When the coffin was deposited in its place in the vault, the herald went down and placed the coronet and cushion on the lid.

He was succeeded in his title and estates by his son Edward, who became the 13th Earl.

Edward George Stanley, 14th Earl of Derby 1799–1869

Born in March 1799 at Knowsley Hall, Edward was the eldest son of 13th Earl and his wife Charlotte Margaret, née Hornby, whom he married in 1798. Edward's childhood at Knowsley as part of an extended family was dominated by the powerful influence of his grandfather. The family included his four sisters and two brothers, as well as three children from his grandfather's second marriage to Elizabeth Farren. From his gregarious grandfather, Edward inherited an early commitment to Whig politics and from his mother an austere evangelicalism, reflected in some of his childhood poems. Edward's father, who was devoted to zoology and ornithology, had less of an influence on him. In 1817, he went up to Christ Church, Oxford, as a gentleman commoner to continue his classical studies, which included the classical Greek historian Herodotus. After university he went into politics. In May 1825, Edward married Emma Wilbraham, daughter of Edward Bootle-Wilbraham, 1st Baron Skelmersdale. By 1830, he was Chief Secretary for Ireland, and in 1833 he was transferred to the Colonial Office, where he drew up the bill for the abolition of slavery. In 1851, he succeeded to the title as 14th Earl of Derby and the following year he became Prime Minister. In 1864, at the age of sixty-five, he translated Homer's *The Iliad*. Aged and ill, he resigned from the premiership in 1868, handing the office on to Disraeli.

Edward died at Knowsley and was buried on 29 October 1869. Throughout his life he was devoted to the study of the classics, as well as being a passionate sportsman. He was the first British statesman to become Prime Minister three times and remains the longest serving Conservative Party leader. His statue in Parliament Square was unveiled by Disraeli in 1874.

The author's mother, Cecily Beatrice (née Squire), is related to the Stanley family, and amongst the family possessions is a leather-bound handwritten volume of Edward Stanley's poems. Composed between 1809 and 1825, many of these poems have never been published; see Appendix P. The Stanley family are related to the Spencer-Churchill family through the present Duke of Marlborough's mother, Mary Cadogan. Her sister Cybil Louise Beatrice is a grandmother of the present Earl of Derby, also named Edward Stanley. The 18th Earl of Derby established the safari park at Knowsley in 1971 and was succeeded by his nephew Edward Richard William Stanley, the 19th Earl, in 1994.

Edward Strong 1676–1741
A stonemason, Strong had the mason's contract for the building of Greenwich Hospital in 1696 and for Blenheim Palace in 1705, for which he used Taynton stone from quarries he had inherited near Burford. In 1708, with the assistance of Sir Christopher Wren's son, he built the lantern that sits atop the dome of St Paul's Cathedral.

George Stubbs 1724–1806
Stubbs was best known for his painting of horses. At the age of fifteen he worked for the Warrington portrait painter Hamlet Winstanley in copying the portraits at Knowsley for the 11th Earl of Derby. Stubbs' friend and fellow artist was Ozias Humphry, who wrote a short biography of his life. In it he compared the prices charged by both Reynolds and Stubbs, and it appears that Stubbs charged more than Reynolds, especially after 1759, when he had the patronage of the Duke of Richmond for whom he painted three commissions. For George Spencer, the 4th Duke of Marlborough, Stubbs painted the portrait of a Bengal tigress that had been given by Clive of India and formed part of the menagerie at Blenheim. It is said that Stubbs painted the animal with such skill that dogs were frightened on seeing it. In her book *Blenheim and The Churchill Family*, Lady Henrietta Spencer-Churchill wrote that it was her favourite painting, because the eyes of the animal followed you as you

moved. By the 1790s, Stubbs had the patronage of the Prince of Wales. When Stubbs died, he left everything to his common law wife Mary Spencer.

Frederick Benjamin Twisleton 1799–1887
The Revd Frederick Twisleton became the 16th Lord Saye and Sele after the deaths of both his uncle and cousin. He was curate of Adlestrop from 1823 to 1825, then rector of Adlestrop and Broadwell until 1852. He was also Prebendary of Hereford in 1825, Canon Residentiary in 1840, and Archdeacon of Hereford from 1863 to 1887. His first wife Emily, the second daughter of Richard Wingfield, 4th Viscount Powerscourt, died in 1837, and twenty years later he married Caroline, the third daughter of Chandos Leigh, 1st Baron Leigh of Stoneleigh.

Sir John Vanbrugh 1664–1726
Vanbrugh was a dramatist and architect, who popularised the English baroque style of architecture. He worked with the Nicholas Hawksmoor at Castle Howard in Yorkshire, as well as at Blenheim Palace. His play *The Provok'd Husband* was finished after his death by Colley Cibber.

John Vanderbank 1694–1739
A painter and book illustrator of Dutch extraction, following the death of Sir Godfrey Kneller he became famous for portraiture in the reign of George I. Among his works are portraits of Charles Spencer, later the 3rd Duke of Marlborough, (1719) and Queen Caroline (1736), which now hangs at Goodwood House.

George Villiers, 2nd Duke of Buckingham and Cliveden 1628–1687
Statesman, wit, writer and notorious libertine, Villiers had a house built at Cliveden as a hunting lodge. Designed by William Winde, it was situated beside the River Thames near Taplow in Buckinghamshire. Cliveden was sold to the Earl of Orkney in 1696, and in 1795 the house was destroyed in a fire, except for two wings. In 1849, the 2nd Duke of Argyll bought the new Cliveden, which was again destroyed by a fire. The Cliveden we know today, designed by Charles Barry and standing in 300 acres of parkland, was sold first to the Duke of Westminster and then, in 1893, to William Waldorf, who was created 1st Viscount Astor in 1916.

Horace Walpole 4th Earl of Orford 1717–1797
Walpole was an art historian, man of letters, antiquarian and politician, largely remembered for his Gothic revival house at Strawberry Hill and for his printing press. He was a close friend of Anne Seymour Damer, to whom he left his house.

Charlotte Wattell 1770–1812
The daughter of John Wattell and the niece of Sir John Stonehouse of Radley, Charlotte was eighteen when she met nineteen-year-old Thomas James Twisleton, second son of the 7th Lord Saye and Sele. On 9 May 1788, they acted together in Robert Jephson's tragedy *Julia*

at The Freemasons' Hall in London. By 1793, Charlotte and Thomas were acting together in Liverpool under the impresario J. G. Holman. The following year, Thomas left his wife, who continued in her acting career and was divorced on the grounds of adultery in 1798, Thomas settling an annuity on her of £100. On 11 July 1799, Charlotte married the actor Thomas Sandon at St George's church in Hanover Square and changed her acting name to Stanley. In 1800, she acted in York with her new husband, but by 1803 they were both in the debtors' prison at The Fleet in London. What happened to Thomas Sandon after Charlotte was discharged is unknown. However, by 1806, she was at Boston in America, and she acted in New York in 1808, before moving back to Boston the following year. By 1811, she was in Halifax, Nova Scotia, and died in Burlington, Vermont, on 26 December 1812.

Lady Elizabeth Webster 1771–1845

Her family made their money in the New World from the slave trade and New England plantations. At the age of fifteen in 1786, she married Sir Godfrey Webster of Battle Abbey, Sussex, who was forty-nine. Her husband, who was a depressive and jealous of his young wife, took to gambling and drinking. Elizabeth persuaded him to travel abroad and in 1791 they started on the Grand Tour. However, on reaching Nice, Sir Godfrey returned to England, leaving his wife and their three-year-old son. While in Nice, Elizabeth met the Duchess of Devonshire, Georgiana and her friend Lady Elizabeth Foster together with Georgiana's mother (Lady Spencer) and her sister Lady Harriet, who was married to Lord Duncannon, Harriet and Elizabeth becoming good friends. The following year, Elizabeth met Lord Henry Spencer in Dresden and in Vienna (see Appendix E). In 1794, in Florence, Elizabeth met Stephen Fox, 2nd Baron Holland, and on her return to England her husband divorced her on the grounds of adultery. Elizabeth married Henry Richard Fox, 3rd Baron Holland, in 1797. Their London home, Holland House, became a political centre to rival Devonshire House, and the scandalous couple regularly threw extravagant parties. Not long before she died Elizabeth was invited by 'Charles Dickens to attend Miss Kelly's theatre, Dean Street, to see Ben Johnson's *Every Man in His Humour*, performed by amateurs, including Dickens and the staff of Punch.'[12]

James Wyatt 1746–1813

Wyatt was a rival of Robert Adam's Neo-classical style and sprang to fame with his building of The Pantheon in 1772, which has since been demolished. He also designed Fonthill Abbey in Wiltshire for William Beckford.

Charles Watkin Williams Wynn 1775–1850

Charles was the brother of Sir Watkin Williams Wynn, 4th Baronet of Wynnstay. Both brothers were tutored by Robert Nares, Edward Nares' cousin. Charles was the first president of the Royal Asiatic Society, now known as the Royal Society for Asian Affairs. His theatre at Wynnstay was designed by James Gandon, who was responsible for many of Dublin's best known houses. Charles's brother William was a patron of Batoni and a man-about-town who dressed as a Macaroni. His town house at 20 St James's Square, London, was built by Robert Adam. In 1771, he married George Grenville's daughter Charlotte, and commissioned 'Capability' Brown to landscape his estate of Wynnstay, near Ruabon in Denbighshire. Here he planted a great avenue of trees and had a lake dug out with a cascade. The grounds of Wynnstay were formally opened in 1784.

John Yenn 1750–1821

A notable architect and a student of the Royal Academy, Yenn became a full academician in 1791. He was a pupil of Sir William Chambers and in the 1770s succeeded him as the Duke of Marlborough's architect at Blenheim Palace. In 1789, he designed the Temple of Health at Blenheim to celebrate the recovery of George III. Yenn was also Clerk of Works at Richmond Park, Kensington Palace, Buckingham House and the Royal Mews.

Appendix H: Facsimile page from Edward Nares' journals

Since life is above all things precarious And God! only knows how long I may live, and as I have at present children so young that though it shd. please God to spare their lives, I may not live to see them come to maturity; and as it is reasonable to think, that when they grow up they will be anxious to know who they descended from, and yet have none to tell them; For these reasons, and no other, I have resolv'd to put together such particulars of my life and connections so may satisfy their enquiries, and serve to inform them, who and what their Father was, as far as such knowledge can be honestly and correctly communicated by frail man. I was born on the 26th of March 1762 in my Fathers House in Carey Street, London being the 3rd son of George [afterwards the Honourable Sir George] Nares, One of the judges of the court of common Pleas. My Mother was the Daughter of the Right Hon.ble Sir John Strange Knight sometime solicitor general to his Majesty George II and afterwards Master of the Rolls, a Privy Counsellor, and I think member of Parliament at the same time, for Totnes in Devonshire.

Sir John Strange died in 1754. My Grandmother Lady Strange was one of the 4 Daughters & Co-heiresses of Mr. Edwd. Strong – a very eminent Mason, who was particularly concerned in the building St. Pauls, of which he laid the last Stone upon the Lantern, Oct 26 1708. The first stone having been 33 yrs. before laid by his elder Brother Thomas. Mr. Strong was also engaged in the building of the Churches erected by act of Parliament, after the fire of London, Greenwich Hospital, and many of the first Houses in the Kingdom.

Appendix I: Letter from I. Pigot to Duchess Caroline from Althorp, 1785

The letter was written from Ranger's Lodge, which today is called The Falconry. It was built in 1613 as a hunting stand in the deer park at Althorp.

My Dearest Duchess
Hope you have all recovered your fatigue and are quite well. We had the pleasure of Lord Blandford's company while we were at Oxford, he looks and is very well and enquired much after

you all. I have made my appointment with Mr. Austin for Monday morning if a fine day if not for Tuesday and will certainly write you a whole account the next day. Nothing can exceed the beauty of the country. Blenheim looks divinely. I wish you were there. My sweet Duchess, Be so good to recollect that when you send the dinners it must come by Wards Chipping Norton Waggon which sets out from the Green Man and still very early every Thursday morning. The things must be there on the Wednesday night. We had upon the whole a pleasant journey and I feel very happy to be got here. But to my sorrow shall not be able to ride for a week as I can't get my horse till then. Pray my dearest take care of not fatiguing yourself in hot weather. Hope you will not be much in London. All here join in their compliments. My love to the young ladies not forgetting My Dear and believe me my dearest Duchess your very affectionate and grateful friend. I. Pigot

Appendix J: Extracts from the diaries of Caroline Powys relating to Blenheim and to private theatricals, 1759–1805

In her diary covering 1756–1808, Caroline Powys wrote extensively about her life. The diary was edited in 1899 by a descendant of hers, Emily Climenson:

1759

We lay at Woodstock the evening we left Oxford, and the next morning went to the Palace (or Castle), of Blenheim, the seat of his Grace the Duke of Marlborough, the royal gift of Queen Anne, who built and gave it to the family in commemoration of the battle of Blenheim in France. It cost near £300,000. On entering the park thro' a portal of Corinthian order, the magnificent pile strikes the eye, and gives one the idea of grandeur from a view so superb. Then the Rialto bridge, the lake, its valley, and other beautiful scenes are not less delightful. Here you are about half a mile distant from the house, and have only an oblique prospect of it, but on a nearer approach you find the front a semi-circle, its centre a portico elevated on massy columns; over the door is the figure of Pallas.

1771

Near Woodstock you see at one view Blenheim, Lord Lichfield's and Sir James Dashwood's. The first, as I told you, we intended to spend some time at. The inside of the house I've given a description in a former journal. The new piece of water is a grand design by Brown tho' I think one too plainly sees that 'tis only a piece of water, which I should have thought might have been conceal'd by a genius so great as Mr. Brown's in design.

1788, 23 May

Mr. Powys and myself were at the play at Richmond House (Lord R's). It was the first night of performing 'False Appearances', a piece General Conway translated from the French of Les Dehors Trompeurs. The prologue and epilogue were both very clever; wrote by General Conway and spoke with great spirit by Lord Derby.

1805

Mr. Powys and myself went to the play at Henley, bespoke by Lady Elizabeth Fane. A very full house. Sheridan's play of 'The Rivals', an excellent one, and vastly well perform'd.

Appendix K: Epilogue to *High Life Below Stairs* sent to the Duchess of Marlborough in March 1774 and signed 'Elizabeth Craven, Nov. 28, 1773', and poetic extracts relating to the Margravine of Anspach

Lest, Sirs, you should mistake me by my Dress
I am – a Muse – which you would never guess
My figure is a strong one, I confess
Deputed by my sisters post I came
To save these infant actresses from shame.
At 'Nassus to me says Melpomene,
'The folks at Blenheim only play at Domino,
I think the game too trifling for her Grace
Some greater play becomes her noble race'
Says I 'Lord Sister something they must do.'
'Ay something,' she returned, 'but something new,
So take a hack, and tell the Party there,
To look unlike themselves and make fools stare,
And you, to add to all the fools surprize
Must take some very human like disguise.'
A jockey of Queen Bessy's female reign
I come – and seriously maintain
That all grave politicians are but Asses
Compared with those who represent these farces.

A sonnet written by the Revd Charles Jenner and inscribed to the Rt. Hon. Lady Craven:

I saw fair Craven sit in state
To smooth her verse, and from her air
The Graces at her toilet wait
The Muses hover round her chair.
A Muse began, with skill profound,
To teach her all the critic art,
The fair one lent an ear, but found
A better tutor in her heart.
Cupid look'd on, with that warm look
Which at his Psyche's feet he wears,
From his own wing a pen he took,
And dipp'd it in a lover's tears.

Jenner died in 1774. There is a monument to his memory in the churchyard of Claybrooke, Leicestershire, on which Lady Craven had this epitaph engraved.
(Extracts from Broadley's *The Beautiful Lady Craven.*)

Appendix L: The Biddenden Maids, Kent

THE BIDDENDEN MAIDS

CHULKHURST CHARITY

The annual distribution of Bread and Cheese takes place on Easter Monday Morning from the Old Workhouse.

This Custom originated with a bequest of the Biddenden Maids, Elisa and Mary Chulkhurst, the famous twin sisters, who in the year 1100 were born joined together at the hips and shoulders.

These sisters lived together thus joined for 34 years, when one of them was seized with a fatal illness and died, the other, refusing to be separated, was so affected by her sister's death did not long survive her, dying in fact only six hours later.

A poem has been found in the old Charity Documents which shows where they were buried:

'The moon on the east oriel shone
Through slender shafts of shaply stone
The silver light so pale and faint,
Shewed the twin sisters and many a saint
Whose images on the glass were dyed:
Mysterious maidens side by side
The moonbeam kissed the holy pane
And threw on the pavement a mystic stain.'

By their will they left their property to the poor of Biddenden.

This property consists of about twenty acres of land, upon which now stands the Old Workhouse, the remainder consists of allotments and a small holding called The Bread & Cheese Land, the rent from which enables the trustees to distribute one pound of cheese and two 4lb. loaves of bread to every poor parishioner.

To keep in remembrance the charitable pair. Biscuits bearing the impress of the Twin Maids, their names, age and year of birth are given away at the same time to all who apply —Strangers and Parishioners.

Since 1907 when the Charity Commissioners formed a scheme to consolidate this trust with other Biddenden Charities, the scope of the Charity has been extended to include gifts of money, fuel, etc., also nursing and treatment for the sick and needy.

The Biddenden Maids, Chulkhurst Charity

Appendix M: Publications by Edward Nares

One God, One Mediator, 1801*
Sermons Composed for Country Congregations, 1803
A View of the Evidences of Christianity, 1805
Thinks I to Myself, 1811
I Says, Says I, 1812
Heraldic Anomalies, 1823
Elements of General History, Ancient and Modern, 1825
Memoirs of the Life and Administration of the Right Honourable William Cecil, Lord Burghley, 1828 (3 volumes)
Man, as known to us Theologically and Geologically, 1834
The History of the Reformation of the Church of England, 1849

*Edward debated in this book 'whether the philosophical notion of a Plurality of Worlds was consistent with the New Testament'. What happened to the frontispiece designed by Lady Charlotte is unknown.

Appendix N: Officers of Oxford University, 1818, including Edward Nares

PROFESSORS, &c.   xiii

CHANCELLOR, VICE-CHANCELLOR,
AND OTHER
OFFICERS *of the* UNIVERSITY, PROFESSORS, *&c.*

Chancellor.
1809 Right Hon. William Wyndham, Lord Grenville.
High Steward.
1801 Right Hon. John Scott, Lord Eldon, Lord High Chancellor of England.
Vice-Chancellor.
1818 Rev. Frodsham Hodson, D.D. Principal of Brasennose College.
Proctors.
1818 Rev. Benjamin Parsons Symons, M.A. Wadham Coll.
Rev. William Russell, M.A. Magdalen College.
Representatives in Parliament.
Right Hon. Sir William Scott, Knight, D.C.L. University College.
Right Hon. Robert Peel, D.C.L. Christ Church.
Regius Professor of Divinity.
Rev. William Van Mildert, D.D. Canon of Christ Church.
Regius Professor of Civil Law.
Joseph Phillimore, LL.D. of Christ Church.
Regius Professor of Medicine.
Sir Christopher Pegge, Knight, M.D. of Christ Church.
Regius Professor of Hebrew.
Rev. Richard Laurence, LL.D. Canon of Christ Church.
Regius Professor of Greek.
Rev. Thomas Gaisford, M.A. of Christ Church.
Margaret Professor of Divinity.
Rev. Septimus Collinson, D.D. Provost of Queen's College.

Professor of Natural Philosophy.
Rev. George Leigh Cooke, B.D. of Corpus Christi College.
Savilian Professor of Geometry.
Stephen Peter Rigaud, M.A. of Exeter College.
Savilian Professor of Astronomy.
Rev. Abram Robertson, D.D. of Christ Church.
Camden's Professor of Ancient History.
Rev. Thomas Winstanley, D.D. Principal of Alban Hall.
Prælector of Anatomy.
Sir Christopher Pegge, Knight, M.D. of Christ Church.
Professor of Music.
William Crotch, Doctor of Music.
Archbishop Laud's Professor of Arabic.
Rev. Thomas Winstanley, D.D. Principal of Alban Hall.
Regius Professor of Botany.
George Williams, M.D. of Corpus Christi College.
Professor of Poetry.
Rev. John Josias Conybeare, M.A. of Christ Church.
Regius Professor of Modern History and Modern Languages.
Rev. Edward Nares, D.D. of Merton College.
Anglo-Saxon Professor.
Rev. Thomas Silver, LL.D. St. John's College.
Vinerian Professor of Common Law.
James Blackstone, LL.D. Principal of New Inn Hall.
Lord Lichfield's Clinical Professor.
Martin Wall, M.D. of New College.
b 3

Mavor's *Oxford University and City Guide,* 1820

Appendix O: Portraiture relating to Jane Austen

1. The Berkeley family portrait, oil on canvas, by Ozias Humphry, *c.* 1780, said to include Jane Austen, aged four or five [Berkeley Castle]. (See 'Portraits by Ozias Humphry of the Berkeley and Austen Families' below.)

2. The Rice portrait, oil on canvas, by Ozias Humphry, said to be Jane Austen as a teenager, *c.* 1788–90. This portrait was reprinted as such until the 1930s [private collection].

3. Watercolour of Jane Austen, *c.* 1805 by her sister Cassandra, showing Jane sitting outdoors with her back to the artist [privately owned].

4. The only fully recognised portrait, which portrays Jane Austen sitting with her arms folded facing the artist. It was done as a pencil and watercolour sketch, 4 inches x 3 inches, *c.* 1810. [The National Portrait Gallery, London, purchased this sketch in 1948.]

5. Another sketch, said to be of Jane Austen, done in chalk and plumbago, *c.* 1814–15, portrays Jane as a writer seated at a table with pens and a sheaf of paper. [This portrait is on loan to the Jane Austen House Museum, Chawton.]

6. Today portraiture concerning Jane Austen is highly valuable and of considerable interest. In 2013, a watercolour miniature based on Cassandra's sketch of Jane Austen by James Andrews of Maidenhead (1869) was sold for approximately £164,500. The steel engraving of Andrews' watercolour, which is the most widely reprinted portrait of Jane Austen, is to feature on £10 notes from 2017.

Portraits by Ozias Humphry of the Austen and Berkeley Families
In 1788, Ozias Humphry painted a portrait of Edward Austen Knight, Jane's brother. It shows Edward, aged twenty-one, in front of a large oak tree in the grounds of Godmersham Park, with old temple ruins and gravestones in the background. Humphry also painted a portrait of Jane's older sister Cassandra, aged fifteen, and Jane herself, aged nearly thirteen. The two sisters had been taken by their parents to stay with their great uncle Francis Austen, who lived at the Red House, Sevenoaks, Kent, and was the owner of Godmersham Park. Francis's second wife, also named Jane, was Jane Austen's godmother, though sadly for Jane, her godmother had died. It is said that the portraits of Cassandra and Jane were commissioned by Francis to improve the girls' marriage prospects. The portrait of Jane shows her wearing a white dress and holding a green parasol in an autumnal landscape. Named the Rice Portrait, after the late Henry Rice, a recent Austen family owner of the portrait, the attribution of the sitter has been controversial. At Christie's New York auction in April 2007, the portrait was withdrawn, having failed to reach its estimate.

In the Berkeley family portrait painted in 1780, the youngest child is said to be, or to resemble, Jane Austen, aged nearly five years (see Ozias Humphry, Appendix G). However, it is quite possible that the child in question is Arabella Craven (1774–1819), Elizabeth Craven's daughter. In the portrait, her mother Elizabeth (née Berkeley) is wearing a grey dress. The two boys in the portrait are William, 1st Earl Craven, 7th Baron (1770–1825), standing, and his brother Henry Augustus Craven (1776–1836), who is being carried. The other lady, wearing a white dress, is Elizabeth's sister Georgiana, the Countess of Granard. The two men are George Cranfield Berkeley RN (1753–1818) and Augustus, 5th Earl of Berkeley (1745–1810).

Appendix P: One of the 14th Earl of Derby's poems

(From a privately published edition by Paul Ledger, 2013).

Appendix Q: Extract from Fanny Burney's diary concerning the Oxford visit to the theatre by George III in 1786

August 13th (1786). At six o'clock my hairdresser, to my great satisfaction, arrived. Full two hours was he at work, yet was I not finished, when Swarthy, the Queen's hairdresser, came rapping at my door, to tell me her Majesty's hair was done, and she was waiting for me. I hurried as fast as I could, and ran down without any cap. She smiled at sight of my hasty attire, and said I should not be distressed about a hairdresser the next day, but employ Swarthy's assistant, as soon as he had done with the Princesses: 'You should have had him,' she added, 'to-day, if I had known you wanted him.'

When her Majesty was dressed, all but the hat, she sent for the three princesses; and the King came also. I felt very foolish with my uncovered head; but it was somewhat the less awkward, from its being very much a custom, in the Royal Family, to go without caps; though none that appear before them use such a freedom.

As soon as the hat was on: 'Now, Miss Burney,' said the Queen, 'I won't keep you; you had better go and dress too.'

And now for the Oxford expedition.

How many carriages there were, and how they were arranged, I observed not sufficiently to recollect; but the party consisted of their Majesties, the princesses Royal, Augusta, and Elizabeth, the Duchess of Ancaster, Lord and Lady Harcourt, Lady Charlotte Bertie, and the two Miss Vernons.

These last ladies are daughters of the late Lord Vernon, and sisters of Lady Harcourt.

General Harcourt, Colonel Fairly, and Major Price, and Mr Hagget, with Miss Planta and myself, completed the group. Miss Planta and I, of course, as the only undignified persons, brought up the rear. We were in a chaise of Lord Harcourt.

The city of Oxford afforded us a very noble view on the road, and its spires, towers, and domes soon made me forget all the little objects of minor spleen that had been crossing me as I journeyed towards them; and indeed, by the time I arrived in the midst of them, their grandeur, nobility, antiquity, and elevation impressed my mind so forcibly, that I felt for the first time since my new situation had taken place a rushing in of ideas that had no connection with it whatever.

The roads were lined with decently dressed people, and the high street was so crowded we were obliged to drive gently and carefully, to avoid trampling the people to death. Yet their behaviour was perfectly respectful and proper. Nothing could possibly be better conducted than the whole of this expedition.

At the outward gate of the theatre, the Vice-Chancellor, Dr Chapman, received their Majesties. All the Professors, Doctors, etc., then in Oxford, arrayed in their professional robes, attended him. How I wished my dear father amongst them!

The Vice-Chancellor then conducted their Majesties along the inner court to the door of the theatre, all the rest following; and there, waiting their arrival, stood the Duke and Duchess of Marlborough, the Marquis of Blandford, in a nobleman's Oxford robe, and Lady Caroline and Lady Elizabeth Spencer.

After they had all paid their duties, a regular procession followed, which I should have thought very pretty, and much have liked to have seen, had I been a mere looker-on; but I was frequently at a loss what to do with myself, and uncertain whether I ought to proceed in the suite, or stand by as a spectator; and Miss Planta was still, if possible, more fearful.

Appendix R: Verses from the Prologue to *All for Love*, acted at Blenheim in 1718–19

This heap of stones, which Blenheim's palace frame,
Rose in this form, a mon'ment to thy name:
This heap of stones must crumble into sand,
But thy great name shall through all ages stand.
In fate's dark book I see they long-liv'd name,
And thus the certain prophecy proclaim:
'One shall arise who shall thy deeds rehearse,
Not in arch'd roofs, or in suspected verse;
But in plain annals of each glorious year,
With pomp of truth the story shall appear;
Long after Blenheim's walls shall moulder'd lie,
Or, blown by winds, to distant countries fly,
By him shall thy great actions all survive
And by thy name shall his be taught to live.'

These verses are from *A hasty prologue to All for Love* by Dryden, acted at Blenheim in 1718. The prologue was written by Bishop Hoadly and the words were spoken by Lady Anne Churchill, who married Lord William Bateman in 1720. She acted the part of Cleopatra. John Churchill, the 1st Duke of Marlborough, to whom the prologue is addressed, was in the audience with his wife Sarah.

Appendix S: Lady Charlotte Spencer's drawings, sketches and silhouettes

These were recently discovered in Blenheim Palace Library and are part of her portfolio, which shows Lady Charlotte to be a skilful and talented artist, an example being a coloured drawing of a spiral shell, entitled *The Orange Flat*, 1793. Some of her drawings are of local Blenheim scenes, including *The New Bridge*, 1788, or *The Monument with the statue of the 1st Duke of Marlborough*, 1791, while a fully signed drawing of a Roman head is possibly taken from one of her father's intaglio collection.

Lady Charlotte's silhouette drawing notebook with a red hardback cover and her name on the inside cover was found with her portfolio. Her silhouettes were in the main drawn between 1780 and 1800, a time when silhouette portraiture was fashionable. Among

Fig. 11 Signed and dated *1784 G : Charlotte Spencer*. It portrays a girl named Charlotte, from the *Sorrows of Young Werther*, by Goethe. Drawn by Lady Charlotte aged fifteen.

Fig. 12 Sketch by Lady Caroline Russell, aged eleven, drawn at Woburn Abbey of Signoria Caterina Galli, a noted soprano and singing teacher for Lady Caroline Russell.

examples of family and friends is a silhouette of the Prince of Wales, later George IV. The family silhouettes include her father, mother and her youngest sister Amelia, and her own silhouette, drawn on 31 October 1788, at the height of the private theatrical performances at Blenheim. Some of the silhouettes in her red notebook have been cut out, possibly to be given to friends, including one of Edward Nares that eventually found its way to Merton College Library. This silhouette, with others at Merton drawn by Lady Charlotte, include her oldest sister Lady Caroline, later Viscountess Clifden, and two of her younger brother Lord Francis. They had been placed in an envelope inscribed with the name of Miss Nares. This would have been Elizabeth Martha Nares, their only child, who lived into adulthood. It formed part of the Nares memorabilia at Merton left by Edward Nares to his second wife Cordelia, which was afterwards left to his grandson, the Revd George Cecil White in 1868, who published his book on Edward, *A Versatile Professor*, in 1903. Amongst Lady Charlotte's portfolio is a sketch of seven fashionable ladies with plumed head-dresses standing round their Italian dancing master seated on a stool. Below these ladies, written by Lady Charlotte, are the words 'and their fond hearts to steal away Italian sonnets to sing'. In October 1787, the actor Frederick Reynolds had described in his diary the dancing and the Italian air sung by Lady Charlotte, which 'she sang most delightfully'. No doubt her mother Duchess Caroline would have been equally delighted, as it may have reminded her of her own dancing and singing lessons at Woburn Abbey, where she grew up under the watchful eyes of her own mother, the Duchess of Bedford.

Appendix T: Epitaph on Lady Holland's dog 'Pierrot'

In 1799, Elizabeth Holland's dog 'Pierrot' died. In her journal Elizabeth wrote, 'He was the gift of Ld. Henry [Spencer]. He faithfully maintained the love for me his master felt whilst living.' Ever mindful of her distress, Elizabeth's husband composed her little dog's epitaph:

> Pierrot, of race, of form, of manners rare,
> Envied alike in life and death lies here.
> Living he proved the favourite of the fair,
> And dying drew from beauty's eye a tear.[13]

Appendix U: Extracts from the diary of the Revd Francis Witts

Extract concerning his visit to the Derby family vault of Ormskirk's parish church, 6 June 1809:

> There is a Chapel of the Derby family, which is their principal place of interment; decorated with Banners & Escutcheons; two or three mutilated marble monumental statues represent Ancestors of the Derby family: on one of these I observed the axed legs, the arms of the Isle

of Man. The crest of the Derby family is also sculptured as an eagle standing above an infant swathed: this crest is frequent as a Sign on Inns in Cheshire & Lancashire. The vault is neither spacious nor deep; it is indecorously & negligently closed, & made an object of curiosity. Many leaden coffins have probably been removed from Burscough Abbey, as also the monumental statues above name: we remarked the mouldering coffin of the Earl of Derby beheaded at Bolton in this County by order of the parliament for his adherence to the cause of Charles the 1st – the coffin of a member of the family, who died at Venice; the coffin of an unusual form, not being shaped to the outline of the corpse: – the coffin containing the remains of a member of the family, who died abroad & whose embalmed bowels are contained in a separate chest. The sister of the present Earl, who died lately, directed, that her remains should not be brought hither, as she scorned to lie in a vault, in which at some time she should be elbowed by the corpse of an Actress: the present Lady Derby was the inimitable Miss Farren. The Vicarage of Ormskirk is extensive, Lathom, Burscough, Scarisbrick &c. are townships within its compass. Its income is small in comparison with other valuable livings in the Patronage of the Derby family. Mr. Stanley, a distant relation of Lord Derby, is Vicar. On our return to Blythe, we walked in the Grounds. After dinner Mrs. Backhouse & Miss Currer arrived from Beck House.[14]

Extracts concerning Daylesford, home of Warren Hastings:

September 3rd 1827

We drove to make our first call on Mrs. Hastings at Daylesford. It has pleased this ancient lady [Warren Hastings' widow], after we have been 18 years settled here, to find us out & visit us: and though we did not particularly covet an introduction, yet we had no disinclination to accept the tardy civility. We found Mrs. H. and her German relative, Miss Chabuzet, at home, and were very politely received. The mistress of the Mansion is a very fine old lady, at a very advanced age, but full of spirit, talent & conversation, graceful & elegant. She must have been very attractive, beautiful & talented, when she engrossed the affections of one of the ablest men of his age, as well as the most ill treated, the quondam Governor General of India.

A veil had better be thrown over some parts of Mrs. Hastings's early life, &, perhaps, few now know accurately the facts, which might admit of extenuation, were the whole truth developed. Thus much is certain, that Mr. H. returning to India from this country made an acquaintance on the voyage with his Lady, then Baroness d'Imhoff, who was also proceeding thither. Baron d'Imhoff, a wild young Saxon Nobleman of slender means, and dissipated habits, had married his beautiful wife from the order of Bourgeois; some rural beauty from the environs of Jena, it has been said; thus he lost caste, & was driven to embrace as a profession the art, which he had pursued as an amusement, portrait painting; by the interest of the German attendants of Queen Charlotte, he was proceeding to the East to follow the profession of an artist: his beautiful wife & two infant sons, I think accompanied him. Mr. Hastings was captivated; Baron d'Imhoff was not particular; an arrangement was made; the German mesalliance was soon broken by the necessary legal measures adopted in the Baron's native country, & the Baroness became the wife of the Governor General of India, retaining her children, one of whom, Sir Charles Imoff, still lives, a Major General in our Service. The Portrait painting scheme thus interrupted, the

Baron returned with a replenished purse to Germany, and at Weimar, as, I believe, I have observed once before, we were well acquainted with his second wife, & son & daughters. On Mr. Hastings's public life, & on his private life in latter years, one most highly to be praised, there is no need of speaking here. The House and grounds at Daylesford were built and laid out by him: the estate, I have heard, had formerly been in his family, but had been sold and passed into other hands; it was his honourable pride to purchase it back, & make it his residence. The situation is very eligible, the structure singular, somewhat in Eastern taste, and striking; the views from the principal apartments extensive, over Adlestrop, Oddington &c. towards Stow; the grounds are well planted; the flower gardens near the House well laid out; there is a winding sheet of water at some distance in a valley; it looks well from the house, but is out of repair. The house contains a handsome suite of apartments; the library is a very enjoyable room, out of it on one hand is a drawing room; a second, rather a passage room, on the other side of the library, communicates with a good dining room, and this with a breakfast room. There are some good & striking paintings; in the library a very curious piece by Zoffani, a painter, who went to India, & succeeded admirably in a critically exact delineation of portraits, costume &c. It represents a cock-fight, there are many Europeans, (Mr. Hastings, probably, among them), and all, doubtless, portraits; many Asiatics, equally portraits, in various costumes, & mostly busy in watching the progress of the combating birds, or engaged in the pursuit. In the drawing room is a very large landscape, representing the fortress of Gwlior, which yields to British valour under the administration of Mr. Hastings. The library contains a marble bust of Mr. H; an admirable resemblance. The breakfast room, in which we had refreshments, has some good Flemish paintings, and others worthy of more minute examination than I could give them; of this number are a Madonna & child, the mother in the act of suckling the infant; the angel appearing to Jacob &c. There are portraits of the Duke & Duchess of Gloucester, and a large landscape representing a scene in Mrs. Hastings' life. She had heard of her husband's illness at Calcutta, when she was absent from him, at a considerable distance up the Ganges; she was bent upon resorting to his bed side; but everything was forbidding; the friends, with whom she was staying, endeavoured in vain to dissuade her; the season of the year, the appearance of the weather, the state of the river, all were unfavourable; but she was resolute, & obtaining a boat with requisite crew, she embarked & reached her husband in safety; tho' not without great apprehensions & terrors; for as she landed, a furious tempest was rising, which shortly after raged tremendously, so that much shipping & many lives were lost: the painter, whom the grateful husband employed to record the fidelity and attachment of his wife, has seized and embodied on his canvas the moment, when the strange looking Eastern barge, with its wild copper coloured mariners directing it thro' the lashed waves & surge, is striving to gain the land; the storm is rushing on behind a frightful rainbow, which the angry elements have formed. The day was fine, our drive agreeable, & we returned home pleased.[15]

September 21st 1827

Yesterday we were to have dined with Mrs. Hastings at Daylesford, but our horses disappointed us, not coming till an hour after the time fixed for our setting out. We were, therefore, obliged to send our servant on horseback with our apology.

September 25th 1827

Mrs. Hastings most politely invited us this day to make up for the disappointment on Thursday last, and we reached Daylesford by six o clock. We had arrived first of the guests not staying in the house, & were received in one of the drawing rooms through the library, remarkable for its suite of ivory chairs & sofas, curious articles of luxury, but not to be used by the male creation. There was a large party: Mrs. & Miss Barton, staying in the family; accomplished, travelled, high bred, & conversible, especially the Mother; for the daughter is somewhat of a beauty and knows it. Mr. Winter officiated as chaplain & carved the haunch of venison. Miss Chabuzet agreeable & obliging & unaffected. Mr. and Mrs. Twisleton from Adlestrop were accompanied by Mrs. T's mother, the Lady Powerscourt, and her sister; the two sisters in the evening sang pleasingly together, without music, or with the mere accompaniment of the guitar played by Miss Wingfield; but the voices unaccompanied by the tinkling pleased me best'.[16]

Appendix V: The Witts family and the diaries of Agnes Witts and her son, Francis Witts

Edward Witts' main love in life appears to have been travel. He was a JP, a deputy Lieutenant for Oxfordshire and, in 1779, High Sheriff of the county. Edward and his wife Agnes had three sons, Francis, George and Edward. Francis wrote a diary of his life, first published in 1978, *The Diary of a Cotswold Parson: Reverend F. E. Witts, 1783–1854*. His mother also wrote detailed diaries of her life in the Cotswolds, published in 2008, *The Complete Diary of a Cotswold Lady*. In 1809, Francis Witts took up residence at the rectory in Upper Slaughter, purchasing the Lordship of the Manor in 1852. Subsequent generations of the Witts family lived in the house until 1969, and it was converted into the 'Lords of the Manor' hotel in 1972.

By reading the diaries of Agnes Witts and Francis, her son, an intriguing picture appears of certain families that lived in the Cotswolds during the eighteenth and nineteenth centuries, in particular the Savages of Tetbury and the Wiltshires of Bathford. These, as the Witts family, appear to have been fond of travelling, as was Jane Austen. The Savages and Wiltshires were related, as Charlotte Savage was the daughter of Walter Wiltshire of Shockerwick House at Bathford in Somerset. It is probable that the friendship between the Savages and the Witts family was due to the Cotswolds business of wool-stapling, both families having made their fortunes in wool trading. Edward Witts had inherited the business in Chipping Norton, although, sadly for his wife Agnes and their children, he bankrupted the family business by his fondness for travel and by living above his means.

In 1790, Edward and his family were forced to sell up the family home at Swerford Park and move into rented accommodation, Bownham House at Rodborough near Stroud in Gloucestershire, partly to be near their friends, the Savages. Bownham House was also conveniently near to Edward's business contacts in the cloth trade. When they moved to Bownham House, Edward sent his oldest son Francis to Elmore Court School near Gloucester, the two younger sons remaining in the nursery until August 1792, when they were settled as day scholars at Cheltenham. To assist financially with his sons' education, Edward approached family members for financial support, including his wealthy sister Lady Apphia Lyttelton (see the Witts family group portrait). Lady Apphia was Edward's favourite sister and was a wealthy and influential woman, particularly after the death of her two husbands. In his letter to her, Edward writes about his elder brother Broome, who lived at nearby Nibley House at North Nibley as a gentleman farmer with his wife Amelia. Edward's business failure had caused considerable family friction, as revealed in the letter dated 21 March 1793:

> … the Settlement, my Brother had the hardness to tell my Wife to her face, was too much for her – perhaps you are a stranger to. It is £2500 of my personalty & my Estate at Chip Norton which now produces – about £110 – in all perhaps £210. Besides the Annuity for my Life of ye D. of Malbro', which if my Brother had had the happiness of being a Father; he would not think too much for their maintainance & Education, so far different am I in that respect, that any bounty will be thankfully received by me; to extend that Education, beyond the narrow limits I am now engaging in – I confess I am much hurt, My Wife presses her kind Regards to those of your affectionate
> Friend & Brother
> Edwd: Witts.[17]

Whether this annuity from the Duke of Marlborough was part of his marriage settlement Edward does not reveal. In 1793, the Witts family moved to Edinburgh, which was then a cheaper place to live.

During the 1780s, the paths of the Witts and Savage families seem to have crossed at the private theatricals at Blenheim and at Adlestrop. Although Agnes does not refer to her friend Charlotte Savage acting in the Blenheim private theatricals, she enjoyed watching the theatricals in 1788, the year that Charlotte was to have played a role in the theatricals but had to withdraw from the production. However, she did appear in other theatrical productions at Blenheim. Agnes Witts was important enough to be invited to the Public Day at Blenheim, which was overseen by Duchess Caroline. The Witts family were also fond of driving through the park at Blenheim in their coach on their journeys from Swerford to Oxford or London. On occasions the two families stayed in each other's homes and enjoyed each other's company, whether it was socialising or playing cards together, or travelling to see other friends and relations. Their oldest sons even went to the same private school and on occasions both boys would be taken there in the same carriage. The families often met up in Cheltenham or Bath, where they enjoyed the Regency spa life of balls, concerts, theatres and taking the waters. When they were in Bath they liked to meet up with the Wiltshires.

It seems, however, that their visits to private or public theatres were their greatest diversion. The plays they attended were all well known at that time, especially to discerning families such as theirs, and they saw some of England's finest actors perform in London, Bath and Cheltenham. However, if they did not enjoy the performances they were quick to say so.

The Witts family also enjoyed going to the races, whether at Epsom, Oxford, Burford or Cheltenham. In 1837, they attended the annual Cheltenham steeplechase. Another important family they enjoyed meeting up with were the Leighs of Adlestrop, and on numerous occasions they visited nearby Daylesford House, the home of Warren Hastings.

Agnes Witts' son Francis took his ecclesiastical duties seriously. On one occasion he went to hear Edward Nares give a 'vague discourse' on Sunday 17 March 1805 at St Mary's, the parish church, in High Street, Oxford. At the time, Edward was the Bampton Lecturer for Oxford University and had travelled there from Biddenden in Kent. This was only three years after the death of his first wife. Francis also attended the church of St Peter-in-the-East, Oxford, where Edward had once been the curate, to listen to a 'sermon on miracles by Dr. Finch that was ridiculous'.

Another enjoyment of the Witts family was reading and belonging to book clubs. In March 1789, one of the books they read was Elizabeth Craven's *A Journey through the Crimea to Constantinople*, which had just been published. Whether Edward Witts would have liked to have travelled as far as Turkey, with Agnes at his side, Agnes does not recount in her diaries. However, they did undertake extensive tours throughout England, Wales, Ireland and the Channel Islands. Possibly Agnes at times would have preferred a quieter life, giving her more time to correspond with her many friends, acquaintances and relatives. Her last entry is for Christmas Day 1824, just two weeks before her death at the age of seventy-six. Agnes would be missed by many, including the Rollinson family of Chadlington, the Tyrwhitts, and the Penystons, who were related to Warren Hastings. There was also a family connection to the Travell family and the Tracy-Kecks, which included Susan Keck, later to become Lady Elcho of Stanway. The Witts were also related to the Tracy family of Swell Bowl, near Stow-on-the-Wold; to the Cavendish-Bentinck family, the Dukes of Portland; and the Dutton family, Lords of Sherborne in Gloucestershire.

Possibly the most exciting travels for Edward and Agnes during their married life was when they lived in Weimar and visited Leipzig and Dresden before returning to England via Copenhagen. They had to stay in Denmark until evacuated along with other British subjects prior to Nelson's attack in the battle of Copenhagen, 2 April 1801.

Appendix W: The Savage family of Tetbury

The family was descended from the Savages of the Ards, and it was Sir John Savage who led the charge of the left wing of Henry Tudor's army at the Battle of Bosworth in August 1485, resulting in the death of Richard III. After the battle Sir John, with his uncle Thomas Stanley, afterwards the 1st Earl of Derby, successfully promoted Henry Tudor to the throne as Henry VII. For this, the King made him a Knight of the Garter. Sir John, who married Catherine, the daughter and heiress of Thomas Stanley, was killed at the Siege of Boulogne in France in 1492.

It appears that since 1594 the Savage family had owned land in and around Tetbury, where they were the Lords of the Manor and lived in a house called the Old Priory. By 1837, the building was known as Church House, and when it was sold in 1850 to Joseph Woods, a local banker, the house became known as Tetbury Close. Eventually it became a hotel in the 1960s.

In the eighteenth century, the Revd John Savage was the rector of Beverston and Westonbirt. He was one of the trustees of the Manor of Tetbury and of other lands which belonged to Tetbury at the annual meeting of the Court Leet held on 10 October 1796, probably at the seventeenth-century market building in the centre of the town. John Savage had married Charlotte Wiltshire of Shockerwick House, and when he died in 1803, aged fifty-six, he left his house and property situated in and near Tetbury for the use of his widow for her life. After her death the property was to pass to his eldest son, also called John. Charlotte died in 1846, aged ninety-two, and was buried at the parish church of St Mary Magdalen in Tetbury on 18 September 1846. On the south side of the altar is a stone monument to the Revd John Savage, which states that he died at Bath, was buried on 26 March 1803, and was the rector of Beverston.

Appendix X: Extract from the diary of Francis Witts concerning Anthony Thomas Lefroy, the Chief Constable of Gloucestershire

March 18th 1852

Left Gloucester by rail at 4 P.M. and arrived at the Police Station at Cheltenham in less than twenty minutes, where I found Lefroy's open carriage waiting to convey me to his house at Swindon. Drove thither by the back road passing Maule's Elms; all very much altered in a lapse of years by the increase of building in the suburbs of Cheltenham, by improved roads, and by the line of railway. The village of Swindon with its Manor House, occupied by Mr. Sherlock Willis, its ancient Church restored, its parsonage now tenanted by a new Incumbent, the Revd. Lewis Griffiths, & two or three lesser residences, the property of Mr. Surman, in one of which the Chief Constable resides, is a pretty, rural, quiet hamlet, embosomed in trees. – Lefroy was fortunate in selecting this residence, on his marriage; it is within half an hour's walk, or ten minutes' drive of his constabulary office at Cheltenham, and the distance is enough to detach him and Mrs. L. from the hurry of town gaieties, while the lady is likely to be more comfortable at a little distance from a worthless father and a Mother who has winked at her husband's irregularities, than if she resided in the same town with them. The rent of the house is moderate; there are three sitting rooms, and four good bedrooms, sufficient offices, garden, stable and coach house: they are near the Church and contiguous to the principal residents of the place. Of these the wealthiest is Mr. Surman, one of the legatees of the miser banker of Gloucester, Jemmy Wood; S's name was Goodlake, and he is unmarried, a sister living with him, a pleasing person. It is strange how women accommodate themselves to a change of circumstances better than men. Miss G. looks the lady, Mr. S. does not look the gentleman. He was clerk to his kinsman, the banker; and now possesses at Swindon, a good estate with a handsome and large house, for the most part newly built, situate in very enjoyable pleasure grounds, bordered at a distance by the Bristol and Birmingham Railway, and commanding a beautiful view of the surrounding hills, Cleeve Hill, Prestbury, Battledown hills with Prestbury, Southam, Cleeve &c. more or less forming features in the landscape. – In these grounds I walked with Lefroy, who introduced me to Mr. Surman, whom we found playing billiards with Mr. Agg in an iron billiard room in the grounds at a little distance from the house. Mr. and Mrs. Agg were staying at the Lefroy's: they have let their place, Hewletts, and are going for a twelvemonth to sea bathing places, wintering at Southampton: with a son, an officer in India, and a daughter, married to a clergyman, living at a distance from Cheltenham, they may find this kind of wandering life agreeable, perhaps convenient. – At half past six Lefroy's small dining room contained a large party including Lady Steele, wife of an Irish Baronet, a magistrate, to whom Cheltenham is more pleasant as a residence than the manor house at Mickleton, which fell to his lot with the heiress Miss Graves; who, perhaps, would prefer the country to the town abode. Cards and music in the evening.[18]

Anthony Thomas Lefroy, was a nephew of Tom Lefroy, whose family lived at Ashe Rectory, near Steventon and with whom Jane Austen enjoyed flirting.

Appendix Y: Frances Fitzroy and the Pigot-Fitzroy family

Admiral Hugh Pigot (1722–1792) lived in Wychwood Forest, Oxfordshire. He was a good friend of the Prime Minister, the 3rd Duke of Grafton. In 1769, the Duke of Grafton married Elizabeth Wrothesley, the sister of Admiral Pigot's second wife Frances Wrothesley. Lady Frances Fitzroy, daughter of the 3rd Duke of Grafton, married the 1st Baron Churchill of Wychwood, Francis Almeric Spencer, the youngest son of the 4th Duke of Marlborough, on 25th November 1801. The baronetcy was created in 1815 for Lord Francis, whose portrait greets visitors as they enter the private east wing at Blenheim Palace in the undercroft.

Appendix Z: Highgrove, Tetbury

Highgrove was built between 1796 and 1798 for John Paul Paul, a local landowner, who later bought the Manor House and the estate of the nearby village of Doughton in 1818. The Paul family were Huguenots who had settled in and around Tetbury and had prospered in the cloth trade, and lived at Highgrove until 1860. From the house, probably designed by the architect Anthony Keck, there is a fine view of the spire of the parish church of St Mary Magdalen. In 1980, HRH Prince Charles bought Highgrove from Maurice Macmillan. When the gardens at Highgrove were opened to the public in the 1990s, a visitor centre called the Orchard Room was built, designed by Charles Morris, who simulated the seventeenth-century market building in the centre of Tetbury by the inclusion of clumpy Tuscan columns. This building is dedicated to the memory of Paddy Whiteland, who worked at Highgrove for nearly fifty years and is depicted in a bas-relief in the entrance hall carved by Nick Cuff, a sculptor from Tetbury who knew Paddy. It is a fine memorial to a great Irish character, who was such a stalwart of HRH Prince Charles during his first years at Highgrove.

Notes

Introduction
1. W. Scott, *The Georgian Theatre*, p. 15

Act I
1. M. Fowler, *Blenheim: Biography of a Palace*, p. 74

Act II
1. S. Rosenfeld, *Temples of Thespis*, p. 10
2. R. Baird, *Goodwood*, p. 75
3. M. Girouard, *A Country House Companion*, p. 97
4. Duchess of Devonshire, *The House: A Portrait of Chatsworth*, pp. 195–96

Act III
1. Lord Granville, *Private Correspondence*, ii, p. 17
2. Everyman Library, *The Diary of Fanny Burney*, p. 137
3. H. Montgomery-Massingberd, *Blenheim and the Churchills*, p. 81
4. W. Mavor, *A Guide to Blenheim*, p. 167

Act IV Scene I
1. F. Reynolds, *The Life and Times of Frederick Reynolds*, p. 150
2. S. Rosenfeld, *Temples of Thespis*, p. 112
3. J. Curthoys, *The Cardinal's College*, p. 183
4. Lord Granville, *Private Correspondence*, ii, p. 251
5. A. Witts, *The Complete Diary of a Cotswold Lady*, vol. 1, 17 October 1788
6. *Ibid.*, 18 August 1789
7. M. Fowler, *Blenheim: Biography of a Palace*, p. 117
8. H. Montgomery-Massingberd, *Blenheim and the Churchills*, p. 73
9. Lord Granville, *Private Correspondence*, ii, p. 20
10. *Ibid.*, ii, p. 36
11. Lady H. Spencer-Churchill, *Blenheim and the Churchill Family*, p. 130
12. W. Mavor, *Oxford University and City Guide*, p. 159

Act IV Scene II

1. S. Rosenfeld, *Temples of Thespis*, p. 79
2. M. Fowler, *Blenheim: Biography of a Palace*, p. 118
3. F. E. Witts, *The Diary of a Cotswold Parson*, p. 175
4. M. J. Barber, *A Man of Many Parts: Professor or Bishop?* p. 17
5. T. Luscombe, *Mansfield Park*, adapted play, p. 21

Act V

1. A. M. Broadley, *The Beautiful Lady Craven*, p. 251
2. M. Fowler, *Blenheim: Biography of a Palace*, p. 106
3. J. Brown, *The Omnipotent Magician*, p. 251
4. A. M. Broadley, *The Beautiful Lady Craven*, p. 252
5. F. Reynolds, *The Life and Times of Frederick Reynolds*, p. 52

Act VI Scene I

1. A. Witts, *The Complete Diary of a Cotswold Lady*, vol. 1, 9 January 1789
2. *Ibid.*, 21 January 1789
3. *Ibid.*, 10 August 1789
4. *Ibid.*, 12 August 1789
5. *Ibid.*, 14 October 1789
6. F. Witts, *The Diary of a Cotswold Parson*, D. Verey edition, p. 194
7. *Ibid.*, p. 194, note 117
8. P. Byrne, *The Real Jane Austen*, p. 169
9. J. Austen, *Mansfield Park*, Wordsworth Classics, p. 237
10. P. Byrne, *The Real Jane Austen*, p.216

Act VI Scene II

1. D. Le Faye, *Austen Papers*, Eliza de Feuillide to Philadelphia Walter

Act VI Scene III

1. P. Byrne, *The Real Jane Austen*, p.141
2. D. Le Faye, *Jane Austen: A Family Record*, p. 133
3. P. Byrne, *The Real Jane Austen*, p. 140
4. *Ibid.*, p.144, letter 112, November 1814
5. F. E. Witts, *The Complete Diary of a Cotswold Parson*, vol. 2, p. 263

Act VI Scene IV

1. J. Austen, *Mansfield Park*, Wordsworth Classics, p. 120
2. G. Hart, *A History of Cheltenham*, p. 124

Appendices

1. S. Keppel, *The Sovereign Lady*, p. 371
2. J. Stawell, *The Burford and Bibury Racecourses*, p. 160
3. F. E. Witts, *The Diary of a Cotswold Parson*, D. Verey edition, p. 502
4. R. Baird, *Goodwood*, pp. 136–37
5. *Ibid.*, p. 100

6–11. Woburn Archives, HMC8, vols 24 & 45; folio Nos 90, 174, 190 & 216

12. S. Keppel, *The Sovereign Lady*, p. 369
13. *Ibid.*, p. 370
14. F. E. Witts, *The Complete Diary of a Cotswold Parson*, vol. 2, p. 182
15. *Ibid.*, vol. 3, p. 364
16. *Ibid.*, vol. 3, p. 368
17. A. Witts, *The Complete Diary of a Cotswold Lady*, vol. 1, 21 March 1793
18. F. E. Witts, *The Diary of a Cotswold Parson*, D. Verey edition, p. 209

Sources

Warmest thanks go to all those who have guided my journey in the footsteps of Edward and Charlotte in their search for love and happiness. References have been kept to a minimum, as many of the passages quoted come either from the memoirs of Edward Nares, from George Cecil White's *A Versatile Professor*, or from Adrian White's *Reminiscences of an Oxford Divine*, published by the Parson Woodforde Society.

Blenheim Palace Archives

Lady Charlotte Spencer's drawings and silhouettes, the Scharf Catalogue and the Residuary Accounts of the 6th Duke of Marlborough

British Library, London

G. C. White Mss 31022 fols 94, 96, 98
G. C. White Mss Add 40407 fols 150, 152, 280
G. C. White Mss Add 50261 fols 71, 159–60
The Charles Burney Collection relating to playbills and newspaper reports, Mss 61678, shelf mark 937.g.96

Merton College, Oxford

Silhouettes: E2.39c/1-4
Play tickets: E2.39c/6-7
Play bills: E2.39/1-3
First volume of Edward Nares' memoirs: E2.41
Portrait of Edward Nares: McPO20

Woburn Archives

HMC8, vols 24 & 45, and the drawing by Lady Caroline Russell of Signorina Galli

Other Sources

Bodleian Library
Jane Austen Society reports, 1966–1985
Evelyn M. Howe, vol. 5, pp. 221–74
Betty Askwith, vol. 6, pp. 268–84
Edward Nares' notebooks on political economy, 1817–20

Hereford County Library and Archives
Unpublished diary of Lady Anne Bateman

OxHistory Centre of Local Studies
Letter of I. Pigot: CG/4.1.4/1820

The Wellcome Library, London
Edward Nares' Commonplace Book

Magazines, guides and reference books (British Library)
The Annual Register for 1787, London, J. Dodsley, 1788
Bell's British Theatre, 90 vols, London, 1793
A Biographical Dictionary of Actors 1660–1800, P. Highfill, K. Burnim & E. Langhans, Southern Illinois University Press, 1973
The British National Biographical Dictionaries, 1801
Encyclopaedia New Britannica, vol. 28, Oxford University Press, 1997
The Gentleman's Magazine, February 1744, vol. 44, pp. 87–88
The International Directory of Theatre, St James Press, 1996
Mavor's Oxford University and City Guide, 1817
The Oxford Companion to the Theatre, Oxford University Press, 1995
The Oxford Dictionary of National Biography, Oxford University Press, 2004
The Sporting Magazine, vol. X, second series, No. LVII, December 1834
Town and Country Magazine or Universal Repository of Knowledge, Instruction and Entertainment, 1787, vol. 19, pp. 437–78 'Blenheim House Theatre'
The Cambridge Companion to British Theatre, 1730–1830, Cambridge University Press, 2007

Further Reading

The following are recommended for Blenheim and the Spencer family:
David Green's *Blenheim Palace and the Churchills of Blenheim*, 1967
Hugh Montgomery-Massingberd's *Blenheim and the Churchills*, 2004
Henrietta Spencer-Churchill's *Blenheim and the Churchill Family*, 2005

On theatre:
Mark Girouard's *Life in the French Country House*, 2000
Sybil Rosenfeld's *Temples of Thespis*, 1978
Ian Thompson's *The Sun King's Garden*, 2000

On Jane Austen:
Deirdre Le Faye's *Jane Austen: A Family Record*, 1989
Lord David Cecil's *A Portrait of Jane Austen*, 1978
Syrie James's novel *The Lost Memoirs of Jane Austen*, 2008

On Edward Nares:
Nigel Aston's *Life of Nares* with bibliography in the Oxford Dictionary of National Biography

On Elizabeth Farren, the 12th Earl of Derby and Anne Damer:
Suzanne Bloxam's *Walpole's Queen of Comedy*, 1988
Emma Donoghue's novel, *Life Mask*, 2004

Bibliography

Adeane, J.; *Girlhood of Maria Josepha Holroyd*, Longmans, Green & Co., 1896

Allen, N.; *Broughton Castle and the Fiennes Family*, Wykeham Press, 2010

Baird, R.; *Goodwood*, Frances Lincoln, 2007

Barber, M. J.; *A Man of Many Parts: Professor or Bishop?* Holywell Press, 2009

Bird, W.; *Drawings and Sketches of Oxford*, Salamander Press, 1983

Blakiston, G.; *Woburn and the Russells*, Constable, 1980

Bleackley, H.; *The Beautiful Duchess*, Bodley Head, 1907

Bloxam, S.; *Walpole's Queen of Comedy*, S. Bloxam, 1988

Bodanis, D.; *Passionate Minds: The Great Enlightenment Love Affair*, Little, Brown, 2006

Bolster, R.; *Marie d'Agoult: The Rebel Countess*, Yale University Press, 2000

Broadley, A. M.; *The Beautiful Lady Craven*, John Lane, 1914

Brown, J.; *The Omnipotent Magician*, Chatto & Windus, 2011

Brown, J.; *The Pursuit of Paradise*, Harper Collins, 1999

Burn, J. S.; *A History of Henley on Thames*, Longman & Co., 1861

Byrne, P.; *Jane Austen and the Theatre*, Hambledon Press, 2002

Byrne, P.; *The Real Jane Austen*, Harper Press, 2013

Cecil, D.; *A Portrait of Jane Austen*, G. Rainbird, 1978

Chapman, R. W.; *The Novels of Jane Austen*, Oxford University Press, 1988

Climenson, E. J.; *Passages of the Diaries of Mrs. Philip Lybbe Powys A.D. 1756 to 1808*, Longmans, Green & Co., 1899

Collins, I.; *The Parson's Daughter*, Hambledon Press, 1998

Cornforth, J.; *Early Georgian Interiors*, Yale University Press, 2004

Coxe, W.; *Memoirs of John Duke of Marlborough*, Longman, Hurst, Rees, Orme and Brown, 1819

Curthoys, J.; *The Cardinal's College*, Profile Books, 2012

Day, M.; *Voices from the World of Jane Austen*, David & Charles, 2006

Devonshire, Duchess of; *The House: A Portrait of Chatsworth*, Macmillan, 1982

Dolan, B.; *Ladies of the Grand Tour*, Harper Collins, 2001

Douglas-Home, J.; *Stately Passions*, Michael O'Mara, 2006

Edgcumbe, R.; *Musical Reminiscences of an Old Amateur*, W. Clarke, 1773–1823

Ellis, K.; *Star of the Morning: The Extraordinary Life of Lady Hester Stanhope*, Harper Collins, 2008

Fiennes, R.; *Mad Dogs and Englishmen*, Hodder & Stoughton, 2009

Fisher, C. T. (ed.); *A Passion for Natural History: The Life and Legacy of the 13th Earl of Derby*, NMGM, 2002

Foreman, A.; *Georgiana's World*, Harper Collins, 2001

Fowler, M.; *Blenheim: Biography of a Palace*, Viking, 1989

Gibbs, L. (ed.); *The Diary of Fanny Burney*, Dent, 1971

Girouard, M.; *A Country House Companion*, Pothecary Ltd, 1987

Girouard, M.; *Life in the English Country House*, Yale University Press, 1978

Girouard, M.; *Life in the French Country House*, Cassell, 2000

Green, D.; *Blenheim Palace and the Churchills of Blenheim*, Collins, 1967

Gross, J.; *The Life and Letters of Lady Melbourne*, Rice University Press, 1997

Hart, G.; *A History of Cheltenham*, Alan Sutton Publishing, 1981

Hibbert, C.; *The Marlboroughs*, Viking, 2002

Highfill, P., K. Burnim & E. Langhans; *A Biographical Dictionary of Actors 1660–1800*, Southern Illinois University Press, 1973

Hill, C.; *Juniper Hall*, Bodley Head, 1903

Hodgson, E.; *A History of Tetbury*, Alan Sutton Publishing, 1976

Holland, F.; *Journal of Elizabeth Lady Holland*, Ilchester Edition, 2 vols, Longmans, Green & Co., 1908

HRH The Prince of Wales & Charles Clover, *Highgrove: Portrait of an Estate*, Chapmans, 1993

HRH The Prince of Wales & Candida Lycett Green, *The Garden at Highgrove*, St Martin's Press, 2000

Hubert, M.; *Jane Austen's Christmas*, History Press, 2009

Humphry, O.; *A Memoir of George Stubbs*, Pallas Athene, 2005

Hutton, W.; *Burford Papers*, Archibald Constable & Co., 1905

Huxley, V.; *Jane Austen & Adlestrop: Her Other Family*, Windrush, 2013

Jacques, D.; *Georgian Gardens: The Reign of Nature*; Batsford, 1990

Jago, L.; *Regency House Party*: BBC, 2004

James, L.; *Aristocrats*, Abacus, 2009

Johnson, J; *Excellent Cassandra: The Life and Times of the Duchess of Chandos*, Alan Sutton Publishing, 1981

Kennedy, J.; *The Changing Faces of Yarnton with Cassington and Begbroke*, Robert Boyd, 1999

Keppel, S.; *The Sovereign Lady*, Hamish Hamilton, 1974

Lane, M.; *A Charming Place: Bath in the Life and Novels of Jane Austen*, Millstream, 1988

Laski, Marghanita; *Jane Austen and Her World*, Thames & Hudson, 1969

Lee, A.; *The History of the Town and Parish of Tetbury*, Henry & Parker, 1857

Le Faye, D.; *Jane Austen: A Family Record*, British Library, 1989

Lefroy, H.; *Jane Austen*, Sutton Publishing, 1997

Leveson-Gower, Lord Granville; *Private Correspondence, 1781–1821*, John Murray, 1916

Leveson-Gower, Hon. F. (ed.); *Letters of Harriet Countess Granville 1810–1845*, 2 vols, Longmans, Green & Co., 1894

Luscombe, T.; *Mansfield Park*, adapted play, Oberon Books, 2012

Mavor, W. F.; *New Description of Blenheim, 1787–1846 and Oxford University and City Guide*, Munday and Slatter, 1820

Montgomery-Massingberd, H.; *Blenheim and the Churchills*, Jarrold, 2004

Munson J.; *Maria Fitzherbert: The Secret Wife of George IV*, Constable, 2001

McCalman, I. (ed.); *An Oxford Companion to the Romantic Age*, Oxford University Press, 2000

McIntyre, I.; *Garrick*, Allen Lane, 1999

Miller, J.; *Hidden Treasure Houses*, John Murray, 2006

Noakes, V.; *Edward Lear: The Life of a Wanderer*, Collins, 1968

Nokes, D.; *Jane Austen*, Fourth Estate, 1997

Nussbaum, F.; *Rival Queens*, University of Pennsylvania Press, 2010

Perry, G.; *Spectacular Flirtations: Viewing the Actress in British Art and Theatre, 1768–1820*, Yale University Press, 2007

Pollard, W.; *The Stanleys of Knowsley*, Frederick Warne & Co., 1869

Pfuell, I.; *A History of Shobdon*, I. Pfuell, 1994

Plumb, J. H.; *Georgian Delights*, Weidenfeld & Nicolson, 1980

Reynolds, F.; *The Life and Times of Frederick Reynolds*, 2 vols, Henry Colburn, 1826

Rosenfeld, S.; *Temples of Thespis*, Society for Theatre Research, 1978

Russell, G.; *The Theatres of War: Performance, Politics and Society*, Clarendon Press, 1995

Scott, W. S.; *The Georgian Theatre*, Westhouse, 1946

Shields, C.; *Jane Austen*, Weidenfeld & Nicolson, 2001

Sloman, S.; *Gainsborough in Bath*, Yale University Press, 2002

Soames, M.; *The Profligate Duke*, Collins, 1987

Spence, J.; *Becoming Jane Austen*, Hambledon Continuum, 2003

Spencer, C.; *Impressions of Althorp*, Quiller, 2013

Spencer-Churchill, H.; *Blenheim and The Churchill Family*, CICO Books, 2005

Stawell, J.; *The Burford and Bibury Racecourses*, Hindsight, 2000

Sutton, A. (ed.); *The Complete Diary of a Cotswold Lady*, Amberley, 2008

Thompson, I.; *The Sun King's Garden*, Bloomsbury, 2006

Thomson, G. S.; *The Russells in Bloomsbury, 1669–1771*, Jonathan Cape, 1940

Tucker, J.; *Jane Austen the Woman*, Robert Hale, 1994

Verey, D. (ed.); *The Diary of a Cotswold Parson*, Alan Sutton Publishing, 1978

Vickery, A.; *The Gentleman's Daughter*, Yale University Press, 1998

White, G. C.; *A Versatile Professor: Reminiscences of the Reverend Edward Nares*, R. Brimley Johnson, 1903

Williamson, G. C.; *History of Portrait Miniatures*, George Bell & Sons, 1904

Wood, M.; *Nancy Lancaster: English Country House Style*, Frances Lincoln, 2005

Wraxall, N. W.; *Historical Memoirs of My Own Time*, Cadell and Davies, 1815